Essays on Heidegger and others

Essays on Heidegger and others

Philosophical papers

VOLUME 2

RICHARD RORTY

University Professor of Humanities
University of Virginia

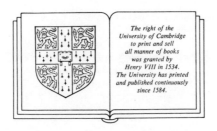

The right of the
University of Cambridge
to print and sell
all manner of books
was granted by
Henry VIII in 1534.
The University has printed
and published continuously
since 1584.

CAMBRIDGE UNIVERSITY PRESS

CAMBRIDGE

NEW YORK   PORT CHESTER   MELBOURNE   SYDNEY

Published by the Press Syndicate of the University of Cambridge
The Pitt Building, Trumpington Street, Cambridge CB2 1RP
40 West 20th Street, New York, NY 10011, USA
10 Stamford Road, Oakleigh, Melbourne 3166, Australia

First published 1991
Reprinted 1991 (twice)

Printed in the United States of America

Library of Congress Cataloging-in-Publication Data
Rorty, Richard.

Essays on Heidegger and others / Richard Rorty.

p. cm. – (Philosophical papers ; v. 2)

Includes bibliographical references and index.

ISBN 0-521-35370-X. – ISBN 0-521-35878-7 (pbk.)

1. Philosophy, Modern – 20th century.   I. Title.   II. Series:
Rorty, Richard, Philosophical papers : 2.

B945.R52   1991   vol. 2
[B804]
191 s – dc20

[190]   90-20328
CIP

British Library Cataloguing in Publication Data
Rorty, Richard

Essays on Heidegger and others : philosophical papers,
vol. 2.

1. German philosophy. Heidegger, Martin, 1889–1976
I. Title
193

ISBN 0-521-35369-6 hardback (volume 1)
ISBN 0-521-35877-9 paperback (volume 1)
ISBN 0-521-35370-X hardback (volume 2)
ISBN 0-521-35878-7 paperback (volume 2)
ISBN 0-521-40476-2 hardback (set)
ISBN 0-521-40915-2 paperback (set)

To Kevin

Contents

Acknowledgments

"Philosophy as Science, as Metaphor, and as Politics" was a contribution to a symposium held at the University of Vienna in celebration of the 50th anniversary of Husserl's *Krisis der Europäischen Wissenschaften*. A German translation was published in *Die Krise der Phänomenologie und die Pragmatik des Wissenschaftsfortschritts*, Michael Benedikt and Rudolf Burger, eds. (Vienna: Verlag der Österreichischen Staatsdruckerei, 1986), pp. 138–149. A revised and enlarged version of the English original (the version reprinted here) appeared in *The Institution of Philosophy*, Avner Cohen and Marcello Dascal, eds. (La Salle: Open Court, 1989), pp. 13–33.

"Heidegger, Contingency, and Pragmatism" is published here for the first time. It will also appear in *Reading Heidegger*, Hubert Dreyfus and Harrison Hall, eds. (Oxford: Blackwell, forthcoming). It includes passages from "Heidegger wider den Pragmatisten," *Neue Hefte für Philosophie* 23 (1984), pp. 1–22. The latter was a version of a lecture given at Haverford College, and has appeared only in German translation.

"Wittgenstein, Heidegger, and the Reification of Language" was a contribution to a symposium celebrating the 100th birthdays of Heidegger and Wittgenstein held at the J. W. Goethe-Universität, Frankfurt am Main, in April 1989. It has not previously been published in English, but will appear also in *The Cambridge Companion to Heidegger*, Charles Guignon, ed. (forthcoming).

"Heidegger, Kundera, and Dickens" was given as a lecture at the Sixth East-West Philosophers' Conference, held at the University of Hawaii in August 1989. It will appear in the proceedings of that conference.

"Deconstruction and Circumvention" began as a lecture called "Now that we have deconstructed metaphysics, do we have to deconstruct literature too?" given at the Summer School of Criticism and Theory held at Northwestern University in 1983. A revised version was published in *Critical Inquiry* 11 (September 1984), pp. 1–23. It is reprinted by permission of The University of Chicago Press.

"Two Meanings of 'Logocentrism' " was written in reply to Christopher Norris's "Philosophy as *Not* Just a 'Kind of Writing': Derrida and the Claim of Reason," which was partly in response to "Philosophy as a Kind of Writing" (included in my *Consequences of Pragmatism*). Norris's essay and my reply were published in *Redrawing the Lines: Analytic Philosophy, Deconstruction and Literary Theory*, Reed Way Dasenbrock, ed. (Minneapolis: University of Minnesota Press, 1989), pp. 204–216.

ix

"Is Derrida a Transcendental Philosopher?" appeared in *Yale Journal of Criticism*, April 1989. It is reprinted here by permission.

"De Man and the American Cultural Left" is a revised version of the last of three Romanell Lectures given at the University of Virginia in January 1989. It borrows some paragraphs from my "Two Cheers for the Cultural Left," *South Atlantic Quarterly* 89, pp. 227–234, and some others from my "Deconstruction," in *The Cambridge History of Literary Criticism*, vol. 8 (forthcoming).

"Freud and Moral Reflection" was given in 1984 as an Edith Weigert Memorial Lecture at the Forum for Psychiatry and the Humanities in Washington, D.C. It appeared in *Pragmatism's Freud: The Moral Disposition of Psychoanalysis*, Joseph H. Smith and William Kerrigan, eds. (Baltimore: Johns Hopkins University Press, 1986), pp. 1–27.

"Habermas and Lyotard on Postmodernity" appeared in *Praxis International* 4 (April 1984), pp. 32–44. It is reprinted here by permission.

"Unger, Castoriadis, and the Romance of a National Future" appeared in *Northwestern University Law Review* 82 (Winter 1988), pp. 335–351. It is reprinted here by permission.

"Moral Identity and Private Autonomy: The Case of Foucault" was given at a conference in memory of Foucault, organized by François Ewald and held in Paris in January 1988. It appeared in French translation in the proceedings of this conference: *Michel Foucault Philosophe: Rencontre Internationale* (Paris: Éditions du Seuil, 1989), pp. 385–394. A slightly curtailed version of the English original was published as "Foucault/Dewey/Nietzsche" in *Raritan* 4 (Spring 1990), pp. 1–8.

I am grateful to the organizers of the conferences, institutes, and symposia at which these papers were presented, and to the publishers of the various journals and collections in which they appeared. I should also like to express my continuing gratitude to the John D. and Catherine T. MacArthur Foundation. The majority of the papers in this and the previous volume were written while I held a MacArthur Fellowship.

Introduction:
Pragmatism and post-Nietzschean philosophy

This is the second volume of a collection of papers written during the 1980s. Volume 1 is made up of papers that discuss themes and figures within analytic philosophy. In contrast, most of this volume is about Heidegger and Derrida. Part I is made up of four papers on Heidegger – the fruits of an abortive, abandoned attempt to write a book about him. Part II contains three papers on Derrida, together with a pendant piece that discusses the uses to which Paul de Man and his followers have put certain Derridean ideas.

Part III is more miscellaneous. Of the four papers in this part, the first and most ambitious is called "Freud and Moral Reflection." It picks out and plays up certain aspects of Freud's work which fit in with Quine's and Davidson's picture of the self as a centerless web of beliefs and desires – a picture I employed in chapter 2 of my *Contingency, Irony, and Solidarity*. The remaining three papers are discussions of the social theories and political attitudes of various contemporary figures (Habermas, Lyotard, Unger, Castoriadis, Foucault); these papers amplify the sociopolitical views presented in Part III of Volume 1.

In the remainder of this introduction, I shall offer some general remarks about the relation between the post-Nietzschean tradition of Franco-German thought which these essays discuss and the antirepresentationalist, pragmatist tradition within analytic philosophy discussed in Volume 1.

Heidegger and Derrida are often referred to as "postmodern" philosophers. I have sometimes used "postmodern" myself, in the rather narrow sense defined by Lyotard as "distrust of metanarratives." But I now wish that I had not. The term has been so over-used that it is causing more trouble than it is worth. I have given up on the attempt to find something common to Michael Graves's buildings, Pynchon's and Rushdie's novels, Ashberry's poems, various sorts of popular music, and the writings of Heidegger and Derrida. I have become more hesitant about attempts to periodize culture – to describe every part of a culture as suddenly swerving off in the same new direction at approximately the same time. Dramatic narratives may well be, as MacIntyre has suggested, essential to the writing of intellectual history. But it seems safer and more useful to periodize and dramatize each discipline or genre separately, rather than trying to think of them all as swept up together in massive sea changes.

In particular, it seems best to think of Heidegger and Derrida simply as post-

Nietzschean philosophers – to assign them places in a conversational sequence which runs from Descartes through Kant and Hegel to Nietzsche and beyond, rather than to view them as initiating or manifesting a radical rupture. Though I unreservedly admire the originality and power of both men, neither can hope to avoid being fitted into contexts by his readers. The most that an original figure can hope to do is to recontextualize his or her predecessors. He or she cannot aspire to produce works that are themselves uncontextualizable, any more than a commentator like myself can aspire to find the one "right" context into which to fit those works.

The context in which my essays put post-Nietzschean philosophy is, predictably enough, pragmatism. I see Nietzsche as the figure who did most to convince European intellectuals of the doctrines which were purveyed to Americans by James and Dewey. A lot of what Nietzsche had to say can be viewed as following from his claim that " 'knowledge in itself' is as impermissible a concept as 'thing-in-itself' "[1] and his suggestion that "[the categories of reason] represent nothing more than the expediency of a certain race and species – their utility alone is their 'truth'."[2] His famous description of "How the 'True World' Became a Fable" in *Twilight of the Idols* is, except for the sneers at Christianity, pretty close to Dewey's vision of Europe's intellectual progress.

Nietzsche's version of pragmatism had, to be sure, little to do with the social hopes characteristic of James and Dewey. His perspectivalism, his refusal to admit the notion of a truth disconnected from interests and needs, was part of a striving for private perfection, for what he thought of as spiritual cleanliness. Nietzsche disliked both his country and his century, so the Emersonian combination of self-reliance and patriotism found in James and Dewey is alien to him.[3] All he took from Emerson, so to speak, was the self-reliance; there is no analogue in his writings to Emerson's American sense of a new kind of social freedom. When Nietzsche read Emerson's abolitionist polemics, he presumably regarded them as merely the unfortunate residue of Christian weakness in an otherwise strong man.

Despite this difference, Nietzsche was as good an anti-Cartesian, antirepresentationalist, and antiessentialist as Dewey. He was as devoted to the question "what difference will this belief make to our conduct?" as Peirce or James. If all you are interested in is epistemology and philosophy of language, as opposed to moral and

---

1 *The Will to Power*, trans. Kaufmann (New York: Random House, 1967), sec. 608.
2 Ibid., sec. 515. There are "pragmatist" passages spotted throughout Nietzsche's works, but the best source is secs. 480–544 of *The Will to Power*. In a forthcoming book on Nietzsche's theory of truth, Maudmarie Clark gives a very convincing and lucid account of his gradual turn to a purer and more consistent version of pragmatism.
3 Cornel West's *The American Evasion of Philosophy: A Genealogy of Pragmatism* (Madison: University of Wisconsin Press, 1989) is very useful for an understanding of Emerson's relation to Dewey. What West calls "the Deweyan project of an Emersonian culture of radical democracy" (p. 128) would have been unintelligible to Nietzsche, who thought that if you were going to be democratic, to go with the herd, you could not be radical.

social philosophy, it will not make much difference to your subsequent conduct whether you read Nietzsche or the classical pragmatists. Further, it is as easy to graft the later, linguistified pragmatists — Quine, Putnam, Davidson — onto Nietzsche as it is to graft them onto Dewey. Indeed, when you switch over from Deweyan talk of experience to Quinean-Davidsonian talk of sentences, it becomes easier to get the point of Nietzsche's famous remark, in "Truth and Lie in an Extra-Moral Sense," that truth is "a mobile army of metaphors."

I interpret this remark along the lines of my discussion of Davidson's treatment of metaphor in Part II of Volume 1. I take its point to be that sentences are the only things that can be true or false, that our repertoire of sentences grows as history goes along, and that this growth is largely a matter of the literalization of novel metaphors. Thinking of truth in this way helps us switch over from a Cartesian-Kantian picture of intellectual progress (as a better and better fit between mind and world) to a Darwinian picture (as an increasing ability to shape the tools needed to help the species survive, multiply, and transform itself).

To see Darwin lying behind both Nietzsche and Dewey (and thus, at one remove, behind what, in Volume 1, I describe as Davidson's nonreductive physicalism) helps one see post-Nietzschean European philosophy and postpositivistic analytic philosophy converging to a single, pragmatist account of inquiry — roughly the account offered in "Inquiry as Recontextualization" in Volume 1. On this account, language is a set of tools rather than a set of representations — tools which, because of what Dewey called "the means–ends continuum", change their users and the products of their use. Abandoning the notion of representation means getting rid of the cluster of problems about realism and antirealism which I discuss in the Introduction to Volume 1.

Sentences as tools, however, is a notion one associates with Wittgenstein rather than with Heidegger and Derrida. Despite the pragmatism of *Being and Time* (brought out by Mark Okrent and discussed in Part I below), and despite the Derrida–Wittgenstein parallels brought out by Henry Staten and the Davidson–Derrida parallels brought out by Samuel Wheeler (discussed in Part II below), Heidegger and Derrida share a tendency to think of language as something *more* than just a set of tools. The later Heidegger persistently, and Derrida occasionally, treat Language as if it were a quasi-agent, a brooding presence, something that stands over and against human beings.

My criticisms of Heidegger in Part I and of Derrida in Part II center around their failure to take a relaxed, naturalistic, Darwinian view of language. I see both men as still, to a certain extent, under the influence of the Diltheyan distinction between *Geist* and *Natur* which I criticized in Part I of Volume 1. So in "Wittgenstein, Heidegger, and the Reification of Language" I criticize the later Heidegger for succumbing to the urge to make language a quasi-divinity. In "Is Derrida a Transcendental Philosopher?" I criticize Rodolphe Gasché's attempt to portray Derrida as offering "conditions of possibility" for the use of language. Both sets of criticisms are protests against letting "Language" become the latest substitute for "God" or "Mind" — something mysterious, incapable of being described in the same terms in which we describe tables, trees, and atoms.

The trouble with making a big deal out of language, meaning, intentionality, the play of signifiers, or *différance* is that one risks losing the advantages gained from appropriating Darwin, Nietzsche, and Dewey. Once one starts reifying language, one begins to see gaps opening between the sorts of things Newton and Darwin describe and the sorts Freud and Derrida describe, instead of seeing convenient divisions within a toolbox — divisions between batches of linguistic tools useful for various different tasks. One begins to be enthralled by phrases like "the unconscious is structured like a language," because one begins to think that languages must have a *distinctive* structure, utterly different from that of brains or computers or galaxies (instead of just agreeing that some of the terms we use to describe language might, indeed, usefully describe other things, such as the unconscious). One takes the irreducibility of the intentional — the irreducibility of descriptions of sentential attitudes such as beliefs and desires to descriptions of the motion of elementary particles — as somehow more philosophically significant than the irreducibility of house descriptions to timber descriptions, or of animal descriptions to cell descriptions.

As I argued in Volume 1, a pragmatist must insist that both redescribability and irreducibility are cheap. It is never very hard to redescribe anything one likes in terms that are irreducible to, indefinable in the terms of, a previous description of that thing. A pragmatist must also insist (with Goodman, Nietzsche, Putnam, and Heidegger) that there is no such thing as the way the thing is in itself, under no description, apart from any use to which human beings might want to put it. The advantage of insisting on these points is that any dualism one comes across, any divide which one finds a philosopher trying to bridge or fill in, can be made to look like a mere difference between two sets of descriptions of the same batch of things.

"Can be made to look like," in this context, does not contrast with "really is." It is not as if there were a procedure for finding out whether one is really dealing with two batches of things or one batch. Thinghood, identity, is itself description-relative. Nor is it the case that language *really* is *just* strings of marks and noises which organisms use as tools for getting what they want. That Nietzschean-Deweyan description of language is no more the real truth about language than Heidegger's description of it as "the house of Being" or Derrida's as "the play of signifying references." Each of these is only one more useful truth about language — one more of what Wittgenstein called "reminders for a particular purpose."

The particular purpose served by the reminder that language can be described in Darwinesque terms is to help us get away from what, in the Introduction to Volume 1, I called "representationalism" and thus from the reality–appearance distinction. Unsurprisingly, I see the best parts of Heidegger and Derrida as the parts which help us to see how things look under nonrepresentationalist, nonlogocentrist descriptions – how they look when one begins to take the relativity of thinghood to choice of description for granted, and so starts asking how to be useful rather than how to be right. I see the worst parts of Heidegger and Derrida as the parts which suggest that they themselves have finally gotten language right, represented it accurately, as it really is. These are the parts that tempted Paul de Man to say things like "literature . . . is the only form of language free from the fallacy of unmediated expression"[4] and Jonathan Culler to insist that a theory of language ought to answer questions about "the essential nature of language."[5] These are also the parts that prompt a whole generation of American literary theorists to talk about "the discovery of the nonreferential character of language," as if Saussure, or Wittgenstein, or Derrida, or somebody, had shown that reference and representation were *illusions* (as opposed to being notions which, in certain contexts, might usefully be dispensed with).

If one treats it simply as a reminder, rather than as a metaphysics, then I think the following is a good way of bringing together the upshot of both the Quine-Putnam-Davidson tradition in analytic philosophy of language and the Heidegger-Derrida tradition of post-Nietzschean thought. Consider sentences as strings of marks and noises emitted by organisms, strings capable of being paired off with the strings we ourselves utter (in the way we call "translating"). Consider beliefs, desires, and intentions – sentential attitudes generally – as entities posited to help predict the behavior of these organisms. Now think of those organisms as gradually evolving as a result of producing longer and more complicated strings, strings which enable them to do things they had been unable to do with the aid of shorter and simpler strings. Now think of *us* as examples of such highly evolved organisms, of our highest hopes and deepest fears as made possible by, among other things, our ability to produce the peculiar strings we do. Then think of the four sentences that precede this one as further examples of such strings. Penultimately, think of the five sentences that precede this one as a sketch for a redesigned house of Being, a new dwelling for us shepherds of Being. Finally, think of the last six sentences as yet another example of the play of signifiers, one more example of the way in which meaning is endlessly alterable through the recontextualization of signs.

Those last seven sentences are an attempt to hold animals, Dasein, and *différance* in a single vision: to show how one can modulate from Darwinian through Heideggerian to Derridean without much strain. They are also an attempt to show that what is important about both traditions, the one that runs up to Davidson and the one that runs up to Derrida, is not what they say but what they do *not* say, what they avoid rather than what they propound. Notice that neither

4 Paul de Man, *Blindness and Insight,* 2nd edition (Minneapolis: University of Minnesota Press, 1983), p. 17.
5 Jonathan Culler, *On Deconstruction: Theory and Criticism After Structuralism* (Ithaca, N.Y.: Cornell University Press, 1982), p. 118.

tradition mentions the knowing subject nor the object of knowledge. Neither talks about a quasi-thing called language which functions as intermediary between subject and object. Neither allows for the formulation of problems about the nature or possibility of representation or intentionality. Neither tries to reduce anything to anything else. Neither, in short, gets us into the particular binds into which the Cartesian-Kantian, subject-object, representationalist tradition got us.

Is that *all* that both traditions are good for? Are all these eminent thinkers *simply* showing us the way out of a dusty fly-bottle, out of a dilapidated house of Being? I am strongly tempted to say, "Sure. What more did you *think* you were going to get out of contemporary philosophy?" But this may sound reductive. So it would be, if I were denying that the works of these people are indefinitely recontextualizable, and so may turn out to be useful in an endless variety of presently unforeseen contexts. But it is not reductive to say: do not underestimate the effects of batting around inside that particular fly-bottle. Do not underestimate what might happen to us, what we might become, as a result of getting out of it. Do not underestimate the utility of merely therapeutic, merely "deconstructive" writing.

Nobody can set any *a priori* limits to what change in philosophical opinion can do, any more than to what change in scientific or political opinion can do. To think that one can know such limits is just as bad as thinking that, now that we have learned that the ontotheological tradition has exhausted its possibilities, we must hasten to reshape everything, make all things new. Change in philosophical outlook is neither intrinsically central nor intrinsically marginal – its results are just as unpredictable as change in any other area of culture. The essays in this and the preceding volume do not try to predict what the effects of the adoption of the pragmatism common to these two traditions might be. My essays should be read as examples of what a group of contemporary Italian philosophers have called "weak thought"[6] – philosophical reflection which does not attempt a radical criticism of contemporary culture, does not attempt to refound or remotivate it, but simply assembles reminders and suggests some interesting possibilities.

6   See Gianni Vattimo and Pier Aldo Rovatti, eds., *Il pensiero debole* (Milan: Feltrinelli, 1983).

PART I

Philosophy as science, as metaphor, and as politics

Beyond scientific philosophy

Three answers have been given, in our century, to the question of how we should conceive of our relation to the Western philosophical tradition, answers which are paralleled by three conceptions of the aim of philosophizing. They are the Husserlian (or 'scientistic') answer, the Heideggerian (or 'poetic') answer and the pragmatist (or 'political') answer. The first answer is the most familiar, and was common to Husserl and his positivist opponents. On this view, philosophy is modeled on science, and is relatively remote from both art and politics.

The Heideggerian and pragmatist answers are reactions to this familiar 'scientistic' answer. Heidegger turns away from the scientist to the poet. The philosophical thinker is the only figure who is on the same level as the poet. The achievements of the great thinkers have as little to do with either mathematical physics or statecraft as do those of the great poets. By contrast, pragmatists such as Dewey turn away from the theoretical scientists to the engineers and the social workers – the people who are trying to make people more comfortable and secure, and to use science and philosophy as tools for that purpose. The Heideggerian thinks that the philosophical tradition needs to be reappropriated by being seen as a series of poetic achievements: the work of Thinkers, people who "have no choice but to find words for what a being *is* in the history of its Being."[1] The pragmatist thinks that the tradition needs to be utilized, as one utilizes a bag of tools. Some of these tools, these 'conceptual instruments' – including some which continue to have undeserved prestige – will turn out no longer to have a use, and can just be tossed out. Others can be refurbished. Sometimes new tools may have to be invented on the spot. Whereas the Heideggerian sees Husserl's "faith in the possibility of philosophy as a task, that is, in the possibility of universal knowledge"[2] as a scientistic, mathematizing misunderstanding of the greatness of the tradition, the pragmatist thinks of it as sentimental nostalgia, an

---

1 Heidegger, *Nietzsche II* (Pfullingen: Neske, 1962), 37. Translated in Heidegger, *Nietzsche*, vol. IV, trans. F. A. Cappuzi (New York: Harper and Row, 1982), 7.
2 Husserl, *The Crisis of European Sciences and Transcendental Phenomenology*, trans. David Carr (Evanston: Northwestern University Press, 1970), 17.

attempt to keep old slogans and strategies alive after they have outlived their practical utility.[3]

Husserl thought the suggestion that we drop the ideal of universal, ahistorical, foundational philosophical knowledge, a suggestion common to pragmatism and to Nietzsche, was the final stage of a disastrous "change which set in at the turn of the past century in the general evaluation of the sciences."[4] On his view, "the total world-view of modern men, in the second half of the nineteenth century, let itself be determined by the positive sciences and be blinded by the 'prosperity' they produced" and this in turn produced "an indifferent turning-away from the questions which are decisive for a genuine humanity."[5]

Husserl thought of traditional rationalism and of empiricist skepticism as two sides of the same 'objectivist' coin.[6] He tried to place both within the framework of his own transcendental phenomenology. Heidegger agreed with Husserl about the relative unimportance of the empiricist-rationalist distinction, and also about the dangers of a technologized, pragmatic culture. But Heidegger thought of pragmatism and transcendental phenomenology as merely two further products of the 'objectivist' tradition. He tried to place both pragmatism's abjuration of 'spirit' and Husserl's attempt to reclaim it within his own account of 'Western metaphysics'. He agreed with Husserl that

an autonomous philosopher with the will to liberate himself from all prejudices . . . must have the insight that all the things he takes for granted *are* prejudices, that all prejudices are obscurities arising out of a sedimentation of the tradition . . . and that this is true even of the great task and idea which is called 'philosophy.'[7]

But Heidegger thought that neither Husserl nor the pragmatists were radical enough in their criticism of their predecessor's self-understanding. He distrusted the pragmatist attempt to replace the Platonic-Cartesian idea of "universal knowledge" with the Baconian dream of maximal control over nature. But he also distrusted Husserl's attempt to see Galilean *techne* as 'founded' in something 'transcendental'. For Heidegger, projects of 'founding' culture – either upon concrete human needs or upon transcendental subjectivity – were simply further expressions of the 'prejudices' which needed to be overcome.

Although Heidegger's assessment of our century's dangers was closer to Husserl's, his actual philosophical doctrines were closer to Dewey's. Like Husserl,

---

3 My failure to discuss Marxism in what follows, and to use it, rather than American pragmatism, to represent the "political" conception of the activity of philosophizing, is due to the conviction that Marxism is an inconsistent mixture of the pragmatism of the 'Theses on Feuerbach' with the scientism common to Marxism and positivism. Kolakowski's history of Marxism shows how every attempt to make Marxism more pragmatic and less scientistic has been firmly suppressed by the institutions which Marxism has created.
4 Ibid., 5.
5 Ibid., 6.
6 See ibid., 83, on Descartes and Hobbes.
7 Ibid., 72.

Heidegger thought that "the European crisis has its roots in a misguided rationalism."[8] But he thought that a demand for foundations was itself a symptom of this misguided rationalism. *Sein und Zeit* is filled with criticisms of the doctrines which Husserl shared with Descartes. The treatment in that book of 'objective scientific knowledge' as a secondary, derivative form of Being-in-the-World, derivative from the use of tools, is of a piece with Dewey's Baconianism.[9] Heidegger's dissolution of philosophical pseudo-problems through letting social practice be taken as a primary and unquestioned datum, rather than an explanandum, exemplifies what Robert Brandom has called "the ontological primacy of the social."[10]

Another way in which Heidegger and pragmatism belong together is in their deep distrust of the visual metaphors which link Husserl to Plato and Descartes. Husserl and Carnap shared the traditional Platonic hope to ascend to a point of view from which the interconnections between everything could be seen. For both, the aim of philosophy is to develop a formal scheme within which every area of culture can be placed. Both are philosophers of what Hilary Putnam has called "the God's-eye view." Heidegger's term for such attempts at a God-like grasp of the realm of possibility, attempts to have a pigeonhole ready for every actual event which might occur, is 'the mathematical'. He defines *ta mathēmata* as "that 'about' things which we really already know."[11] The search for the mathematical, for a formal ahistorical scheme, was, in Heidegger's view, the hidden link between Husserlian phenomenology, Carnapian positivism, and the objectivist tradition.

Dewey's insistence on the subordination of theory to practice, and his claim that the task of philosophy is to break the crust of convention, expresses the same distrust of the contemplative ideal, and of attempts to have an a priori place prepared for everything that may happen. But Heidegger's and Dewey's conceptions of philosophy were nevertheless very different. Their common opposition to foundationalism and to visual metaphors took radically different forms. In what follows I want to discuss these differences under two headings: their different treatments of the relationship between the metaphorical and the literal, and their different attitudes towards the relation between philosophy and politics. By turning from Dewey to a philosopher whose work seems to me to be the best

---

8   Ibid., 290.
9   As Hubert Dreyfus and John Haugeland make clear, Husserl's reaction to this portion of *Sein und Zeit* was the assumption that the *zuhanden* was as much grist for the phenomenological mill as the *vorhanden,* and specifically that a *Zeug* was "something identical, something identifiable again and again," and so something which would exhibit a universal essence. See Dreyfus and Haugeland, 'Husserl and Heidegger: Philosophy's Last Stand' in Michael Murray, ed., *Heidegger and Modern Philosophy* (New Haven: Yale University Press, 1978), 222–238 (especially the quotation from a fragmentary manuscript of Husserl's labeled "das ist gegen Heidegger" at p. 233).
10 Robert Brandom, 'Heidegger's Categories in *Being and Time*', *The Monist,* vol. 66 (1983), 389.
11 Heidegger, *What is a Thing?,* trans. Barton and Deutsch (South Bend: Gateway, 1967), 74.

current statement of a pragmatist position – Donald Davidson – I hope to be able to bring out the relevance of a theory of metaphor to the critique of foundationalism. By focusing on Heidegger's assimilation of philosophy to poetry, I hope to bring out the difference between what I have called the 'political' and the 'poetic' answers to the question of our relationship to the philosophical tradition.

Metaphor as the growing point of language

Let me open up the topic of metaphor by making a curt, dogmatic claim: there are three ways in which a new belief can be added to our previous beliefs, thereby forcing us to reweave the fabric of our beliefs and desires – viz., perception, inference, and metaphor. Perception changes our beliefs by intruding a new belief into the network of previous beliefs. For example, if I open a door and see a friend doing something shocking, I shall have to eliminate certain old beliefs about him, and rethink my desires in regard to him. Inference changes our beliefs by making us see that our previous beliefs commit us to a belief we had not previously held – thereby forcing us to decide whether to alter those previous beliefs, or instead to explore the consequences of the new one. For example, if I realize, through a complicated detective-story train of reasoning, that my present beliefs entail the conclusion that my friend is a murderer, I shall have to either find some way to revise those beliefs, or else rethink my friendship.

Both perception and inference leave our language, our way of dividing up the realm of possibility, unchanged. They alter the truth-values of sentences, but not our repertoire of sentences. To assume that perceptions and inference are the *only* ways in which beliefs ought to be changed is to adopt what Heidegger identified as the 'mathematical' attitude. It is to assume that the language we presently speak is, as it were, all the language there is, all the language we shall ever need. Such a conception of language accords with the idea that the point of philosophy is what Husserl took it to be: to map out all possible logical space, to make explicit our implicit grasp of the realm of possibility. It supports the claim, common to Husserlian phenomenology and to analytic philosophy, that philosophizing consists in clarification, in patiently making explicit what has remained implicit.

By contrast, to think of metaphor as a third source of beliefs, and thus a third motive for reweaving our networks of beliefs and desires, is to think of language, logical space, and the realm of possibility, as open-ended. It is to abandon the idea that the aim of thought is the attainment of a God's-eye view. The philosophical tradition downgraded metaphor because recognizing metaphor as a third source of truth would have endangered the conception of philosophy as a process culminating in vision, *theoria,* contemplation of what is *vorhanden.* Such visual metaphors contrast with the auditory metaphors which Heidegger preferred (e.g., *Ruf des Gewissens, Stimme des Seins*). The latter are better metaphors for metaphor, because they suggest that cognition is not always recognition, that the acquisition of truth is not always a matter of fitting data into a preestablished scheme. A metaphor is, so to speak, a voice from outside logical space, rather than an empirical filling-up of a portion of that space, or a logical-philosophical clarification of the structure of that space. It is a call to change one's language and one's life, rather than a proposal about how to systematize either.

Such a view of metaphor requires that we follow Davidson in rejecting the claim that "a metaphor has, in addition to its literal sense or meaning, another sense or meaning,"[12] Davidson's point is that it is misleading to interpret the expression 'the metaphorical use of language' as implying that lots of 'metaphorical meanings', in addition to lots of 'literal meanings', are already *vorhanden* in our language. On such a view, metaphor cannot expand logical space, for to learn the language is already to have learned all the possibilities for metaphor as well as all the possibilities for fact. A language is not changed by the invention of metaphor, since metaphorical speech is not invention but simply utilization of tools already at hand. By contrast, Davidson's view is that there is a strict distinction between meaning (the property which one attributes to words by noting standard inferential connections between the sentences in which they are used and other sentences) and use, and that "metaphor belongs exclusively to the domain of use."[13]

Davidson says that "most metaphors are false" but it would be better to say that most metaphors take the form of sentences which seem, *prima facie,* obviously false. Later on, however, these same sentences may come to be thought of as literally true. To take a trivial case, mentioned by Davidson, "Once upon a time . . . rivers and bottles did not, as they do now, literally have mouths."[14] To take more important cases, the first time someone said 'Love is the only law' or 'The earth moves around the sun' the general response would have been 'You must be speaking metaphorically'. But, a hundred or a thousand years later, these sentences become candidates for literal truth. Our beliefs were, in the interval, rewoven to make room for these truths – a process which was indistinguishable from the process of changing the meanings of the words used in these sentences in such a way as to make the sentences literally true.

Notice that the claim I have just made – that large-scale change of belief is indistinguishable from large-scale change of the meanings of one's words – follows from the definition of 'meaning' which I inserted parenthetically above. This definition of meaning encapsulates the Quine-Davidson approach to philosophy of language. This approach makes meanings neither Platonic essences nor

---

12 Donald Davidson, *Inquiries into Truth and Interpretation* (Oxford: Clarendon Press, 1984), 246.

13 Ibid., 247. See also p. 259: "No theory of metaphorical meaning or metaphorical truth can help explain how metaphor works. Metaphor works on the same familiar linguistic tracks that the plainest sentences do. . . . What distinguishes metaphor is not meaning but use – in this it is like assertion, hinting, lying, promising, or criticizing."

14 Ibid., 252.

Husserlian noemata but rather patterns of habitual use – what Sellars calls 'linguistic roles'. It thereby makes the Carnapian quest for 'analysis' of meanings seem a misleading 'formal' and 'transcendental' way of describing the project of charting the behavior of a group of language-users. *Mutatis mutandis,* it does the same for the Husserlian project of 'grounding' culture through an inspection of noemata. More generally, it undermines any scientistic philosophical project, any project which depends upon the ahistorical version of what Davidson calls 'the dualism of scheme and content'. This version is the claim that philosophy can make explicit a scheme, a permanent neutral matrix of possibilities, which lies in the background of all our inquiries and practices.

I have argued elsewhere that Davidson's attack on this distinction is the best current expression of the pragmatist attempt to break with the philosophical tradition.[15] Here I want to present this attack as paralleling Heidegger's attack on the tradition's attempt to 'mathematize' the world (in the specifically Heideggerian sense of 'mathematical' mentioned above). To think of metaphorical sentences as the forerunners of new uses of language, uses which may eclipse and erase old uses, is to think of metaphor as on a par with perception and inference, rather than thinking of it as having a merely 'heuristic' or 'ornamental' function.[16] More specifically, it is to think of truth as something which is *not* already within us. Rather, it is something which may only become available to us thanks to an idiosyncratic genius. Such a conception of truth legitimizes auditory metaphors: a voice from far off, a *Ruf des Gewissens,* a word spoken out of the darkness.

Another way of putting this point is to say, with Davidson, that "the irrational" is essential to intellectual progress. In a paper on Freud, Davidson notes that "mental causes which are not reasons" – that is, beliefs and desires which play a role in determining our behavior but which do not fit into the scheme of beliefs and desires which we would claim as ours – are needed not only to explain "deviant" behavior (as Freudian psychoanalytic theory employs them) but also to "explain our salutary efforts, and occasional successes, at self-criticism and self-improvement."[17]

15 See 'Pragmatism, Davidson and Truth' in Volume I.
16 But this is not to say that it has a 'cognitive' function, if this means 'telling' us something, answering a previously formulated question. Its contribution to cognition is rather to give us a sentence which we are tempted to try to 'literalize' by changing the truth-values of, so to speak, various surrounding sentences. Davidson says about attempts to give 'cognitive content' to metaphors: "But in fact there is no limit to what a metaphor calls to our attention, and much of what we are caused to notice is not propositional in character. When we try to say what a metaphor 'means', we soon realize that there is no end to what we want to mention" (*Inquiries,* p. 263). He goes on to analogize metaphors to pictures and to say that "words are the wrong currency to try to exchange for a picture." The attempt to think of metaphors as telling us something is the attempt to think of pictures or metaphors as being interchangeable with a set of sentences, instead of as providing (as do surprising perceptual data) a challenge to (a) redistribute truth-values among familiar sentences, and (b) invent further unfamiliar sentences.
17 Davidson, 'Paradoxes of Irrationality', in Richard Wollheim and James Hopkins, *Philosophical Essays on Freud* (Cambridge: Cambridge University Press, 1982), 305.

Davidson's insistence in that paper on the importance of "mental causality that transcends reason" is focused on self-criticism and self-improvement in individual human beings, but I think his point is even more striking and plausible for the self-criticism of cultures. The "irrational" intrusions of beliefs which "make no sense" (i.e., cannot be justified by exhibiting their coherence with the rest of what we believe) are just those events which intellectual historians look back upon as 'conceptual revolutions'. Or, more precisely, they are the events which spark conceptual revolutions – seemingly crazy suggestions by people who were often without honor in their own countries, suggestions which strike *us* as luminous truths, truths which must always have been latent in 'human reason'. These events are the words spoken by the people Heidegger calls "Thinkers." From a point of view common to Heidegger and Davidson, the philosophical tradition is a long sequence of attempts to exhibit intellectual history as exhibiting a 'hidden rationality', as achieved by *die List der Vernunft,* where 'Vernunft' names something that has been there all the time, rather than simply some recently literalized metaphors.

Heidegger is concerned to deny that there is a topic of ahistorical inquiry called 'human reason' or 'the structure of rationality' or 'the nature of language' which has been the object of philosophical inquiry in all ages. Even in the '20s, before the 'Kehre', Heidegger was contradicting Husserl's criticism of historicism[18] by saying such things as

Construction in philosophy is necessarily destruction, that is to say, a de-constructing (Abbau) of traditional concepts carried out in a historical recursion to the tradition. . . . Because destruction belongs to construction, philosophical cognition is essentially at the same time, in a certain sense, historical cognition.[19]

In the '40s he was to conclude that in *Sein und Zeit* he had not yet been historicist enough to accomplish this destruction. Referring to that early book he says "This destruction, like 'phenomenology' and all hermeneutical-transcendental questions, has not yet been thought in terms of the history of Being."[20] Heidegger identified 'human reason', 'rationality', and 'sound common sense', as these terms are used by philosophers, with the unselfconscious, *uneigentlich,* unquestioning use of an inherited language. Philosophy is not simply the utilization of that tradition – not simply the distribution of truth-values over a range of sentences

---

18   In, e.g., *Philosophie als strenge Wissenschaft.*
19   Heidegger, *The Basic Problems of Phenomenology,* trans. Hofstadter (Bloomington: Indiana University Press, 1982), 23. The original is at *Grundprobleme der Phänomenologie* (Frankfurt: Klostermann, 1975), 31.
20   Aber diese Destruktion ist wie die 'Phänomenologie' und alles hermeneutisch-transzendentale Fragen noch nicht seinsgeschichtlich gedacht: Heidegger, *Nietzsche* II, p. 415. I am grateful to Hubert Dreyfus for calling my attention to this passage. The English translation is from Heidegger, *The End of Philosophy,* ed. and trans. Joan Stambaugh (New York: Harper and Row, 1973), 15.

which are already "present" in the language – because "all essential philosophical questioning is necessarily untimely. . . . Philosophy is essentially untimely because it is one of those few things that can never find an immediate echo in the present."[21]

We may identify what finds no echo in the present with the sort of metaphor which is *prima facie* a pointless falsehood, but which nevertheless turns out to be what Heidegger calls "a word of Being," one in which "the call of Being" is heard. Consider, in the light of this identification, two pregnant sentences in which Heidegger describes "the task of philosophy":

. . . the ultimate business of philosophy is to preserve the *force of the most elemental words* in which Dasein expresses itself, and to keep the common understanding from leveling them off to that unintelligibility which functions in the end as a source of pseudo-problems.[22]

It is the authentic function of philosophy to challenge historical being-there (Dasein) and hence, in the last analysis, Being (Sein) pure and simple.[23]

These sentences express what I am calling Heidegger's 'poetic' answer to the question of our relation to the tradition. On his account the aim of philosophical thought is to free us from the language we presently use by reminding us that this language is not that of 'human reason' but is the creation of the thinkers of our historical past. These thinkers are the poets of Being, the transcribers of "Being's poem – man."[24] To remind us of these thinkers, and to permit us to feel the force of their metaphors in the days before these had been leveled down into literal truths, before these novel uses of words were changed into familiar meanings of words, is the *only* aim which philosophy can have at the present time – not to facilitate but only to make more difficult, not to reweave our fabric of belief and desires but only to remind us of its historical contingency. Heidegger thinks that our time cannot profit from redistributing truth-values among the sentences currently in our repertoire. But he holds out little hope of a new prophetic age, one in which new words will be spoken, words which will enlarge this repertoire in unexpected ways. The most he will say is that such hopes will not be fulfilled without the preparatory work of restoring force to "the most elementary words" in which Dasein has expressed itself in the past. Our relation to the tradition must

---

21 Heidegger, *Einführung in die Metaphysik* (Tübingen: Niemeyer, 1953), 6. The English translation is at *Introduction to Metaphysics,* trans. Manheim (New Haven: Yale University Press, 1959), 8.

22 . . . ist es am Ende das Geschäft der Philosophie, die *Kraft der elementarsten Worte*, in denen sich das Dasein ausspricht, davor zu bewahren, dass sie durch den gemeinen Verstand zur Unverständlichkeit nivelliert werden, die ihrerseits als Quelle für Scheinprobleme fungiert. Heidegger, *Sein und Zeit* (Tübingen: Niemeyer, 1979), 220. English translation at *Being and Time,* trans. John Macquarrie and Edward Robinson (New York: Harper and Row, 1962), 262.

23 Heidegger, *Einführung in die Metaphysik*, p. 9 (*Introduction to Metaphysics,* p. 11).

24 From Heidegger's prose-poem *Aus der Erfahrung des Denkens*. Translated in Heidegger, *Poetry, Language, Thought,* trans. Hofstader (New York: Harper and Row, 1971), 4: "We are too late for the gods and too early for Being. Being's poem, just begun, is man."

be a rehearing of what can no longer be heard, rather than a speaking of what has not yet been spoken.

Poetry and politics

To see the difference between Heidegger's 'poetic' view of our relation to the tradition and the 'political' view which I wish to attribute to American pragmatism, consider the distinction between 'pseudo-problems' and 'real' problems which Heidegger shares with Carnap. On the pragmatist view, as on Carnap's, a pseudo-problem is one which there is no point in discussing because, as William James put it, it turns upon a difference which "*makes* no difference." It is a "merely verbal problem" — that is, one whose resolution would leave the rest of our beliefs unchanged. This is close to Heidegger's own meaning, as is shown by the fact that some of his examples of pseudo-problems ("other minds," "the external world") are the same as Carnap's.

But there is a crucial difference. Whereas Carnap and the pragmatists think of traditional philosophy as pseudo-science, Heidegger thinks of it as hackneyed poetry — poetry so banal as to be unconscious self-parody. That is, he thinks of the pseudo-problems of the philosophical tradition as pointless reenactments of cliché situations. His objection to them is not that, unlike the real (technologically-oriented) problems solved by scientists, considering them will do us no practical good. Rather, it is that they debase a genre — the genre called 'philosophy'. He is complaining that this genre, which should be the one in which everything is made more difficult, has become an easy game, one which any fool can play. He despises the suggestion, found in scientistic philosophers like Husserl and Carnap, that philosophers might cooperate in the way that engineers do, that they should divide up the work that needs to be done into bite-sized chunks and assign one to each member of a team for 'linguistic analysis' or 'phenomenological description'.

The pragmatist would grant Heidegger's point that the great thinkers are the most idiosyncratic. They are the people like Hegel or Wittgenstein whose metaphors come out of nowhere, lightning bolts which blaze new trails. But whereas Heidegger thinks that the task of exploring these newly suggested paths of thought is banausic, something which can be left to hacks, the pragmatist thinks that such exploration is the pay-off from the philosopher's work. He thinks of the thinker as serving the community, and of his thinking as futile unless it is followed up by a reweaving of the community's web of belief. That reweaving will assimilate, by gradually literalizing, the new metaphors which the thinker has provided. The proper honor to pay to new, vibrantly alive metaphors, is to help them become dead metaphors as quickly as possible, to rapidly reduce them to the status of tools of social progress. The glory of the philosopher's thought is not that it initially makes everything more difficult (though that is, of course, true), but that in the end it makes things easier for everybody.

Because the pragmatist rejects scientism just as Heidegger does, he or she rejects the scientistic idea that some new metaphor, some new philosophical idea, might reveal the permanent neutral matrix of inquiry, a matrix which now simply needs to be filled in by systematic teamwork. The reweaving of the community's fabric of belief is not to be done systematically; it is not a research program, not a matter of filling in what Heidegger calls a *Grundriss*.[25] It is a matter of scratching where it itches, and only where it itches. But whereas Heidegger thinks of this scratching, this liberating of culture from obsolete vocabularies through the work of weaving new metaphors into our communal web of beliefs and desires, as a process of banalization, the pragmatist thinks of it as the only suitable tribute to render the great philosopher. Without this utilization of his work, the great philosopher would have no social role to play, no political function. The pragmatist and Heidegger can agree that the poet and the thinker (in Heidegger's special 'elitist' senses of these terms) are the unacknowledged legislators of the social world. But whereas Heidegger thinks of the social world as existing for the sake of the poet and the thinker, the pragmatist thinks of it the other way round. For Dewey as for Hegel, the point of individual human greatness is its contribution to social freedom, where this is conceived of in the terms we inherit from the French Revolution.

So the crucial difference between the Heideggerian and the pragmatist attitude towards the philosophical tradition stems from a difference in attitude towards recent political history. The basic motive of pragmatism, like that of Hegelianism, was, I have argued elsewhere, a continuation of the Romantic reaction to the Enlightenment's sanctification of natural science.[26] Once scientistic rhetoric (which persists in both Hegel and Dewey, and obscures their more basic Romanticism) is cleared away, both Hegelianism and pragmatism can be seen as attempts to clear the ground for the kind of society which the French Revolution hoped to build: one in which every human potentiality is given a fair chance. In the terms I have been using in this paper, this aspiration amounts to the hope that every new metaphor will have its chance for self-sacrifice, a chance to become a dead metaphor by having been literalized into the language. More specifically, it is the hope that what Dewey calls "the crust of convention" will be as superficial as possible, that the social glue which holds society together – the language in which we state our shared beliefs and hopes – will be as flexible as possible.

One can only have such a hope if one thinks that, despite the fears of Husserl, Julien Benda, and contemporary communitarian critics of political liberalism, a

---

25 See Heidegger, 'Die Zeit des Weltbildes' in *Holzwege*, p. 71.
26 This claim may, in the light of Dewey's obsessive 'scientistic' rhetoric, seem paradoxical. I have tried to defend it in 'Nineteenth Century Idealism and Twentieth Century Textualism', in my *Consequences of Pragmatism* (Minneapolis: University of Minnesota Press, 1982); in 'Pragmatism Without Method', in Volume I; and in 'Reply to Sleeper and Edel', *Transactions of the C. S. Peirce Society*, vol. 21 (1985).

democratic society can get along without the sort of reassurance provided by the thought that it has 'adequate philosophical foundations' or that it is 'grounded' in 'human reason'. On this view, the most appropriate foundation for a liberal democracy is a conviction by its citizens that things will go better for everybody if every new metaphor is given a hearing, if no belief or desire is held so sacred that a metaphor which endangers it is automatically rejected. Such a conviction amounts to the rejection of the claim that we, the democratic societies of the West, know what we want in advance – that we have more than a tentative and revisable *Grundriss* for our social projects. One task of the intellectuals in these societies will be to help their fellow citizens live with the thought that we do not yet have an adequate language, and to wean them from the idea that there is something out there to be 'adequate' to. This amounts to suggesting that we try to eschew scientistic pronunciamentos which take for granted that we now have a secure grasp on the nature of society, or of the good. It means admitting that the terms in which we state our communal convictions and hopes are doomed to obsolescence, that we shall *always* need new metaphors, new logical spaces, new jargons, that there will never be a final resting-place for thought, nor a social philosophy which is a *strenge Wissenschaft*.

It will be apparent that, in formulating the pragmatist view in this way, I am trying to turn such Heideggerian notions as 'clearing', 'opening', 'authenticity' and 'historical being-there' to un-Heideggerian purposes. I want to yoke them to political movements which Heidegger himself distrusted. For him, the political life of both the liberal democracies and the totalitarian states was a piece with that 'technological frenzy' which seemed to him the essence of the modern age. The difference between the two did not really matter. By contrast, I want to suggest that we see the democracy-versus-totalitarianism issue as as basic as an intellectual issue can get. We need to eschew the idea, common to Heidegger and Adorno as well as to many contemporary *Marxisant* writers, that there is a phenomenon called "modernity" which encompasses both bourgeois democracy and totalitarianism, and that one can achieve a philosophical grasp of this phenomenon in which the distinction between these two forms of social life is *aufgehoben.*

One way of putting this point is that although Heidegger was only accidentally a Nazi,[27] Dewey was essentially a social democrat. His thought has no point when

27 I would grant that Heidegger was, from early on, suspicious of democracy and of the 'disenchanted' world which Weber described. His thought was, indeed, essentially anti-democratic. But lots of Germans who were dubious about democracy and modernity did not become Nazis. Heidegger did because he was both more of a ruthless opportunist and more of a political ignoramus than most of the German intellectuals who shared his doubts. Although Heidegger's philosophy seems to me not to have specifically *totalitarian* implications, it does take for granted that attempts to feed the hungry, shorten the working day, etc., just do not have much to do with philosophy. For Heidegger, Christianity is merely a certain decadent form of Platonic metaphysics; the change from pagan to Christian moral consciousness goes unnoticed. The 'social gospel' side of Christianity which meant most to Tillich (a social democratic thinker who was nevertheless able to appropriate a lot of Heideggerian ideas and jargon) meant nothing to Heidegger.

detached from social democratic politics.[28] His pragmatism is an attempt to help achieve the greatest happiness of the greatest number by facilitating the replacement of language, customs, and institutions which impede that happiness. Heidegger dismissed this attempt as one which we can no longer take seriously. He thinks that Nietzsche helped us see that

Metaphysics is history's open space, wherein it becomes a destining that the suprasensory world, the Ideas, God, the moral law, the authority of reason, progress, the happiness of the greatest number, culture, civilization, suffer the loss of their constructive force and become void.[29]

But for Dewey, "progress, the happiness of the greatest number, culture, civilization" do not belong on the same list as "the suprasensory world, the Ideas, God, the moral law, the authority of reason." The latter are dead metaphors which pragmatists can no longer find uses for. The former still have a point. The pragmatist does not claim to have an argument against the latter items and for the former items. He is not scientistic enough to think that there is some neutral philosophical standpoint which would supply premises for such an argument. He simply takes his stand within the democratic community and asks what an understanding of the thinkers of the past and of the present can do for such a community.

Heidegger thinks that a non-reductive, non-anachronistic hearing of the word of these thinkers might put us in a position to appreciate where we now are (where, as Heidegger would say, Being now is). The pragmatist agrees, but hears them differently. He hears them as the young Hegel did – as urging us in the direction of greater human freedom, rather than in the direction of technological frenzy, of an age in which "human creativity finally passes over into business enterprise."[30] He agrees with both Husserl and Heidegger (and with Horkheimer and Adorno) that the age of scientific technology *may* turn out to be the age in which openness and freedom are rationalized out of existence. But his reply is that it *might* turn out to be the age in which the democratic community becomes the mistress, rather than the servant, of technical rationality.

---

28 For an account of Dewey as a contributor to social democratic thought, see James T. Kloppenberg, *Uncertain Victory: Social Democracy and Progressivism in European and American Thought, 1870–1920* (New York: Oxford University Press, 1986). For some acute comments on the relation between my own version of pragmatism and political liberalism, see Christopher Norris, *Contest of Faculties: Philosophy and Theory after Deconstruction* (London: Methuen, 1985), chapter 6 ('Philosophy as a Kind of Narrative: Rorty on Post-modern Liberal Culture').

29 Die Metaphysik ist der Geschichtsraum, worin zum Geschick wird, dass die uebersinnliche Welt, die Ideen, Gott, das Sittengesetz, die Vernunftautorität, der Fortschritt, das Glück der Meisten, die Kultur, die Zivilisation ihre bauende Kraft einbüssen und nichtig werden: Heidegger, *Holzwege* (Frankfurt: Klostermann, 1972), 204, trans. W. Lovitt at Heidegger, *The Question Concerning Technology and Other Essays* (New York: Harper and Row, 1977), 65.

30 Heidegger, *Holzwege*, p. 203 (*The Question Concerning Technology . . .* , p. 64).

The present situation

In what precedes I have sketched what I take to be the central metaphilosophical disagreements of recent times. On my account, there are two basic lines of division: one between the scientism common to Husserl and positivism, and the other between two reactions to this scientism. The first reaction – Heidegger's – is dictated by a tacit and unarguable rejection of the project of the French Revolution, and of the idea that everything, including philosophy, is an instrument for the achievement of the greatest happiness of the greatest number. The second – Dewey's – is dictated by an equally tacit and unarguable acceptance of that project and that idea.

By way of a conclusion, I shall try to bring these distinctions to bear on the contemporary situation of the philosophical profession, of philosophy as an institution. One can look at this situation from the inside, and concentrate on the relations, within the profession, of competing philosophical schools. Or one can look at it from the outside, at the relations between the profession and the rest of culture.

Taking the inside view first, it is clear that there are really two institutions rather than one. Analytic philosophy has pretty well closed itself off from contact with non-analytic philosophy, and lives in its own world. The scientistic approach to philosophy which Husserl shared with Carnap lives on, forming a tacit presupposition of the work of analytic philosophers. Even though analytic philosophy now describes itself as post-positivistic, the idea that philosophy 'analyzes' or 'describes' some ahistorical formal 'structures' – an idea common to Husserl, Russell, Carnap, and Ryle – persists. However, there is little explicit metaphilosophical defense or development of this claim. Analytic philosophers are not much interested in either defining or defending the presuppositions of their work. Indeed, the gap between 'analytic' and 'non-analytic' philosophy nowadays coincides pretty closely with the division between philosophers who are not interested in historico-metaphilosophical reflections on their own activity and philosophers who are.

This difference in interests parallels a difference in reading habits, a difference in philosophical canons. If the preeminent figures in one's canon include Berkeley, Hume, Mill, and Frege, one will probably not be much interested in metaphilosophy. If they include Hegel, Nietzsche, and Heidegger, one probably will – not metaphilosophy in the form of methodology, the form it took in Husserl and in Russell, but rather in the form of an historical narrative which places the works of the philosophers within the historical development of the culture.

Most analytic philosophers simply take for granted that such figures as Hume and Frege have isolated central, deep problems – problems which are definatory of the discipline. They see no more need to construct or study historical narratives

than students of physics do to study the history of physics. But some less complacent members of this school (e.g., Cora Diamond, Hilary Putnam, Thomas
Nagel, Stanley Cavell) have a more ambivalent and nuanced relation to the
analytic canon, and a less distant relation to historical narrative. Nagel, for
example, suggests that the familiar textbook 'problems of philosophy' – the problems of which he himself proceeds to treat – are characteristic of 'the childhood of
the intellect'. But he thinks that "a culture that tries to skip it [this stage of
childhood] will never grow up."[31] He cautions against "deflationary metaphilosophical theories like positivism and pragmatism, which offer to raise us above
the old battles."[32] On Nagel's view "Philosophy cannot take refuge in reduced
ambitions. It is after eternal and nonlocal truth, even though we know that is not
what we are going to get."[33]

On the 'non-analytic' side of the divide, by contrast, the realization that we are
not going to get this sort of truth is a reason for dropping old ambitions. For the
tacit presupposition which unites non-analytic philosophers – those philosophers
who reject metaphilosophical scientism – is that Nagel is wrong when he says
that

> philosophy is not like a particular language. Its sources are preverbal and often precultural,
> and one of its most difficult tasks is to express unformed but intuitively felt problems in
> language without losing them.[34]

The mark of intellectual immaturity is, on this alternative account, precisely an
ahistorical account of philosophy such as Nagel's, an account whose grip has only
been broken in the last two hundred years. On the alternative account, philosophy
is very much like a 'particular language' and the idea that a particular philosophical
canon has isolated problems which are 'often precultural' is just the latest version of
the empiricist 'Myth of the Given'. So these philosophers try to place the analysts'
canon, and their list of problems, in history, rather than seeing both as in touch
with something ahistorical, something natural to the species. The reason why
Hegel, Nietzsche, and Heidegger loom so large in the alternative canon is that
these philosophers specialize in narratives which 'place' rival canons.

There is little common ground between these two sets of metaphilosophical
presuppositions, and therefore little possibility of debate between their propo-
nents. The result is that the philosophical profession is divided into two institutionalized traditions which have little contact. Analytic philosophy, in so far as it
takes notice of its rival, views it as an aestheticized and historicized form of
idealism.[35] The 'continental' tradition, by contrast, views the 'analytic' tradition

---

31   Thomas Nagel, *The View from Nowhere* (New York: Oxford University Press, 1986), 12.
32   Ibid., 11.
33   Ibid., 10.
34   Ibid., 11.
35   Nagel, for example, sees those who adopt alternative canons as being less closely in touch with
     reality than those who adopt his own – as 'idealist', in the sense of believing that "what there is

as escaping from history into a dogmatic and outworn realism, but it too takes little notice of the opposition.

Because neither side has much use for the notion that philosophy has a distinctive method, neither is about to offer large metaphilosophical self-descriptions of the sort in which Russell and Husserl indulged. Yet the crucial difference between them is, I think, still caught by the formula which I have used to catch the difference between Husserl on the one hand and Heidegger and Dewey on the other: they differ on the question of whether philosophy has a prelinguistic subject-matter, and thus on the question of whether there is an ahistorical reality to which a given philosophical vocabulary may or may not be adequate. The analytic tradition regards metaphor as a distraction from that reality, whereas the non-analytic tradition regards metaphor as the way of escaping from the illusion that there is such a reality. My hunch is that these traditions will persist side-by-side indefinitely. I cannot see any possibility of compromise, and I suspect that the most likely scenario is an increasing indifference of each school to the existence of the other. In time it may seem merely a quaint historical accident that both institutions bear the same name.[36]

What, then, of the place of the philosophical profession in the culture as a whole? For philosophers who think of themselves as quasi-scientists, this is not an important question. Analytic philosophy has little influence on other academic disciplines, and little interest either for practitioners of those disciplines or for the intellectuals. But analytic philosophers are not distressed by this fact. It is natural, given their scientistic metaphilosophy, that analytic philosophers are content to solve philosophical problems without worrying about the source of those problems or the consequences of their solution.[37]

and how things are cannot go beyond what we could in principle think about" (ibid., 9). They suffer from "an insufficiently robust sense of reality and of its independence of any particular form of human understanding" (ibid., 5). Nagel's attitude toward pragmatism parallels the attitude which Heidegger adopts toward what he calls "humanism" in the 'Letter on Humanism'.

36 Occasionally a university sets up an 'alternative' philosophy department, bowing to the fact that two noncommunicating disciplines are currently going by the same name. This usually creates trouble, because the word 'philosophy' is still an honorific, and both departments resent its use by the other. Eventually some genius will resolve this entirely verbal issue by hitting upon just the right names for the two sorts of philosophy departments, names which will permit peaceful coexistence of the sort which now obtains between classics departments and departments of modern literature. (It is sometimes forgotten that classicists once objected furiously to the creation of departments of the latter sort. On their view, putting recent novels on a syllabus for a degree was a degradation of the university.)

37 There are exceptions. Analytic philosophers who specialize in 'applied ethics' have sometimes claimed that there are special skills associated with analytic philosophy which are useful in resolving policy dilemmas (on such matters as abortion, job discrimination, disarmament, and the like). But it is very hard to isolate any skills employed by philosophy professors who take up such issues which were not routinely employed by people (philosophers like J. S. Mill and non-philosophers like Macaulay) who took up similar issues in the last century, and are not being routinely employed by non-philosophers who write on such topics today. The notion of 'analytic skills' is, I think, a relic of the earlier idea of a special 'method of philosophical analysis'. Analytic

By contrast, non-analytic philosophers typically dislike the thought that philosophy is (or is only) an academic discipline, merely one more *Wissenschaft*. They would like their work to be continuous either with literature on the one hand or with politics on the other, or both. Insofar as they succeed in making their work continuous with literature, they cease to belong to a separate institution: they are simply writers who happen to be familiar with a certain literary tradition (a tradition that starts with Plato and runs up through Hegel to the present). Thus there is little point in drawing institutional lines between the study of Sartre's treatises, of his critical essays, and of his stories. There is equally little point in worrying whether Nietzsche counts as a figure in the history of German literature (as he used to, before Heidegger helped him to a place in the philosophical canon) or in the history of philosophy. Anybody interested in Derrida's treatment of Socrates in *La Carte Postale* is likely also to be interested in Valéry's treatment of him in *Eupalinos* and Nietzsche's in *The Birth of Tragedy,* and is unlikely to know or care that only one among these three great writers earned his bread as a philosophy professor.

When it comes to attempts to make non-analytic philosophy continuous with politics, however, things become more complex and problematic. For non-analytic philosophy is, with some exceptions, dominated by a Heideggerian vision of the modern world rather than a Deweyan one, and by despair over the condition of the world rather than by social hope. Because the typical member of this tradition is obsessed with the idea of 'radical criticism', when he or she turns to politics it is rarely in a reformist, pragmatic spirit, but rather in a mood either of deep pessimism or of revolutionary fury. Except for a few writers such as Habermas, 'continental' philosophers see no relation between social democratic politics and philosophizing.[38] So the only sort of politics with which this tradition is continuous is not the actual political discourse of the surviving democratic nations, but a kind of pseudo-politics reminiscent of Marxist study-groups of the thirties — a sort of continual self-correction of theory, with no conceivable relation to practice.[39]

As Deweyan social democrats, philosophers can be politically useful in the same way as can poets, playwrights, economists, and engineers. Members of these various professions can serve reformist social democratic politics by providing

philosophers have often written very well indeed on current policy dilemmas, but it is not easy to see their work as the product of a distinctive professional ability.

38 Habermas is (despite what are, to my mind, unfortunate residues of scientism in his thought) the contemporary philosopher who most resembles Dewey — not only in doctrine but in his attitude toward his society, and in the role which he has played in the day-to-day, nitty-gritty political debates of his time. Like Dewey, Habermas's thought is dominated by the question 'What sort of philosophical vocabulary and approach would serve human freedom best?" and by the conviction that the modern industrialized technological world is not hopeless, but, on the contrary, capable of continual self-improvement.

39 This is particularly evident in the U.S. and Britain, where there is often thought to be some natural affinity between neo-Heideggerian philosophizing and leftist politics.

piecemeal nudges and cautions in respect to particular projects at particular times. But this sort of retail political utility is not the wholesale sort which Marxists, post-Marxist radicals, and neo-conservatives would like philosophers to have. They see political theory and philosophy as foundational because they see it as penetrating to a reality behind contemporary appearances. By contrast, the Deweyan sees the relevant 'reality' – human suffering and oppression – as already having been made clearly visible in the course of the last two centuries' attempt to realize the ideals of the French Revolution. The Deweyan is ruefully willing to admit that there are always going to be more varieties of suffering and oppression to be exposed (e.g., those endured by women as a class). He sees philosophy's role in exposing them as continuous with that of literature and of the social sciences. But he thinks contemporary democratic societies are *already* organized around the need for continual exposure of suffering and injustice, and that no 'radical critique' is required, but just attention to detail. So he thinks of the philosopher not as exposing the false or corrupt foundations of this society but as playing off the good and the bad features of this society against each other.

To my mind, the persistence on the left of this notion of 'radical critique' is an unfortunate residue of the scientistic conception of philosophy. Neither the idea of penetrating to a reality behind the appearances, nor that of theoretical foundations for politics, coheres with the conception of language and inquiry which, I have been arguing, is common to Heidegger and to Dewey. For both ideas presuppose that someday we shall penetrate to the true, natural, ahistorical matrix of all possible language and knowledge. Marx, for all his insistence on the priority of praxis, clung to both ideas, and they became dominant within Marxism after Lenin and Stalin turned Marxism into a state religion. But there is no reason why either should be adopted by those who are not obliged to practice this religion.

The moral I wish to draw from the story I have been telling is that we should carry through on the rejection of metaphilosophical scientism. That is, we should let the debate between those who see contemporary democratic societies as hopeless, and those who see them as our only hope, be conducted in terms of the actual problems now being faced by those societies. If I am right in thinking that the difference between Heidegger's and Dewey's ways of rejecting scientism is political rather than methodological or metaphysical, then it would be well for us to debate political topics explicitly, rather than using Aesopian philosophical language.

If we did, then I think that we would realize how little theoretical reflection is likely to help us with our current problems. For once we have criticized all the self-deceptive sophistry, and exposed all the 'false consciousness', the result of our efforts is to find ourselves just where our grandfathers suspected we were: in the midst of a struggle for power between those who currently possess it (in our day: the oilmen of Texas or Qatar or Mexico, the *nomenklatura* of Moscow or Bucharest, the generals of Indonesia or Chile) and those who are starving or terrorized because they lack it. Neither twentieth-century Marxism, nor analytical philosophy, nor post-Nietzschean 'continental' philosophy has done anything to clarify this struggle. We have not developed any conceptual instruments with which to operate politically that are superior to those available at the turn of the century to Dewey or Weber.

The vocabulary of social democratic politics – the vocabulary which Dewey and Weber helped cobble together – probably does not require further sophistication by philosophers (though economists and sociologists and historians have done some useful updating). There are no facts about economic oppression or class struggle, or modern technology, which that vocabulary cannot describe and a more 'radical' metaphoric can. The horrors peculiar to the end of our century – imminent nuclear holocaust, the permanent drug-riddled black underclass in the U.S., the impossibility of feeding countries like Haiti and Chad except by massive charity which the rich nations are too selfish to provide, the unbreakable grip of the rich or the military on the governments of most of the Third World, the unbreakable grip of the KGB on the Russian people and of the Soviet army on a third of Europe – are no better describable with the help of more recent philosophical vocabulary than with the vocabulary used by our grandfathers. Nobody has come up with any proposal for ending any of these horrors which draws on new conceptual resources. Our political imagination has not been enlarged by the philosophy of our century. This is not because of the irrelevance or cowardice or irresponsibility of philosophy professors, but because of the sheer recalcitrance of the situation into which the human race has stumbled.[40]

Dewey was lucky. His generation may have been the last which could feel confident of a future in which the race would work out its destiny without needing the religious and scientistic myths which had comforted it in the past – a future in which human freedom was entrusted to as yet undreamt-of metaphors, vocabularies still unborn. As the century has darkened, we find it less and less possible to imagine getting out of our present trap and into such a future. But Dewey was also right. If we ever have the courage to drop the scientistic model of philosophy without falling back into a desire for holiness (as Heidegger did), then, no matter how dark the time, we shall no longer turn to the philosophers for rescue as our ancestors turned to the priests. We shall turn instead to the poets and the engineers, the people who produce startling new projects for achieving the greatest happiness of the greatest number.

40 This paragraph was, obviously, written before Gorbachev. Little did I (or anyone else) dream that a faceless protégé of Andropov's would become the Abraham Lincoln of Central and Eastern Europe.

Heidegger, contingency, and pragmatism

One of the most intriguing features of Heidegger's later thought is his claim that if you begin with Plato's motives and assumptions you will end up with some form of pragmatism. I think that this claim is, when suitably interpreted, right. But, unlike Heidegger, I think pragmatism is a *good* place to end up. In this paper, I shall try to say how far a pragmatist can play along with Heidegger, and then try to locate the point at which he or she must break off.

A suitable interpretation of Heidegger's claim requires defining Platonism as the claim that the point of inquiry is to get in touch with something like Being, or the Good, or Truth, or Reality — something large and powerful which we have a duty to apprehend correctly. By contrast, pragmatism must be defined as the claim that the function of inquiry is, in Bacon's words, to "relieve and benefit the condition of man" — to make us happier by enabling us to cope more successfully with the physical environment and with each other. Heidegger is arguing that if you start with Plato's account of inquiry you will eventually wind up with Bacon's.

The story Heidegger tells about the transition from the one set of goals to the other is summarized in his "Sketches for a History of Being as Metaphysics" in the second volume of his *Nietzsche*.[1] Here is one such sketch, entitled "Being" (*Das Sein*):

Alētheia (apeiron, logos, hen — arche).
Revealing as the order at the start.
Physis, emergence (going back to itself).
Idea, perceivability (*agathon*), causality.
Energeia, workness, assembly, *en-echeia to telos*.
Hypokeimenon, lie present (from *ousia, ergon*).
(presence — stability — constancy — *aei*).
Hyparchein, presencing which rules from what is already present.
Subiectum.
Actualitas: beings — the real — reality
    Creator — ens creatum
    causa prima (ens a se).

1 Martin Heidegger, "Entwürfe zur Geschichte des Seins als Metaphysik," *Nietzsche* II (Pfullingen: Neske, 1961), pp. 455ff. This and the preceding section, "Die Metaphysik als Geschichte des Seins," have been translated by Joan Stambaugh and appear in Heidegger, *The End of Philosophy* (New York: Harper and Row, 1973).

Certitudo – res cogitans.
Vis – *monas (perceptio – appetitus), exigentia essentiae.*
Objectivity.
Freedom
　　will-representation
　　practical reason.
will – as absolute knowledge: Hegel.
As will of love: Schelling.
Will to power: eternal recurrence: Nietzsche.
Action and Organization – pragmatism.
The will to will.
Machination (Enfaming).[2]

This potted history of Western philosophy stretches from the Greek conviction that the point of inquiry is apprehension of *archai,* principles, things greater and more powerful than everyday human existence, to the American conviction that its point is technological contrivance, getting things under control. Heidegger sees this chronological list of abbreviations for philosophers' "understandings of Being" as a downward escalator. Once you have gotten on you cannot get off until you have reached the bottom. If you start off with Plato you will wind up with Nietzsche and, worse yet, Dewey.

Heidegger claims that to understand what is going on here at the bottom of the escalator, in the twentieth century, the age in which philosophy has exhausted its possibilities, "we must free ourselves from the technical interpretation of think-

---

2　*The End of Philosophy,* pp. 65–66 (*Nietzsche* II, pp. 470–471). Stambaugh leaves words untranslated because, as I shall be saying later, Heidegger insists that the sounds of words matter, not just what they have in common with their translations into other languages. (In particular, he thinks that Cicero's translation into Latin of Plato's and Aristotle's Greek was a decisive turn in Western thought.) Nevertheless, I shall list the most common English translations of the Greek and Latin terms here. *Alētheia*-truth; *apeiron*-infinite; *logos*-word, reason, thought; *hen*-one; *arche*-principle; *physis*-nature (derived from *phyein,* to grow, to emerge); *idea*-idea in the Platonic sense of "Idea" or "Form," deriving from *idein* to see, to perceive; *agathon*-the good; *energeia*-actuality (as opposed to potentiality); *en-echeia to telos*-having the end within it, having achieved its purpose (*entelechia* is a word sometimes used synonymously with *energeia* by Aristotle; it too is frequently translated as "actuality"); *hypokeimenon*-substrate (a term applied to matter when Aristotle is discussing metaphysics, and to the subject of predication when he is discussing logic); *ousia*-substance (but also a participle of the verb *einai,* "to be"); *ergon*-work, activity; *aei*-eternity; *hyparchein*-to possess, or (in Aristotle's logic) to have as a property; *subiectum*-Latin translation of, and etymologically equivalent to, *hypokeimenon,* "substrate" – but also, after Descartes, a word for "subject" in both senses – the subject of a sentence and the ego as subject of experience; *actualitas*-Latin translation of *energeia,* "actuality"; *creator*-creator; *ens creatum*-created being; *causa prima*-first cause; *ens a se*-being capable of existing by itself (i.e., God); *certitudo*-certitude; *res cogitans*-thinking thing (Descartes's term for the mind); *vis*-force, power; *monas*-monad (Leibniz's term for the ultimate components of the universe, nonspatiotemporal loci of force, of perception [*perceptio*], of appetite [*appetitus*], and of a need to exist in order to express themselves [*exigentia essentiae*]). Heidegger offers, in one place or another in his writings, alternative translations of each of these terms, designed to restore their force by stripping them of their familiar connotations.

ing." The beginnings of that interpretation, he says, "reach back to Plato and Aristotle."[3] As I read him, his point here is the same as Dewey's: that Plato and Aristotle built what Dewey called "the quest for certainty" into our sense of what thinking is for. They taught us that unless we can make the object of our inquiry *evident* — get it clear and distinct, directly present to the eye of the mind, and get agreement about it from all those qualified to discuss it — we are falling short of our goal.

As Heidegger says, "All metaphysics, including its opponent, positivism, speaks the language of Plato."[4] That is, ever since Plato we have been asking ourselves the question: what must we and the universe be like if we are going to get the sort of certainty, clarity, and evidence Plato told us we ought to have? Each stage in the history of metaphysics — and in particular the Cartesian turn toward subjectivity, from exterior to interior objects of inquiry[5] — has been an attempt to redescribe things so that this certainty might become possible. But, after many fits and starts, it has turned out that the only thing we can be certain about is what we want. The only things that are really evident to us are our own desires.

This means that the only way we can press on with Plato's enterprise is to become pragmatists — to identify the meaning of life with getting what we want, with imposing our will. The only cosmology we can affirm with the certainty Plato recommended is our own (communal or individual) world picture, our own way of setting things up for manipulation, the way dictated by our desires. As Heidegger says:

world picture, when understood essentially, does not mean a picture of the world but the world conceived and grasped as picture. What is, in its entirety, is now taken in such a way

3 Heidegger, "Letter on Humanism," in *Basic Writings* (hereafter abbreviated as *BW*), ed. David Krell (New York: Harper and Row, 1977), p. 194. The original is at Heidegger, *Wegmarken* (hereafter *WM*) (2nd edition, Frankfurt: Klostermann, 1978), p. 312.

4 Heidegger, "The End of Philosophy and the Task of Thinking," *BW*, p. 386. The original is at Heidegger, *Zur Sache des Denkens* (Tübingen: Niemeyer, 1976), p. 74. See also Heidegger, *Nietzsche*, vol. 4, trans. Frank Capuzzi (New York: Harper and Row, 1982), p. 205: "*Metaphysics as metaphysics is nihilism proper.* The essence of nihilism *is* historically as metaphysics, and the metaphysics of Plato is no less nihilistic than that of Nietzsche." The original is at *Nietzsche* II (Pfullingen: Neske, 1961), p. 343.

5 "In the subjectness of the subject, will comes to appearance as the essence of subjectivity. Modern metaphysics, as the metaphysics of subjectness, thinks the Being of that which is in the sense of will." Heidegger, "The word of Nietzsche," in *The Question Concerning Technology and Other Essays* (hereafter *QT*), trans. William Lovitt (New York: Harper and Row, 1977), p. 88. The original is at Heidegger, *Holzwege* (Frankfurt: Klostermann, 1972), p. 225. This quotation summarizes the transition, on the list above, from Being as Cartesian *subiectum* to Being as the Leibnizian *exigentia essentiae* within the monad, and thence to the Kantian conception of the nonphenomenal self as will under the aspect of practical reason. The notion of "will" is then reinterpreted by Hegel and Schelling in a way which quickly brings one to Nietzsche and Dewey. The same transition is formulated at *QT,* p. 128, by saying that with "man becoming subject", gradually "man becomes the relational center of all that is."

that it first is in being and only is in being to the extent that it is set up by man, who represents and sets forth.[6]

To see how the quest of certainty took us down this road, think of Plato as having built the need to overcome epistemological skepticism – the need to answer questions like "What is your evidence?," "How do you know?," "How can you be sure?" – into Western thinking. Then think of the skeptic as having pressed the philosopher back from a more ambitious notion of truth as accurate representation to the more modest notion of truth as coherence among our beliefs. Think of Spinoza and Leibniz as having elaborated proto-coherence theories of truth. Think of the coherence theory of truth becoming philosophical common sense after Kant explained why a "transcendental realist" account of knowledge would always succumb to skeptical attack. Think of Kant as completing the Cartesian turn toward interior objects by replacing the realist story about inner representations of outer originals with a story about the relation between privileged representations (such as his twelve categories) and less privileged, more contingent representations.

As soon as we adopt this Kantian story, however, we begin to drift toward Nietzsche's view that "the categories of reason" are just "means toward the adjustment of the world for utilitarian ends."[7] We begin to see the attractions of Deweyan redefinitions of terms like "truth" and "rationality" in terms of contributions to "satisfaction" and "growth." We move from Kant to pragmatism when we realize that a coherence theory of truth must be a theory about the harmony not just of beliefs, but rather of beliefs *and desires*. This realization leads us to the common element in Nietzsche's perspectivalism and C. I. Lewis's "conceptual pragmatism" – the doctrine that Kantian categories, the forms in which we think, the structures of our inquiries, are malleable. We change them (as, for example, we changed from an Aristotelian to a Newtonian understanding of space and time) whenever such a change enables us better to fulfill our desires by making things more readily manipulable.

Once we take this final step, once human desires are admitted into the criterion of "truth," the last remnants of the Platonic idea of knowledge as contact with an underlying nonhuman order disappear. We have become pragmatists. But we only took the path that leads to pragmatism because Plato told us that we had to take evidence and certainty, and therefore skepticism, seriously. We only became pragmatists because Plato and Aristotle already gave us a technical, instrumental account of what thinking was good for.

Heidegger thinks of himself as having tracked down the assumption common to Plato, the skeptic, and the pragmatists – the assumption that truth has something to do with evidence, with being clear and convincing, with being in

6   *QT,* pp. 129–130; *Holzwege,* p. 81.
7   Nietzsche, *The Will to Power,* trans. Kaufmann (New York: Random House, 1967), sec. 584, p. 314.

possession of *powerful, penetrating, deep* insights or arguments – insights or arguments which will put you in a commanding position vis-à-vis something or somebody else (or vis-à-vis your own old, bad, false self). The West, Heidegger thinks, has been on a power trip ever since, with the Greeks, it invented itself. A metaphysics of the Will to Power (the metaphysics Heidegger ascribed to Nietzsche by taking some of Nietzsche's posthumous fragments to be the "real" Nietzsche) and an antimetaphysical technocratic pragmatism are the destined lost stages of Western thought. This is the ironic result of Plato's attempt to rise above the pragmatism of the marketplace, to find a world elsewhere.

A familiar way to see Plato as power freak – as an example of what Derrida calls "phallogocentrism" – is to emphasize his conviction that mathematical demonstration is the paradigm of inquiry, his awe at the geometers' ability to offer knockdown arguments. But another way is to think of him as convinced that all human beings have the truth within them, that they are already in possession of the key to the ultimate secrets – that they merely need to know themselves in order to attain their goal. This is the basic assumption of what Kierkegaard, in his *Philosophical Fragments,* called "Socratism." To make this assumption is to believe that we have a built-in affinity for the truth, a built-in way of tracking it once we glimpse it, a built-in tendency to get into the right relation to a more powerful Other. In Plato, this assumption was expressed as in the doctrine that the soul is itself a sort of *archē* because it is somehow connate with the Forms. Down here at the bottom of the escalator, it is expressed in the pragmatist's claim that to know your desires (not your deeply buried "inmost," "true" desires, but your ordinary everyday desires) is to know the criterion of truth, to understand what it would take for a belief to "work."

For Kierkegaard, the opposite of Socratism was Christianity – the claim that man is not complete, is not in the truth, but rather can attain truth only by being re-created, by being made into a New Being by Grace. Kierkegaard thought that Socratism was Sin, and that Sin was the attempt by Man to assume the role of God, an attempt which found its *reductio* in Hegel's System. A lot of Heidegger can profitably be read as a reflection on the possibility that Kierkegaard was right to reject Socratism but wrong to accept Christianity – or, more generally, on the possibility that humanism and Pauline Christianity are alternative forms of a single temptation. Suppose that both are expressions of the need to be overwhelmed by something, to have beliefs forced upon you (by conclusive evidence, rational conviction, in the one case, or by Omnipotence re-creating you, in the other). Suppose that this desire to be overwhelmed is itself just a sublimated form of the urge to share in the power of anything strong enough to overwhelm you. One form such sharing might take would be to become identical with this power, through a purificatory askesis. Another would be to become the favored child of this power.

The result of thinking through these suppositions was Heidegger's attempt to struggle free from what he came to think of as the underlying assumption of the West – the assumption that truth is somehow a matter of the stronger overcoming the weaker. This notion of overcoming is what is common to suggestions that intellect can overcome sensual desire, that Grace can overcome Sin, that rational evidence can overcome irrational prejudice, and that the human will can overcome the nonhuman environment. This assumption that power relations are of the essence of human life is, Heidegger thinks, fundamental to what he sometimes calls "the ontotheological tradition."

I take Heidegger to be saying that if one is going to stay within this tradition, then one might as well be a pragmatist. One might as well be a self-conscious, rather than a repressed and self-deceived, power freak. Pragmatism has, so to speak, turned out to be all that the West could hope for, all we had a right to expect once we adopted a "technical" interpretation of thinking. Plato set things up so that epistemological skepticism would become the recurrent theme of philosophical reflection, and pragmatism is, in fact, the only way to answer the skeptic. So if the only choice is between Platonism and pragmatism, Heidegger would wryly and ironically opt for pragmatism.

This qualified sympathy for pragmatism is clearest in *Being and Time,* the book which Dewey described as "sounding like a description of 'the situation' in transcendental German." In Part I of his *Heidegger's Pragmatism,* Mark Okrent has shown, very carefully and lucidly, how to read *Being and Time* as a pragmatist treatise.[8] The crucial point is the one Okrent puts as follows: "it is built into Heidegger's view of understanding that beliefs and desires must be ascribed together."[9] Once understanding is de-intellectualized in the way in which both Dewey and Heidegger wanted to de-intellectualize it – by viewing the so-called "quest for disinterested theoretical truth" as a continuation of practice by other means – most of the standard pragmatist doctrines follow.[10] In particular, it

8   I first learned how much of *Being and Time* can be read as a pragmatist tract from Robert Brandom's seminal "Heidegger's Categories in Being and Time," *Monist* 60 (1983).
9   Mark Okrent, *Heidegger's Pragmatism* (Ithaca, N.Y.: Cornell University Press, 1988), p. 64. See also p. 123: "Husserl conceives of the fundamental form of intentionality as cognitive; Heidegger conceives of it as practical. As a result, Husserl thinks of the horizons in which beings are presented on the model of sensuous fields in which objects are placed before us for our intuitive apprehension, whereas Heidegger thinks of these horizons as fields of activity." One can substitute "the early Russell" or "the early Wittgenstein" for "Husserl," and "Dewey" or "the later Wittgenstein" for "Heidegger," in these sentences *salva veritate.*
      On Heidegger's conception of the relation between cognition and action, see Brandom, "Heidegger's Categories," pp. 405–406. Brandom notes that on the traditional, Platonic account "the only appropriate response to something present-at-hand is an assertion, the only use which can be made of assertion is inference, and inference is restricted to theoretical inference" whereas on the Heideggerian and pragmatist accounts "the only way in which the present-at-hand can affect Dasein's projects is by being the subject of an assertion which ultimately plays some role in practical inference."
10 The difference between pragmatists and nonpragmatists on this point comes out very clearly in an early criticism of Bradley by Dewey. ("The Intellectualist Criterion for Truth," in *Middle*

follows that, as Heidegger puts it, Dasein's Being-in-the-world is "the *foundation* for the primordial phenomenon of truth."[11] It also follows that

Being (not entities) is something which 'there is' only in so far as truth is. And truth is only in so far and as long as Dasein is. Being and truth 'are' equiprimordially.[12]

That is to say: Being, which Plato thought of as something larger and stronger than us, is there only as long as we are here. The relations between it and us are not power relations. Rather, they are relations of fragile and tentative codependence. The relation between *Sein* and *Dasein* is like the relation between hesitant lovers; questions of relative strength and weakness do not arise.[13]

With Okrent, I read Division One of *Being and Time* as a recapitulation of the standard pragmatist arguments against Plato and Descartes. I read Division Two, and in particular the discussion of Hegelian historicism, as recapitulating Nietzsche's criticism of Hegel's attempt to escape finitude by losing himself in the dramas of history. Hegel hoped to find in history the evidence and certainty that Plato hoped to find in a sort of super-mathematics called "dialectic," and that positivism hoped to find in a unified science. But from Heidegger's point of view, Plato, Descartes, Hegel, and positivism are just so many power plays. They are so many claims to have read the script of the drama we are acting out, thus relieving us of the need to make up this drama as we go along. Every such power play is, for Heidegger as for Dewey, an expression of the hope that truth may become *evident,*

Works, vol. 4, pp. 50–75; the quotations that follow are from pp. 58–59.) After quoting Bradley as saying "You may call the intellect, if you like, a mere tendency to a movement, but you must remember that it is a movement of a very special kind. . . . Thinking is the attempt to satisfy a *special* impulse," Dewey comments: "The unquestioned presupposition of Mr. Bradley is that thinking is such a wholly separate activity . . . that to give it autonomy is to say that it, and its criterion, have nothing to do with other activities. . . ." Dewey argues that "intellectual discontent *is* the practical conflict becoming deliberately aware of itself as the most effective means of its own rectification." Compare Heidegger, *Being and Time* (hereafter *BT*), trans. Macquarrie and Robinson (New York: Harper and Row, 1962), p. 95: "The kind of dealing which is closest to use is . . . not a bare perceptual cognition, but rather that kind of concern which manipulates things and puts them to use." (The original is at *Sein und Zeit* – hereafter *SZ* – [Tübingen: Niemeyer, 1963], p. 67.

    In Part I of the first volume of these papers, I criticize Bernard Williams for agreeing with Bradley about the autonomy of truth-seeking, about the destinction between theoretical inquiry and practical deliberation. The assumption of such autonomy is, I think, essential to the intelligibility of Williams's notion of "the absolute conception of reality." The Heideggerian-Deweyan reply to Descartes and Williams on this topic is put by Brandom ("Heidegger's Categories," p. 403) as follows: "the move from equipment, ready-at-hand, fraught with socially instituted significances, to objective things present-at-hand, is not one of decontextualization but of *recontextualization*".

11 Heidegger, *BT*, p. 261; *SZ*, p. 219.

12 *BT*, p. 272; *SZ*, p. 230.

13 To be fair to Kierkegaard, he too realized that something other than power relations were needed to make sense of Christianity. See his claim that "the form of the servant was not something put on" in his discussion of the Incarnation as a solution to a loving God's need not to overwhelm the beloved sinner. *Philosophical Fragments,* trans. Howard and Edna Hong (Princeton, N.J.: Princeton University Press, 1985), p. 32.

undeniable, clearly present to the mind. The result of such presence would be that we should no longer have to have projects, no longer have to create ourselves by inventing and carrying out these projects.

This quest for certainty, clarity, and direction from outside can also be viewed as an attempt to escape from time, to view *Sein* as something that has little to do with *Zeit*. Heidegger would like to recapture a sense of what time was like before it fell under the spell of eternity, what we were like before we became obsessed by the need for an overarching context which would subsume and explain us – before we came to think of our relation to Being in terms of power. To put it another way: he would like to recapture a sense of *contingency,* of the fragility and riskiness of any human project – a sense which the ontotheological tradition has made it hard to attain. For that tradition tends to identify the contingent with the merely apparent. By contrasting powerful reality with relatively impotent appearance, and claiming that it is all-important to make contact with the former, our tradition has suggested that the fragile and transitory can safely be neglected.

In particular, the tradition has suggested that the particular *words* we use are unimportant. Ever since philosophy won its quarrel with poetry, it has been the thought that counts – the proposition, something which many sentences in many languages express equally well. Whether a sentence is spoken or written, whether it contains Greek words or German words or English words, does not, on the traditional philosophical view, greatly matter. For the words are mere vehicles for something less fragile and transitory than marks and noises. Philosophers know that what matters is literal truth, not a choice of phonemes, and certainly not metaphors. The literal lasts and empowers. The metaphorical – that which you can neither argue about nor justify, that for which you can find no uncontroversial paraphrase – is impotent. It passes and leaves no trace.

One way to describe what Heidegger does in his later work is to see him as defending the poets against the philosophers. More particularly, we should take him at his word when, in the middle of *Being and Time,* he says:

In the end, the business of philosophy is to preserve the *force of the most elemental words* in which Dasein expresses itself, and to keep the common understanding from levelling them off to that unintelligibility which functions as a source of pseudo-problems.[14]

I think that we should read "unintelligibility" here as "the inability to attend to a word which is common currency."[15] When a word is used frequently and easily, when it is a familiar, ready-to-hand instrument for achieving our purpose, we can no longer *hear* it. Heidegger is saying that we need to be able to hear the "most elemental" words which we use – presumably the sort of words which make up

---

14 *BT,* p. 262; *SZ,* p. 220. Emphasis in the original.
15 This interpretation coheres with Heidegger's remark at *BT,* p. 23 (*SZ,* p. 4) about the easy intelligibility of "is" in "the sky is blue." He says that "here we have an average kind of intelligibility, which merely demonstrates that this is unintelligible."

the little "Sketch of the History of Being" I quoted above – rather than simply using these words as tools. We need to hear them in the way in which a poet hears them when deciding whether to put one of them at a certain place in a certain poem. By so hearing them we shall preserve what Heidegger calls their "force." We shall hear them in the way in which we hear a metaphor for the first time. Reversing Hobbes, Heidegger thinks that words are the counters of everyday existence, but the money of Thinkers.[16]

Another way of describing Heidegger's later work is to emphasize a line in his own quasi-poem, *Aus der Erfahrung des Denkens:* "Being's poem, just begun, is man."[17] Think of the list of words cited above as a sort of abstract of the first stanza of that poem. Then think of the stanza being abstracted as *us,* the dwellers in the West.[18] To think of that poem that way, we have to think of ourselves as, first and foremost, the people who used – who *just happened* to use – those words. This is hard for us to do, because our tradition keeps trying to tell us that it isn't the words that matter, but the realities which they signify. Heidegger, by contrast, is telling us that the words do matter: that we are, above all, the people who

16 On hearing, see *BT,* p. 228 (*SZ,* p. 183): "But Being 'is' only in the understanding of those entities to whose Being something like an understanding of Being belongs." Heidegger added a marginal note here which reads, "Understanding is to be taken here in the sense of 'hearing'. That does not mean that 'Being' is only 'subjective' but that Being (as the Being of beings) is 'in' Dasein as the thrown is in the throwing" (*SZ,* 15th edition, p. 443). I construe this passage in the light of the passage I quoted earlier about "the force of the most elementary words." See also *BT, p. 209 (SZ,* 163): "Hearing constitutes the primary and authentic way in which Dasein is open for its ownmost potentiality-for-Being – as in hearing the voice of the friend whom every Dasein carries with it."

17 Heidegger, *Poetry, Language, Thought,* trans. Albert Hofstadter (New York: Harper and Row, 1971), p. 4. The original is *Wir kommen für die Götter zu spät und zu früh für das Seyn. Dessen angefangenes Gedicht ist der Mensch.* Heidegger, *Aus der Erfahrung des Denkens* (Pfullingen: Neske, 1954), p. 7.

18 Heidegger often refuses to make a distinction between Dasein, the "Da" of Dasein, and the lighting-up of beings by Dasein's use of language to describe beings. See *BT,* p. 171 (*SZ,* p. 133): "To say that it [Dasein] is 'illuminated' [*erleuchtet*] means that *as* Being-in-the-world it is cleared [*gelichtet*] in itself, not through any other entity, but in such a way that it *is* itself the clearing [*die Lichtung*]." But he also, especially in the later works, refuses to make a distinction between Dasein and Sein. Note the use of *Lichtung* in "Letter on Humanism" (*BW,* p. 216; *WM,* p. 333) where Heidegger says that "Being is essentially broader than all beings because it is the lighting [*Lichtung*] itself." When Heidegger says, at the beginning of "Letter on Humanism," that "Language is the house of Being. In its home man dwells" (*BW,* p. 193; *WM,* p. 145), the suggestion that the two dwellers cannot be distinguished from one another is deliberate. The more you read later Heidegger, the more you realize that the distinctions between language, human beings, and Being are being deliberately and systematically blurred. I read this blurring as a warning, analogous to Wittgenstein's, against trying to get between language and its object, plus a further warning against trying to get between language and its user. In Heidegger's version, the warning says: if you try to come between them – if you try to make the user more than his or her words, and the object described more than its description in words, you risk winding up with some version of the Subject–Object or Human–Superhuman dualisms, and thus being condemned to think in terms of power relations between the terms of these dualisms. Though for purposes of *manipulating* them you may *have* to separate subject and object from each other and from language, remember that there are other purposes than manipulation.

have used those words. We of the West are the people whose project consisted in running down that particular list, in riding that particular escalator. There was no more *necessity* about getting on that escalator than there is about a poet's use of a given metaphor. But once the metaphor is used, the fate of the poet's audience is, Heidegger thinks, determined.

It is important to emphasize at this point that there is no hidden power called Being which designed or operated the escalator. Nobody whispered in the ears of the early Greeks, the poets of the West. There is just us, in the grip of no power save those of the words we happen to speak, the dead metaphors which we have internalized. There is no way, and no need, to tell the dancer from the dance, nor is there any point in looking around for a hidden choreographer. To see that there is *just us* would be simultaneously to see ourselves – to see the West – as a contingency and to see that there is no refuge from contingency. In particular, it would be to accept Heidegger's claim that "Only as long as Dasein is (that is, only as long as an understanding of Being is ontically possible) 'is there' Being."[19] If we could only see *that,* Heidegger thinks, then we might shake off the will to power which is implicit in Plato and Christianity and which becomes explicit in pragmatism.

But if Being is not a hidden choreographer, not a source of empowerment, what is it? So far I have tossed "Being" around insouciantly, spoken Heideggerese. Now, in a brief excursus from my main topic – the relation between Heidegger and pragmatism – I shall try to say something about why Heidegger uses this term, and to offer a quasi-definition of it.

I think that Heidegger goes on and on about "the question about Being" without ever answering it because Being is a good example of something we have no criteria for answering questions about. It is a good example of something we have no handle on, no tools for manipulating – something which resists "the technical interpretation of thinking." The reason Heidegger talks about Being is not that he wants to direct our attention to an unfortunately neglected topic of inquiry, but that he wants to direct our attention to the difference between inquiry and poetry, between struggling for power and accepting contingency. He wants to suggest what a culture might be like in which poetry rather than philosophy-cum-science was the paradigmatic human activity. The question "What is Being?" is no more to be *answered correctly* than the question "What is a cherry blossom?" But the latter question is, nevertheless, one you might use to set the theme of a poetry competition. The former question is, so to speak, what the Greeks happened to come up with when they set the theme upon which the West has been a set of variations.

But doesn't Heidegger's use of "Being" immerse him in the tradition which he

19 *BT*, p. 255.

wants to wriggle free of: the ontotheological tradition, the history of metaphysics? Yes, but he wants to get free of that tradition not by turning his back on it but by attending to it and redescribing it.[20] The crucial move in this redescription, as I read Heidegger, is his suggestion that we see the metaphysician's will to truth as a self-concealing form of the poetic urge. He wants us to see metaphysics as an inauthentic form of poetry, poetry which thinks of itself as antipoetry, a sequence of metaphors whose authors thought of them as escapes from metaphoricity. He wants us to recapture the force of the most elementary words of Being – the words on the list above, the words of the various Thinkers who mark the stages of our descent from Plato – by ceasing to think of these words as the natural and obvious words to use. We should instead think of this list as as contingent as the contours of an individual cherry blossom.

To do this, we have to think of the West not as the place where human beings finally got clear on what was really going on, but as just one cherry blossom alongside actual and possible others, one cluster of "understandings of Being" alongside other clusters. But we also have to think of it as the blossom which *we* are. We can neither leap out of our blossom into the next one down the bough, nor rise above the tree and look down at a cloud of blossoms (in the way in which we imagine God looking down on a cloud of galaxies). For Heidegger's purposes, we are nothing save the words we use, nothing but an (early) stanza of Being's poem. Only a metaphysician, a power freak, would think we were more.

So is Being the leaf, the blossom, the bole, or what? I think the best answer is that it is what elementary words of Being refer to. But since such words of Being – words like *physis* or *subiectum* or *Wille zur Macht* – are just abbreviations for whole vocabularies, whole chains of interlocked metaphors, it is better to say that *Being is what vocabularies are about.* Being's poem is the poem about Being, not the poem Being writes. For Being cannot move a finger unless Dasein does, even though there is nothing more to Dasein than Being's poem.

More precisely, Being is what *final* vocabularies are about. A final vocabulary is one which we cannot help using, for when we reach it our spade is turned. We cannot undercut it because we have no metavocabulary in which to phrase criticisms of it.[21] Nor can we compare it with what it is about, test it for "adequacy" – for there is no nonlinguistic access to Being. To put the point in slightly more Heideggerian language: all we know of Being is that it is what understandings of

---

20 In 1962 Heidegger suggests that he may have done too much redescribing, and needs to start ignoring: "a regard for metaphysics still prevails even in the intending to overcome metaphysics. Therefore our task is to cease all overcoming, and leave metaphysics to itself." *Of Time and Being,* trans. Joan Stambaugh (New York: Harper and Row, 1972), p. 24; *Zur Sache des Denkens,* p. 25. But by 1962 he had put in thirty years struggling to overcome – the years in which he wrote his most intriguing and provocative works.

21 For a fuller explicit definition of "final vocabulary" see my *Contingency, Irony, and Solidarity* (Cambridge: Cambridge University Press, 1989), p. 73. Chapter 4 of that book is a sort of long contextual definition of this term.

Being are understandings of. But that is also all we need to know. We do not need to ask which understandings of Being are better understandings. To ask that question would be to begin replacing love with power.

To see the point of this quasi-definition of "Being," it is essential to realize that Being is not the same thing under all descriptions, but is something different under each. That is why the line between Being and Language is so thin, and why Heidegger applies many of the same phrases to both. Heidegger insists that he is writing a History *of Being,* not just a History of Human Understandings of Being. An imperfect analogy is that every description of space given by the definitions and axioms of a geometry is a description of a different space (Euclidean space, Riemannian space, etc.), so there is no point in asking whether the space was there before the geometry, nor in asking which geometry gets space-in-itself right. A History of Geometry would also be a History of Space. The analogy is imperfect because we construct geometries for particular purposes, but we do not *construct* final vocabularies. They are always already there; we find ourselves thrown into them. Final vocabularies are not tools, for we cannot specify the *purpose* of a final vocabulary without futilely twisting around inside the circle of that very vocabulary.

The metaphysical thinker thinks that if you can just get the right understanding of Being — the one that gets Being right — then you are home. Heidegger thinks that the notion of "the right understanding of Being" is a confusion of Being with beings. You can relate beings to other beings (e.g., points in space to other points in space) in more or less useful ways — indeed, such relating is what Being-in-the-world consists of. But you cannot relate some beings — and in particular, some words — to Being any more than they are already related by the wimpy, impotent relation of "aboutness." In particular, Being is not the sort of thing which one can master, or which masters one. It is not related by the power relationships, the means-end relationships, which relate *beings* to one another.

The metaphysician, as Heidegger tells us in "On the Essence of Truth," regularly confuses truth with correctness. He confuses the relation of a vocabulary to Being with the relation of a sentence like "the sky is blue" to the color of the sky. There are criteria of correctness for deciding when to use that sentence to make a statement, but there are no criteria of correctness for final vocabularies.[22] If I am

---

22 See Okrent, *Heidegger's Pragmatism,* p. 286: "It seems possible to raise the question of which 'language,' which 'vocabulary,' which intentional horizon is the right or correct one. In fact, this is the very question that metaphysics in Heidegger's sense was designed to raise and answer. . . . But according to both American neopragmatism and Heidegger as we have interpreted him, there is no determinate answer to this question, because being cannot be seen as grounding and justifying a particular intentional horizon." I agree with what Okrent says in this passage, but disagree with much of what he goes on to say at pp. 289–297 about the status of pragmatism as a doctrine. Okrent thinks that one should avoid "Heidegger's own desperate recourse to the view that assertions concerning the truth of being are not really assertions at all" (p. 292). I am not sure that one should; if pragmatism is to be viewed as saying something about the "truth of

right in interpreting *Seinsverständnis* as "final vocabulary" and *Sein* as what final vocabularies are about, then one would expect Heidegger to say that no understanding of Being is more or less an understanding of Being, more or less true (in the sense of truth-as-disclosedness – *aletheia, Erschlossenheit, Unverborgenheit, Ereignis*) than any other. No petal on a cherry blossom is more or less a petal than any other.

Sometimes Heidegger does say things like this. For example: "Each epoch of philosophy has its own necessity. We simply have to acknowledge that philosophy is the way it is. It is not for us to prefer one to the other, as is the case with regard to various *Weltanschauungen*."[23] But often, as his use of the term "Forgetfulness of Being" suggests, he seems to be saying the opposite. For he makes all sorts of invidious comparisons between the less forgetful people at the top of the escalator – the Greeks – and the more forgetful ones at the bottom, us. The question of whether he has any business making such comparisons is the question of whether he has any business disliking pragmatism as much as he does. So now I return from my excursus on Being to the main topic of this paper.

The question of Heidegger's relation to pragmatism can be seen as the question: does Heidegger have any right to nostalgia? Any right to regret the golden time before Platonism turned out to be simply implicit pragmatism? Is there any room in his story for the notion of belatedness, for the notion of a *downward* escalator? To put it another way, should we read him as telling a story about the contingency of vocabularies or about the belatedness of our age? Or rather: since he is obviously telling both stories, can they be fitted together? I do not think they can.

To get this issue about contingency and belatedness in focus, consider the preliminary problem of whether Heidegger's early "ontological" enterprise can be fitted together with his later attempt to sketch the "history of Being." The reader of *Being and Time* is led to believe that the Greeks enjoyed a special relationship to Being which the moderns have lost, that they had less trouble being ontological than we do, whereas we moderns have a terrible time keeping the difference between the ontological and the ontic in mind. The reader of the later work, however, is often told that Descartes and Nietzsche were as adequate expressions of what Being was at their times as Parmenides was of what Being was at his time. This makes it hard to see what advantage the Greeks might have enjoyed over the moderns, nor how Parmenides and Nietzsche could be compared in respect of the "elementariness" of the "words of Being" with which they are associated. Since

---

Being" (a phrase which Okrent finds more intelligible than I do), then I should like it to take the form of a proposal ("Let's try it this way, and see what happens") rather than an assertion. My disagreement with Okrent here is connected with my doubts about Okrent's claim that "all pragmatism either must be based on a transcendental semantics or be self-contradictory" (p. 280). See Okrent's "The Metaphilosophical Consequences of Pragmatism" in *The Institution of Philosophy,* ed. Avner Cohen and Marcello Dascal (Totowa, N.J.: Rowman and Littlefield, 1988), for his defense of this latter claim and for criticism of some of my own views.

23 *BW,* p. 375; *Zur Sache des Denkens,* pp. 62–63.

there is no more to Being than its understanding by Dasein, since Being is not a power over and against Dasein, it is not clear how there could be anything more authentic or primal about the top of the escalator than the bottom. So it is not clear why we should think in terms of an escalator rather than of a level moving walkway.

Although *Being and Time* starts off with what looks like a firm distinction between the ontological and the ontic, by the end of the book the analytic of Dasein has revealed Dasein's historicity. This historicity makes it hard to see how ontological knowledge can be more than knowledge of a particular historical position. In the later work, the term "ontology" drops out, and we are told that what the Greeks did was to invent something called "metaphysics" by construing Being as "presence." What *Being and Time* had called "ontological knowledge," and had made sound desirable, now looks very like the confusion between Being and beings which the later work says is at the heart of the metaphysical tradition. Something seems to have changed, and yet the more one rereads Heidegger's writings of the 1920s in the light of his later essays the more one realizes that the historical story which he told in the 1930s was already in his mind when he wrote *Being and Time*. One's view about what, if anything, has changed, will determine what one makes of the idea that, for example, *logos* is *more* primordial than *Wille zur Macht* (in some honorific sense of "primordial").

Heidegger's own later glosses on *Being and Time* are of little help when it comes to the question of whether "the average vague understanding of Being" which is supposed to be the datum of the "analytic of Dasein" is itself an historical phenomenon, rather than something ahistorical which provides a neutral background against which to portray the differences between the Greeks and ourselves. My own guess is that in the 1920s Heidegger thought that it is ahistorical and that in the 1930s he came to think of it as historically situated.[24] If this guess is right, then the later Heidegger abjures the quest for ahistorical ontological knowledge and thinks that philosophical reflection is historical all the way down. But if it is, then we confront the problem of contingency and belatedness I sketched above. We face the question: is coming to an understanding of what Heidegger calls "what in the fullest sense of Being now is"[25] *simply* a matter of recapturing our historical contingency, of helping us see ourselves *as* contingent by seeing ourselves as historical, or is it, for example, learning that this is a particularly dark and dangerous time?[26]

24 Heidegger would of course deny this. But, as Okrent (*Heidegger's Pragmatism,* p. 223) notes, Heidegger "stubbornly refused to admit that he had changed his mind, made any crucial mistakes in earlier works, or significantly altered terminology over time."

25 "Letter on Humanism," *BW,* p. 221. The original is just as obscure as the English: *was in einem erfüllten Sinn von Sein jetzt ist* (*WM,* p. 338).

26 One should be clear that for Heidegger things like the danger of a nuclear holocaust, mass starvation because of overpopulation, and the like, are not indications that the time is particu-

The $32 question of whether the later Heidegger still believes there is an ahistorical discipline called "ontology" leads fairly quickly to the $64 question of whether he has a right to the nostalgia for which Derrida and others have criticized him, and to the hostility he displays toward pragmatism. Returning now to the former question, I would argue that the "analytic of Dasein" in *Being and Time* is most charitably and easily interpreted as an analytic of *Western* Dasein, rather than as an account of the ahistorical conditions for the occurrence of history.[27] There are passages in *Being and Time* itself, and especially in the roughly contemporary lecture course *The Basic Problems of Phenomenology,* which support this interpretation. These passages seem to make it clear that Heidegger comes down on the historicist side of the dilemma I have sketched. Thus toward the end of *Being and Time* he approvingly quotes Count von Yorck as saying: "it seems to me methodologically like a residue from metaphysics not to historicize one's philosophizing."[28] At the very end of that book he reminds us that the analytic of Dasein was merely preparatory and that it may turn out not to have been the right way to go;[29] he hints that it might be what it later turned out to be: a disposable ladder.

In *Basic Problems of Phenomenology* he says that "even the ontological investigation that we are now conducting is determined by its historical situation." He goes on to say that

These three components of phenomenological method – reduction, construction, destruction – belong together in their content and must receive grounding in their mutual pertinence. Construction in philosophy is necessarily destruction, that is to say, a de-constructing [Abbau] of traditional concepts carried out in a historical recursion to the tradition. . . . Because destruction belongs to construction, philosophical cognition is essentially at the same time, historical cognition.[30]

This seems a proto-Derridean line of thought, in which philosophy becomes identical with historicist ironism, and in which there can be no room for nostalgia.

larly dark and dangerous. These merely ontic matters are not the sort of thing Heidegger has in mind when he says that "the wasteland spreads."

27 The ambiguity between these two alternatives is nicely expressed by a note which Heidegger inserted in the margin at *BT,* p. 28 (*SZ,* p. 8). Having said "This guiding activity of taking a look at Being arises from the average understanding of Being in which we always operate and *which in the end belongs to the essential constitution of Dasein itself [und das am Ende zur Wesensverfassung des Daseins selbst gehört],*" he glosses "in the end [*am Ende*]" with "that is, from the beginning [*d.h. von Anfang an*]". "*Am Ende*" would naturally have been read as meaning "in the nature of Dasein," but "*von Anfang an*" can be read as reminding us that Dasein does not have a nature, but only an historical existence. The question remains whether Heidegger earlier, at the time of writing *Being and Time,* did think that Dasein – not just Western Dasein – had a nature which Daseinsanalytik could expose, or whether he meant the indexical "Da" to express historicity even back then.

28 *BT,* p. 453; *SZ,* p. 402.

29 *BT,* p. 487; *SZ,* pp. 436–437.

30 Heidegger, *The Basic Problems of Phenomenology* (hereafter *BP*), trans. Albert Hofstadter (Bloomington: Indiana University Press, 1982), p. 23. The original is at Heidegger, *Gesamtausgabe,* vol. 24: *Die Grundprobleme der Phänomenologie* (Frankfurt: Klostermann 1975), p. 31.

But there are plenty of passages in which the other horn of the dilemma, the ontological horn, seems to be grasped. In the "Introduction" to *Basic Problems*, from which I have just been quoting, Heidegger says that in our time, as perhaps never before, philosophizing has become "barbarous, like a St. Vitus' dance." This has happened because contemporary philosophy is no longer ontology, but simply the quest for a "world-view." Heidegger defines the latter by contrast with "theoretical knowledge." The definition of "world-view" which he quotes from Jaspers sounds a good deal like my definition of "final vocabulary." Something is equally a world-view whether it is based on "superstitions and prejudice" or on "scientific knowledge and experience."

However, after seeming to contrast ontology and world-view, Heidegger goes on to say the following:

It is just because this positivity – that is, the relatedness to beings, to world that *is*, Dasein that *is* – belongs to the essence of the world-view, and thus in general to the formation of the world-view, that the formation of a world-view cannot be the task of philosophy. To say this is not to exclude but to include the idea that philosophy itself is a distinctive primal form [*eine ausgezeichnete Urform*] of world-view. Philosophy can and perhaps must show, among many other things, that something like a world-view belongs to the essential nature of Dasein. Philosophy can and must define what in general constitutes the structure of a world-view. But it can never develop and posit some specific world-view qua just this or that particular one.[31]

But there is an obvious tension in this passage between the claim that philosophy "is a distinctive primal form of world-view" and that "philosophy . . . can never develop and posit some specific world-view." Heidegger never tells us how we can be historical through and through and yet ahistorical enough to step outside our world-view and say something neutral about the "structure" of all actual and possible world-views. To put the point in my own jargon, he never explains how we could possibly do more than create a new, historically situated, final vocabulary in the course of reacting against the one we found in place. To do something more – something ontological – would be to find a vocabulary which would have what he calls "an elementary and fundamental relation to all world-view formation" – the sort of relation which all the vocabularies of the metaphysical tradition have tried and failed to have. To possess such a vocabulary would, indeed, be to have a "distinctive primal form of world-view." Yet the very *attempt* at such a vocabulary looks like what Yorck called "a residue of metaphysics."

I read this confusing passage about philosophy and world-view as an early expression of the tension between saying that each epoch in the "history of Being" – each stage in the transition from the Greeks to the moderns – is on an ontological par, and saying that the Greeks' relation to Being was somehow closer than ours, that our "forgetfulness of Being" and lack of "primordiality" is responsible for the

31 *BP*, p. 10; *Die Grundprobleme*, pp. 12–13.

42

barbaric and frenzied character of the modern world. In other words, I see the difficulty about the historicity of ontology as a manifestation of the more basic difficulty about whether it can make sense to *criticize* the "understanding of Being" characteristic of one's own age. The early work suggests that the present age can be criticized for its lack of ontological knowledge. The later work continues to criticize the present age but seems to offer no account of the standpoint from which the criticism is made.

In the later work, as I have said, the term "ontology" drops out, as does "Dasein." The pejorative work done by ontic–ontological distinction in *Being and Time* is now done by the distinction between the nonprimordial and the primordial. Yet we are never told what makes for primordiality, any more than we were told how to step outside of our facticity long enough to be ontological. "Primordial" (*ursprünglich*) in the later work has all the resonance and all the obscurity which "ontological" had in the earlier.

This point can be put in other words by saying that Heidegger has two quite different things to say about the way the West is now: that it is contingent and that it is belated. To say that it is contingent it is enough to show how self-deceptive it is to think that things *had* to be as they are, how provincial it is to think that the final vocabulary of the present day is "obvious" and "inescapable." But to say that this vocabulary is belated, to contrast it with something more primordial, one has to give "primordial" some kind of normative sense, so that it means something more than just "earlier."

The only candidate for this normative sense which I can find in Heidegger is the following: an understanding of Being is more primordial than another if it makes it easier to grasp its own contingency. So to say that we in the twentieth century are belated, by comparison with the Greeks, is to say that their understanding of Being in terms of notions like *arche* and *physis* was less self-certain, more hesitant, more fragile, than our own supreme confidence in our own ability to manipulate beings in order to satisfy our own desires. The Greek Thinkers presumably did not think of their "most elementary words" as "simply common sense," but we do. As you go down the list of words for "Being" in the West, the people using those words become less and less able to hear their own words, more and more thoughtless – where "thoughtless" means something like "unable to imagine alternatives to themselves." Something in these words themselves makes it increasingly easy not to hear them.

The importance of appreciating contingency appears most clearly, I think, in a passage from "On the Essence of Truth" in which Heidegger seems to be saying that history, Being's poem, begins when the first ironist has doubts about the final vocabulary he finds in place. It begins when somebody says "maybe we don't have to talk the way we do," meaning not just "maybe we should call this Y rather than X" but "maybe the language-game in which 'X' and 'Y' occur is the wrong one to be playing – not for any particular reason, not because it fails to live up to

43

some familiar criterion, but just because it is, after all, only one among others. Here is the passage:

History only begins when beings themselves are expressly drawn up in their unconceal-ment and conserved in it, only when this conservation is conceived on the basis of questioning regarding beings as such. The primordial disclosure of being as a whole, the question concerning beings as such, and the beginning of Western history are the same.[32]

I interpret this as saying that prehistorical people living in the West may have played sophisticated language-games, written epics, built temples, and predicted planetary motions, but they didn't count either as "thinking" or as "historical" until somebody asked "Are we doing the right things?" "Are our social practices the right ones to engage in?"

Thought, in Heidegger's honorific sense of the term, begins with a willing suspension of verificationism. It begins when somebody starts asking questions such that nobody, including himself or herself, can verify the answers for correct-ness. These are questions like "What is Being?" or "What is a cherry blossom?" Only when we escape from the verificationist impulse to ask "How can we tell a right answer when we hear one?" are we asking questions which Heidegger thinks worth asking. Only then are we Dasein, because only then do have the possibility of being *authentic* Dasein, Dasein which knows itself to be "thrown." For, at least in the West, "Dasein . . . is ontically distinguished by the fact that, in its very Being, that Being is an *issue* for it."[33] So only then is there a *Da,* a clearing, a lighting-up. Before that, we were just animals that had developed complicated practices, practices we explained and commended to one another in the words of a final vocabulary which nobody dreamt of questioning. Afterward, we are divided into inauthentic Dasein, which is still just a complexly behaving animal insofar as it hasn't yet realized that its Being is an issue for it, and authentic Dasein, made up of Thinkers and Poets who know that that there is an open space surrounding present-day social practices.

In Heidegger's mind, the attitude of questioning which he thinks begins historical existence, and thus makes Dasein out of an animal, is associated with an ability to do what he calls "letting beings be." This, in turn, is associated with freedom. In "Letter on Humanism" he says that there is a kind of nonontological thinking which is "more rigorous [*strenger*] than the conceptual"[34] – a phrase which I take to mean "more difficult to achieve than the kind of 'technical,' verificationist thinking which submits to criteria implicit in social practices." "The material relevance [*sachhaltige Verbindlichkeit*]" of such thinking, Heidegger

32 *BW,* p. 129; *WM,* p. 187.
33 See *BW,* p. 32; *SZ,* p. 12. I take it that for *das Man,* for the ordinary person-in-the-street, for *in*authentic Dasein, Being is *not* an issue. If Heidegger means that it is an issue even for inauthentic Dasein, then I have no grasp of what "being an issue" is, what it is *um dieses Sein selbst gehen.*
34 *BW,* p. 235; *WM,* p. 353.

says, is "essentially higher than the validity of the sciences, because it is freer. For it lets Being – be."[35] In "On the Essence of Truth" he says "The essence of truth reveals itself as freedom. The latter is ek-sistent, disclosive letting beings be [*das ek-sistente, entbergende Seinlassen des Seienden*]."[36]

You let beings be when you disclose them, and you disclose them when you speak a language. So how can any language-user be less free, less open, less able to let Being and beings be, than any other? This is a reformulation of my previous question – how can any understanding of Being be preferable to any other, in the mysterious sense of being "more primordial"? The beginning of Heidegger's answer is that

> because truth is in essence freedom, historical man can, in letting beings be, also *not* let beings be the beings which they are and as they are. Then beings are covered up and distorted. Semblance [der Schein] comes to power.

Further, Heidegger claims, this ability to *not* let beings be increases as technical mastery increases. As he says:

> where beings are not very familiar to man and are scarcely and only roughly known by science, the openedness of beings as a whole can prevail more essentially than it can where the familiar and well-known has become boundless, and nothing is any longer able to withstand the business of knowing, since technical mastery over things bears itself without limit. Precisely in the leveling and planning of this omniscience, this mere knowing, the openedness of beings gets flattened out into the apparent nothingness of what is no longer even a matter of indifference but rather is simply forgotten.[37]

But *what* is forgotten when we forget the "openedness of beings"? Heidegger's familiar and unhelpful answer is "Being." A slightly more complex and helpful answer is: that it was Dasein using language which let beings be in the first place. The greater the ease with which we use that language, the less able we are to *hear* the words of that language, and so the less able we are to think of language as such. To think of language as such, in this sense, is to think of the fact that no language is fated or necessitated. So to forget the openedness of beings is to forget about the possibility of alternative languages, and thus of alternative beings to those we know. It is, in the terms I was using before, to be so immersed in inquiry as to forget the possibility of poetry. This means forgetting that there have been other beings around, beings which we are covering up by playing the language-games we do, having the practices we have. (The quarks were covered up by the Olympian deities, so to speak, and then later the quarks covered up the deities.) This forgetfulness is why we Westerners tend to think of poets referring to the same old beings under fuzzy new metaphorical descriptions, instead of thinking

---

35 *BW*, p. 236; *WM*, p. 354.
36 *BW*, p. 30; *WM*, p. 189.
37 *BW*, p. 131; *WM*, 190.

of poetic acts as the original openings up of the world, the acts which let new sorts of beings be.

In "On the Essence of Truth" the sections on freedom as the essence of truth are followed by a section called "untruth as concealing." This section is rather difficult to interpret, and I am by no means certain that I have caught Heidegger's intent. But I would suggest that the heart of Heidegger's claim that "Letting-be is intrinsically at the same time a concealing"[38] is just that you cannot let all possible beings be at once. That is, you cannot let all possible languages be spoken at once. The quarks and the Olympians, for example, would get in each other's way. The result would be chaos. So the best you can do is to remember that you are not speaking the only possible language — that around the openness provided by your understandings of Being there is a larger openness of other understandings of Being as yet unhad. Beyond the world made available by *your* elementary words there is the silence of other, equally elementary, words, as yet unspoken.

If I understand him, Heidegger is saying that the ability to *hear* your own elementary words is the ability to hear them against the background of that silence, to be aware of that silence. To be primordial is thus to have the ability to know that when you seize upon an understanding of Being, when you build a house for Being by speaking a language, you are automatically giving up a lot of other possible understandings of Being, and leaving a lot of differently designed houses unbuilt.

Assuming this interpretation is on the right track, I return to the question of why the Greeks are supposed to have been so good at knowing this, and why we are supposed to be so bad. Heidegger says

However, in the same period in which the beginning of philosophy takes place, the *marked* domination of common sense (sophistry) [Herrschaft des gemeinen Verstandes (die Soph-istik)] also begins.

Sophistry appeals to the unquestionable character of the beings that are opened up and interprets all thoughtful questioning as an attack on, an unfortunate irritation of, common sense.[39]

I take this to say that right after we ceased to be animals, as a result of some Thinker having questioned whether the beings which our practices had opened up were the right beings, we divided up into sophistic and thoughtful Dasein. Sophistic, inauthentic Dasein could not see the point of questioning common sense, whereas thoughtful and authentic Dasein could. But, somehow, sophistry has become easier here in the twentieth century than it was back then. Somehow the beings that have been opened up by the languages we are speaking have become more unquestionable than those which the early Greeks opened up.

38 *BW*, p. 132; *WM*, p. 190.
39 *BW*, p. 138; *WM*, p. 196.

But is it in fact the case that we in the twentieth century are less able to question common sense than the Greeks were? Offhand, one can think of a lot of reasons why we might be *more* able to do so: we are constantly reminded of cultural diversity, constantly witnessing attempts at novelty in the arts, more and more aware of the possibility of scientific and political revolutions, and so on. If one wants complacent acceptance of common sense, one might think, the place to go is a fairly insular society, one which did not know much about what went on beyond its borders, one in which historiography had barely been invented and in which the arts were just getting started – some place like Greece in the 5th century B.C.

Heidegger, of course, would dismiss this suggestion. For him, the very diversity and business of the modern world is proof that it is unable to sit still long enough to hear "elementary words." For Heidegger, cosmopolitanism, technology, and polymathy are enemies of Thinking. But why? Here we face the $64 question in all its starkness, a question which may be rephrased as follows: can we pragmatists appropriate all of Heidegger except his nostalgia, or is the nostalgia integral to the story he is telling? Can we agree with him both about the dialectical necessity of the transition from Plato to Dewey, and about the need to restore force to the most elementary words of Being, while nevertheless insisting that we in the twentieth century are in an exceptionally *good* position to do the latter? Can pragmatism do justice to poetry as well as to inquiry? Can it let us hear as well as use?

Predictably, my own answer to these last two questions is "yes indeed." I see Dewey's pragmatism – considered now not simply as an antirepresentationalist account of experience and an antiessentialist account of nature, but in its wholeness, as a project for a social democratic utopia – as putting technology in its proper place, as a way of making possible social practices (linguistic and other) which will form the next stanza of Being's poem. That utopia will come, as Dewey put it, when

philosophy shall have co-operated with the course of events and made clear and coherent the meaning of the daily detail, [and so] science and emotion will interpenetrate, practice and imagination will embrace. Poetry and religious feeling will be the unforced flowers of life.[40]

I cannot, without writing several more papers, back up this claim that Dewey was as aware as Heidegger of the danger that we might lose the ability to hear in the technological din, though more optimistic about avoiding that danger. But I think that anybody who reads, for example, the section of Dewey's *A Common Faith* called "The Human Abode," or the concluding chapter ("Art and Civiliza-

40 Dewey, *Reconstruction in Philosophy* (Boston: Beacon, 1957), pp. 212–213.

tion") of *Art as Experience,* will see the sort of case that might be made for my claim.[41]

If one asks what is so important about the ability to hear, the ability to have a sense of the contingency of one's words and practices, and thus of the possibility of alternatives to them, I think Dewey's and Heidegger's answers would overlap. They both might say that this ability, and only this ability, makes it possible to feel *gratitude* for and to those words, those practices, and the beings they disclose.

The gratitude in question is not the sort which the Christian has when he or she thanks Omnipotence for the stars and the trees. It is rather a matter of being grateful to the stars and trees themselves – to the beings that were disclosed by our linguistic practices. Or, if you prefer, it means being grateful for the existence of *ourselves,* for our ability to disclose the beings we have disclosed, for the embodied languages we are, but not grateful *to* anybody or anything. If you can see yourself-in-the-midst-of-beings as a *gift* rather than as an occasion for the exercise of power, then, in Heidegger's terms, you will cease to be "humanistic" and begin to "let beings be." You will combine the humility of the scientific realist with the spiritual freedom of the Romantic.

That combination was just what Dewey wanted to achieve. He wanted to combine the vision of a social democratic utopia with the knowledge that only a lot of hard work and blind luck, unaided by any large nonhuman power called Reason or History, could bring that utopia into existence. He combines reminders that only attention to the daily detail, to the obstinacy of particular circumstance, can create a utopia with reminders that all things are possible, that there are no *a priori* or destined limits to our imagination or our achievement. His "humanism" was not the power mania which Heidegger thought to be the only remaining possibility open to the West. On the contrary, it put power in the service of love – technocratic manipulation in the service of a Whitmanesque sense that our democratic community is held together by nothing less fragile than social hope.

My preference for Dewey over Heidegger is based on the conviction that what Heidegger wanted – something that was not a calculation of means to ends, not

---

41   The latter book is full of the kinds of criticisms of aestheticism which Heidegger himself makes. Heidegger would heartily agree with Dewey that "As long as art is the beauty parlor of civilization, neither art nor civilization is secure." *Art as Experience* (New York: Putnam, 1958), p. 344. But Heidegger would not agree that "there is nothing in the nature of machine production *per se* that is an insuperable obstacle in the way of workers' consciousness of the meaning of what they do and work well done" (p. 343). Heidegger thought it in principle impossible that assembly line workers could have what Schwarzwald peasants had. Dewey had some ideas for arranging things so that they might.

In *A Common Faith* (New Haven, Conn.: Yale University Press, 1934), Dewey praises "natural piety" for much the same reasons as Heidegger criticizes "humanism." See, for example, p. 53, in which both "supernaturalism" and "militant atheism" are condemned for lack of such piety, and for conceiving of "this earth as the moral center of the universe and of man as the apex of the whole scheme of things."

power madness — was under his nose all the time. It was the new world which began to emerge with the French Revolution — a world in which future-oriented politics, romantic poetry, and irreligious art made social practices possible in which Heidegger never joined. He never joined them because he never really looked outside of philosophy books. His sense of the drama of European history was confined to the drama of his own "Sketches for a History of Being as Metaphysics." He was never able to see politics or art as more than epiphenomenal — never able to shake off the philosophy professor's conviction that everything else stands to philosophy as superstructure to base. Like Leo Strauss and Alexandre Kojéve, he thought that if you understood the history of Western philosophy you understood the history of the West.[42] Like Hegel and Marx, he thought of philosophy as somehow geared into something larger than philosophy. So when he decided that Western philosophy had exhausted its possibilities, he decided that the West had exhausted its. Dewey, by contrast, never lost the sense of contingency, and thus the sense of gratitude, which Heidegger thought only an unimaginably new sort of Thinking might reintroduce. Because he took pragmatism not as a switch from love to power, but as a switch from philosophy to politics as the appropriate vehicle for love, he was able to combine skill at manipulation and contrivance with a sense of the fragility of human hopes.

In this paper I have been reading Heidegger by my own, Deweyan lights. But to read Heidegger in this way is just to do to him what he did to everybody else, and to do what no reader of anybody can help doing. There is no point in feeling guilty or ungrateful about it. Heidegger cheerfully ignores, or violently reinterprets, lots of Plato and Nietzsche while presenting himself as respectfully listening to the voice of Being as it is heard in their words. But Heidegger knew what he wanted to hear in advance. He wanted to hear something which would make his own historical position decisive, by making his own historical epoch terminal.

As Derrida brilliantly put it, Heideggerian hope is the reverse side of Heideggerian nostalgia. Heideggerian hope is the hope that Heidegger himself, his Thinking, will be a decisive event in the History of Being.[43] Dewey had no similar hope for his own thought. The very idea of a "decisive event" is foreign to Dewey. Pragmatists like Dewey hope that things may turn out well in the end, but their sense of contingency does not permit them to write dramatic narratives about upward or downward escalators. They exemplify a virtue which Heidegger preached, but was not himself able to practice.

42   This preoccupation with philosophy made Heidegger ungrateful to the time in which he lived, unable to realize that it was thanks to living at a certain historical moment (after Wordsworth, Marx, Delacroix, and Rodin) — living in what he sneeringly called the age of the world picture — that he could paint his own picture, and find an appreciative audience for it.

43   See Derrida, "Différance," in *Margins of Philosophy,* trans. Alan Bass (Chicago: University of Chicago Press, 1982), p. 27: "From the vantage of this laughter and this dance, from the vantage of the affirmation foreign to all dialectics, the other side of nostalgia [cette autre face de la nostalgie], what I will call Heideggerian hope [espérance], comes into question."

Wittgenstein, Heidegger, and the reification of language

What Gustav Bergmann christened "the linguistic turn" was a rather desperate attempt to keep philosophy an armchair discipline. The idea was to mark off a space for *a priori* knowledge into which neither sociology nor history nor art nor natural science could intrude. It was an attempt to find a substitute for Kant's "transcendental standpoint." The replacement of "mind" or "experience" by "meaning" was supposed to insure the purity and autonomy of philosophy by providing it with a nonempirical subject matter.

Linguistic philosophy was, however, too honest to survive. When, with the later Wittgenstein, this kind of philosophy turned its attention to the question of how such a "pure" study of language was possible, it realized that it was *not* possible – that semantics had to be naturalized if it were to be, in Donald Davidson's phrase, "preserved as a serious subject." The upshot of linguistic philosophy is, I would suggest, Davidson's remark that "there is no such thing as a language, not if a language is anything like what philosophers . . . have supposed. . . . We must give up the idea of a clearly defined shared structure which language users master and then apply to cases."[1] This remark epitomizes what Ian Hacking has called "the death of meaning" – the end of the attempt to make language a transcendental topic.

I take Frege and the early Wittgenstein to be the philosophers primarily responsible for imposing on us the idea that there *was* such a clearly defined shared structure. In particular, we owe to Wittgenstein the idea that all philosophical problems can in principle be finally solved by exhibiting that structure. I take the later Wittgenstein, Quine, and Davidson to be the philosophers who freed us from the idea that there is any such structure. The early Wittgenstein had defined the mystical as "the sense of the world as a limited whole." By contrast, the latter Wittgenstein triumphed over his younger, more Schopenhauerian self by no longer feeling the need to be mystical, no longer needing to set himself over against the world as "the unsayable limit of the world."

The younger Heidegger, the author of *Being and Time,* was much more free of this Schopenhauerian urge than was the younger Wittgenstein. That book was filled with protests against the idea of philosophy as *theoria.* Heidegger saw that

---

1   Donald Davidson, "A Nice Derangement of Epitaphs," in *Truth and Interpretation: Perspectives on the Philosophy of Donald Davidson,* ed. Ernest LePore (Oxford: Blackwell, 1986), p. 446.

idea as an attempt to rise above the "guilt" and "throwness" which he claimed were inseparable from Dasein's worldly and historical existence, an attempt to escape from the contingency of that existence. The younger Heidegger, had he read the *Tractatus*, would have dismissed that book in the same way as the older Wittgenstein dismissed it – as one more attempt to preserve the philosopher's autonomy and self-sufficiency by letting him picture himself as somehow above, or beyond, the world. The young Heidegger would have seen the linguistic turn recommended by Frege and Wittgenstein as merely one more variation on the Platonic attempt to distance oneself from time and chance.

But although the younger Heidegger worked hard to free himself from the notion of the philosopher as spectator of time and eternity, from the wish to see the world from above "as a limited whole," the older Heidegger slipped back into a very similar idea. The limited whole which that Heidegger tried to distance himself from was called "metaphysics" or "the West." For him, "the mystical" became the sense of himself as "thinking after the end of metaphysics" – as looking back on metaphysics, seeing it as a limited, rounded-off whole – and thus as something we might hope to put behind us. The old Heidegger's final vision was of the West as a single gift of Being, a single *Ereignis,* a chalice with one handle labeled "Plato" and the other "Nietzsche," complete and perfect in itself – and therefore, perhaps, capable of being set to one side.

The young Wittgenstein had said, echoing Kant and Schopenhauer, that

We feel that even when *all possible* scientific questions have been answered, the problems of life remain completely untouched. Of course there are then no questions left, and this itself is the answer. . . . There are, indeed, things that cannot be put into words. They *make themselves manifest.* They are what is mystical.[2]

By contrast, the young Heidegger had no explicit doctrine of things that cannot be put into words, of *das Unaussprechliche.* Dasein was linguistic through and through, just as it was social through and through.[3] What the younger Heidegger tells us about the sociohistorical situation of Dasein is just what the older Wittgenstein tells us about our situation in regard to language – that when we try to transcend it by turning metaphysical we become self-deceptive, inauthentic.

2 *Tractatus Logico-Philosophicus,* trans. D. F. Pears and B. F. McGuiness (London: Routledge and Kegan Paul, 1961), 6.52–6.522.
3 I take the claim in *Being and Time* (trans. John Macquarrie and Edward Robinson [New York: Harper and Row, 1962], p. 318; *Sein und Zeit* [Tübingen: Niemeyer, 1963], p. 273), that "Conscience discourses solely and constantly in the mode of keeping silent" to be not a doctrine of inexpressibility but rather the doctrine that the realization that one must change one's life cannot be backed up with reasons – for such reasons could only be voices from one's past life. See Davidson on this point in his "Paradoxes of Irrationality" in Richard Wollheim and James Hopkins, eds., *Philosophical Essays on Freud* (Cambridge: Cambridge University Press, 1982), p. 305: "The agent has reasons for changing his own habits and character, but those reasons come from a domain of values necessarily extrinsic to the contents of the views or values to undergo change. The cause of the change, if it comes, can therefore not be a reason for what it causes."

But the older Heidegger retreated from sentences and discourse to single words – words which had to be abandoned as soon as they ceased to be hints (*Winke*) and became signs (*Zeichen*), as soon as they entered into relations with other words and thus became tools for accomplishing purposes. The younger – unpragmatical, mystical – Wittgenstein had wanted sentences to be pictures rather than merely tools. By contrast, the pragmatical young Heidegger, the philosopher of inescapable relationality (*Bezüglichkeit*), had been content to let them be tools. But the older, more pragmatical Wittgenstein became content to think of them as tools, about the same time that the older Heidegger decided his early pragmatism had been a premature surrender to "reason [which], glorified for centuries, is the most stiff-necked adversary of thought."[4]

On my reading of them, then, these two great philosophers passed each other in mid-career, going in opposite directions. Wittgenstein, in the *Tractatus*, started from a point which, to a pragmatist like myself, seems much less enlightened than that of *Being and Time*. But, as Wittgenstein advanced in the direction of pragmatism, he met Heidegger coming the other way – retreating from pragmatism into the same escapist mood in which the *Tractatus* had been written, attempting to regain in "thought" the sort of sublimity which the young Wittgenstein had found in logic. The direction in which Wittgenstein was going led him to radical doubts about the very notion of philosophy as a provider of knowledge, and to a detranscendentalized, naturalized conception of philosophy as a form of therapy, as a *technē* rather than as the achievement of *theoria*. Heidegger had himself begun with just such doubts. But he was unable to sustain them, and so in the end he was driven to inventing "Thought" as a substitute for what he called "metaphysics." This led him to speak of language as a quasi-divinity in which we live and move and have our being, and of all previous Thought as a limited whole, a tale that had now been fully told.

So far I have been presenting a brief outline of a story which I shall tell in more detail. I shall begin my longer version with Wittgenstein's attempt to find a new way of doing philosophy.

Any attempt to preserve a method and a topic for armchair philosophy, one which will permit it to look down upon natural science and history, is likely to invoke the Kantian notion of "conditions of possibility." Whereas physics and history find conditions for the existence of actualities by discovering temporally prior actualities, philosophy can achieve autonomy only if it escapes from time by escaping from actuality to possibility. The Kantian strategy for achieving this escape was to replace an atemporal Deity with an atemporal subject of experience. Kant's "possible experience" – the domain whose bounds philosophy was to set –

4 Heidegger, "Nietzsche's Word: 'God is Dead,' " in *The Question Concerning Technology and Other Essays*, trans. W. Lovitt (New York: Harper and Row, 1977), p. 112. The original is at Heidegger, *Holzwege* (Frankfurt: Klostermann, 1972), p. 247.

was purportedly smaller than the broader domain of logical possibility to which Wolff's ontotheology had claimed access. But it was enough for Kant's purposes that it overarched the domains of the scientists and the historians.

The linguistic turn was a second attempt to find a domain which would overarch those of the other professors. This second attempt became necessary because, in the course of the nineteenth century, evolutionary biology and empirical psychology had begun to naturalize the notions of "mind," "consciousness," and "experience."[5] "Language" was the twentieth-century philosopher's substitute for "experience" for two reasons. First, the two terms had an equally large scope – both delimited the entire domain of human inquiry, of topics available to human study. Second, the notions of "language" and "meaning" seemed, at the beginning of the century, immune to the naturalizing process.[6] Wittgenstein's *Tractatus* became the model around which the disciplinary matrix of analytic philosophy was molded. The preface to that book suggested (for the first time, as far as I know) the doctrine which Michael Dummett later put forward explicitly: that philosophy of language was first philosophy.

Philosophy of language, done in the manner of Frege, was supposed to produce conditions of describability, just as Kant had promised to produce conditions of experienceability. Describability, like experienceability, was supposed to be the mark of everything studied or exemplified by all areas of study other than philosophy. Language seemed able to avoid relativization to history, for description was thought to be a single indissoluble activity, whether done by Neanderthals, Greeks, or Germans. If one could give *a priori* conditions of the activity of description, then one would be in a position to offer apodeictic truths. To both Husserl and Frege, Brentano's thesis of the irreducibility of the intentional

5 After Darwin, it became increasingly difficult to use the notion of "experience" in the sense Kant had tried to give it. For Darwin, by making Spirit continuous with Nature, completed the historicizing process which Hegel had begun. So those who wanted to preserve the notion of philosophy as a nonempirical science *relativized* the Kantian *a priori*, in the manner common to Dilthey, Collingwood, Croce, and C. I. Lewis. They tried to keep intact the notion of a distinction between the formal and the material – the domain of philosophy and the domain of natural science. But this relativizing cast doubt on the notion of a "transcendental standpoint," and thus on the notion of "possible experience" as something the conditions of which could be specified. For a plurality of forms of experience or forms of consciousness looks much like a plurality of actualities, each of which may be presumed to have causal, naturalistically explicable conditions. Further, if the *a priori* could change, then it is no longer *a priori* enough, for philosophical arguments can no longer culminate in immutable, apodeictic truths.

In this situation, what was needed was to find something which looked as much like an indissoluble unity as Kant had thought "experience" to be, but which could not be subjected to relativization. For Husserl, this need was met by the realm which opened itself up to those highly trained professionals capable of performing transcendental-phenomenological reductions. For Frege and the young Wittgenstein, it was met by the notion of a language, construed in the sense condemned by Davidson, as referring to a "clearly defined shared structure."

6 What Hacking describes as the "death of meaning" brought about by Davidsonian holism I should prefer to describe as the naturalization of Fregean meaning. This description preserves the parallel with Darwin's naturalization of Kantian experience.

seemed to guarantee that the Kantian distinction between the *a priori* and apodeictic and the *a posteriori* and relative would remain secure. For even though the evolutionary transition from organisms which do not exhibit linguistic behavior to those which do could be explained naturalistically, linguistic behavior could not be adequately characterized in the terms used to characterize everything else in the universe. So the irreducibility of the intentional seemed to guarantee the autonomy of philosophy.[7]

The young Wittgenstein saw, however, what Frege and the young Russell had not seen: that the search for nonempirical truth about the conditions of the possibility of describability raises the self-referential problem of its own possibility. Just as Kant had faced the problem of rendering the possibility of transcendental philosophy consistent with the restrictions on inquiry which such philosophy purports to have discovered, so Frege and Russell had trouble explaining how knowledge of what they called "logic" was possible. The problem was that logic seemed to be an exception to the conditions which it itself laid down. The propositions of logic were not truth-functional combinations of elementary statements about the objects which make up the world. Yet "logic" seemed to tell us that only such combinations had meaning.

Russell had tried to solve this problem by reinventing the Platonic Forms. He had postulated a realm of otherworldly logical objects and a faculty of intellectual intuition with which to grasp them. But Wittgenstein saw that this led to a new version of the "third man problem" which Plato had raised in the *Parmenides* – the problem of how the entities designed to explain knowledge are known. Russell's logical objects, the Kantian categories, and the Platonic Forms were all supposed to make another set of objects – the empirical objects, the Kantian intuitions, or the Platonic material particulars – knowable, or describable. In each case, we are told the latter objects need to be related by the former objects before they become available – before they may be experienced or described.

Call the lower-level entities, those which stand in need of being related in order to become available, entities of type B. These are entities which require relations but cannot themselves relate, require contextualization and explanation but cannot themselves contextualize nor explain. The Platonic Forms, the Kantian categories, and the Russellian logical objects are examples of what I shall call type A entities. These entities contextualize and explain but cannot, on pain of infinite regress, be contextualized or explained.

<hr />

7 I have argued elsewhere, following leads provided by Quine and Davidson, that the irreducibility of one vocabulary to another is no guarantee of the existence of two distinct sets of objects of inquiry. On the current state of debate about the nature and importance of intentional ascriptions, see Daniel Dennett's suggestion that the great divide within contemporary philosophy of mind and philosophy or language comes between those who believe in "intrinsic intentionality" (Searle, Nagel, Fodor, Kripke, et al.) and those who do not (Dennett, Davidson, Putnam, Stich, et al.). Dennett develops this suggestion in chapters 8 and 10 of his *The Intentional Stance* (Cambridge, Mass.: MIT Press, 1987).

Those who postulate type A objects are always faced with the following self-referential problem: if we claim that no entity is available which remains unrelated by a form of relationship which cannot hold between unaided type B entities, then we have problems about the availability of the type A entities we postulate to lend the necessary aid. For if we are allowed to say that type A entities are their own *rationes cognoscendi,* or their own conditions of linguistic accessibility – that they make themselves available without being related to one another or to anything else – then we are faced with the question of why type B entities cannot themselves have this obviously desirable feature.

This dilemma is familiar from theology: if God can be *causa sui,* why should not the world be? Why not just identify God and nature, as Spinoza did? All type A entities, all unexplained explainers, are in the same situation as a transcendent Deity. If we are entitled to believe in them without relating them to something which conditions their existence or knowability or describability, then we have falsified our initial claim that availability requires being related by something other than the relata themselves. We have opened up the question of why we ever thought that there was a problem about availability in the first place. We have thereby questioned the need for philosophy, insofar as philosophy is thought of as the study of conditions of availability.

I shall define "naturalism" as the view that *anything* might have been otherwise, that there can be no conditionless conditions.[8] Naturalists believe that all explanation is causal explanation of the actual, and that there is no such thing as a noncausal condition of possibility. If we think of philosophy as a quest for apodicticity, for truths whose truth requires no explanation, then we make philosophy inherently antinaturalistic and we must agree with Kant and Husserl that Locke and Wundt operate at a subphilosophical level. Wittgenstein's *Tractatus* can be read as a heroic attempt to save philosophy from naturalism by claiming that type A objects must be ineffable, that they can be shown but not said, that they can never become available in the way that type B objects are.

As David Pears has pointed out in his admirable *The False Prison,* there is an analogy between Wittgenstein's discussion of the mysterious "objects" of the *Tractatus* and "the *via remotionis* in theology."[9] Of these objects, which form what he called "the substance of the World," Wittgenstein wrote as follows:

If the world had no substance, then whether a proposition had sense would depend on whether another proposition was true.
In that case we could not sketch out any picture of the world (true or false).[10]

No intrinsically simple objects, no pictures, and no language. For if analysis could not end with such objects, then whether a sentence had sense would

8   Historicism is a special case of naturalism, so defined.
9   See David Pears, *The False Prison* (Oxford: Oxford University Press, 1988), I:67.
10   *Tractatus,* 2.0211–2.0212.

depend, *horribile dictu,* upon whether another sentence were true – the sentence which specifies that two simpler objects making up a composite stand in the relevant compositional relationship. But when one asks what would be so horrible about *that,* Wittgenstein has no obvious answer.

On Pears's account, which seems to me right, what would be horrible about this situation would be that it would violate Wittgenstein's doctrine that "sense-conditions are ineffable." But, Pears sensibly continues, this just makes us wonder why they have to be ineffable.[11] His answer to this latter question is that if they were not ineffable we should have to give up the notion of "the limits of language," and therefore give up the doctrine that there is something which can be shown but not said.[12] Pears rightly takes this "doctrine of showing" to be the one closest to Wittgenstein's heart. He sums it up as follows:

[Wittgenstein's] leading idea was that we can see further than we can say. We can see all the way to the edge of language, but the most distant things that we see cannot be expressed in sentences because they are the pre-conditions of saying anything.[13]

Another way in which Pears formulates this point is by saying that "if factual language could contain an analysis of its conditions of application, the language in which it analysed them would itself depend on further conditions. . . ."[14] This chimes with the following passage:

Objects can only be *named.* Signs are their representatives. I can only speak *about* them: I cannot *put them into words.* Propositions can only say *how* things are, not *what* they are. The requirement that simple signs be possible is the requirement that sense be determinate.[15]

To sum up, if there were no objects, if the world had no substance, if there were no "unalterable form of the world,"[16] then sense would not be determinate, we would not be able to make ourselves pictures of the world, and description would be impossible. So the condition of the possibility of description must itself be indescribable. By way of parallel arguments, Plato concluded that the conditions of the possibility of the material world must be immaterial, and Kant that the conditions of the phenomenal world must be nonphenomenal.

The later Wittgenstein dropped the notion of "seeing to the edge of lan-

11 Pears, *False Prison,* I:71–72.
12 More exactly, his answer is that ". . . we cannot give a complete account of the sense of any factual sentence. The reason . . . is that such an account would have to use language in order to identify the possibility presented by the sentence, and there is only one way for language to latch on to this possibility and that is to exploit the same method of correlation. . . . There is only one way in which the ultimate grid of possibilities [the array of objects which form the substance of the world] imposes its structure on all factual languages, and in this case it has been pre-empted by the original sentence." (Ibid., I:144.)
13 Ibid., I:146–147.
14 Ibid., I:7.
15 *Tractatus,* 3.221–3.23.
16 See ibid., 2.026–2.027: "There must be objects if the world is to have an unalterable form. Objects, the unalterable, and the subsistent are one and the same."

guage." He also dropped the whole idea of "language" as a bounded whole
which had conditions at its outer edges, as well as the project of transcendental
semantics – of finding nonempirical conditions for the possibility of linguistic
description. He became reconciled to the idea that whether a sentence had sense
did indeed depend upon whether another sentence was true – a sentence about
the social practices of the people who used the marks and noises which were the
components of the sentence. He thereby became reconciled to the notion that
there was nothing ineffable, and that philosophy, like language, was just a set of
indefinitely expansible social practices, not a bounded whole whose periphery
might be "shown." At the time of the *Tractatus* he had thought that the
assemblage of philosophical problems formed such a whole, and that he had
solved all these problems at once by drawing the consequences of the statement
which, he claimed, "summed up the whole sense of [his] book": "what can be
said at all can be said clearly, and what we cannot talk about we must pass over
in silence."[17] He thought of philosophy as coextensive with an investigation of
the possibility of meaning, and of that investigation as culminating in the
discovery of the ineffable.

As Michael Dummett rightly says, if one adopts the point of view of Wittgenstein's *Philosophical Investigations,* there can be no such thing as a "systematic
theory of meaning for a language." If one believes, with Dummett, that philosophy of language is first philosophy, then it follows that philosophy can never be
more than therapeutic – can never set out positive conclusions.[18] As Thomas
Nagel rightly says, Wittgenstein's later position "depends on a position so radical
that it . . . undermines the weaker transcendent pretensions of even the least
philosophical of thoughts." This position entails, as Nagel puts it, "that any
thoughts we can form of a mind-independent reality must remain within the
boundaries set by our human form of life."[19] Dummett and Nagel both see the
later Wittgenstein as endangering philosophy by casting aside the picture which
had held him captive when he wrote the *Tractatus* – the picture which Davidson

17 Ibid., "Foreword."
18 See Michael Dummett, *Truth and Other Enigmas* (Cambridge, Mass.: Harvard University Press,
    1978), p. 453, and compare Dummett's "What Is a Theory of Meaning? (II)," in *Truth and
    Meaning,* ed. Gareth Evans and John McDowell (Oxford: Oxford University Press, 1976), p.
    105. In the latter essay Dummett traces our philosophical problems back to "our propensity to
    assume a realistic interpretation of all sentences of our language, that is, to suppose that the
    notion of truth applicable to statements of this kind is determinately either true or false,
    independently of our knowledge or means of knowing" (p. 101). In contrast, Davidson is
    inclined to trace them back to the antiholistic implications of the assumption which Dummett
    (p. 89) calls "principle C," viz., "if a statement is true, there must be something in virtue of
    which it is true." Dummett mistakenly believed, at the time of writing this paper, that this
    principle was accepted by both himself and Davidson. Dummett's acceptance of this principle
    and his insistence on the need for an "atomic or molecular theory of meaning," as opposed to a
    thoroughgoing holistic one, stands to Davidson's view roughly as the *Tractatus* stands to the
    Philosophical Investigations.
19 Thomas Nagel, *The View from Nowhere* (Oxford: Oxford University Press, 1986), pp. 106–107.

has labeled the distinction of scheme and content. This is the distinction between what I have called type A entities and type B entities.

I would argue that this A-versus-B distinction is the least common denominator of the Greek distinction between universals and particulars, the Kantian distinction between concepts and intuitions, and the Tractarian distinction between the available and effable world and the unavailable and ineffable "substance of the world." The last version of this distinction is the most dramatic and the most revealing, since it sets out starkly the contrast between atomism and holism – between the assumption that there can be entities which are what they are totally independent of all relations between them, and the assumption that all entities are merely nodes in a net of relations.

Both Nagel and Dummett see a need to resist holism in order to preserve the possibility of philosophy. Both think of Davidson as endangering philosophy by embracing a thoroughgoing holism. They are right to do so, since Davidson's account of human linguistic behavior takes for granted, as the later Wittgenstein also did, that there are no linguistic entities which are intrinsically relationless – none which, like the "simple names" of the *Tractatus*, are by nature relata. But Davidson's holism is more explicit and thoroughgoing than Wittgenstein's, and so its antiphilosophical consequences are more apparent. Whereas in the *Philosophical Investigations* Wittgenstein still toys with the idea of a distinction between the empirical and the grammatical, between nonphilosophical and philosophical inquiry, Davidson generalizes and extends Quine's refusal to countenance either a distinction between necessary and contingent truth or a distinction between philosophy and science. Davidson insists that we not think either of language in general or a particular language (say, English or German) as something which has edges, something which forms a bounded whole and can thus become a distinct object of study or of philosophical theorizing. Bjorn Ramberg is right in saying that Davidson's principal motive is to avoid the reification of language.[20] So Davidson has no use for the idea that philosophical therapy is a matter of detecting "nonsense," of spotting "violations of language." Rather, it is a matter of spotting unproductive and self-defeating philosophical behavior – the sort of behavior which sends one, over and over again, down the same blind alleys (e.g., alleys labeled "realism," "idealism," and "antirealism").

Instead, Davidson asks us to think of human beings trading marks and noises to accomplish purposes. We are to see this linguistic behavior as continuous with nonlinguistic behavior, and to see both sorts of behavior as making sense just insofar as we can describe them as attempts to fulfill given desires in the light of given beliefs. But the realm of belief and desire – the so-called "realm of the intentional" – does not itself form an object of philosophical inquiry. Davidson

---

20 See Bjorn Ramberg, *Donald Davidson's Philosophy of Language: An Introduction* (Oxford: Blackwell, 1989), p. 2 and chapter 8, *passim*.

agrees with Quine that neither the practical indispensability of the intentional idiom nor its Brentanian irreducibility to a behavioristic idiom gives us reason to think that there are type A entities called "intentions" or "meanings" which serve to relate type B entities.[21]

So much, for the moment, for Wittgenstein's and Davidson's attempts to escape from the idea that there is a discipline – philosophy – which can study conditions of possibility rather than merely conditions of actuality. I turn now to the early Heidegger's attempt to escape from this same idea – the idea of a discipline which lets us stand over and against the world of everyday practice by seeing it as God sees it, as a limited whole. I interpret the pragmatism of the first Division of *Being and Time* – the insistence on the priority of the ready-to-hand, the *Zuhanden,* over the present-at-hand, the *Vorhanden,* and on the inseparability of Dasein from its projects and its language – as a first attempt to find a nonlogocentric, nonontotheological way of thinking of things. It was a holistic attempt to eschew the scheme–content distinction, to replace a distinction between entities of type A and those of type B with a seamless, indefinitely extensible web of relations.

From the point of view of both *Philosophical Investigations* and *Being and Time,* the typical error of traditional philosophy is to imagine that there could be, indeed that there somehow *must* be, entities which are atomic in the sense of being what they are independent of their relation to any other entities (e.g., God, the transcendental subject, sense-data, simple names). For the later Wittgenstein, the best example of this mistake is his own earlier hope to discover the "unalterable

---

21 See Quine's remark about Brentano at *Word and Object* (Cambridge, Mass.: MIT Press, 1960), p. 221, and Davidson's treatment of Brentanian irreducibility in "Mental Events," included in his *Essays on Actions and Events* (Oxford: Oxford University Press, 1980).

My picture of Quine and Davidson as taking the holism of the *Philosophical Investigations* to its limits helps bring out the frequently cited analogies between Wittgenstein and Derrida. See Henry Staten, *Wittgenstein and Derrida* (Lincoln: University of Nebraska Press, 1984). For analogies between Derridean and Davidsonian doctrines, see Samuel Wheeler, "Indeterminacy of French Interpretation: Derrida and Davidson," in *Truth and Interpretation: Perspectives on the Philosophy of Donald Davidson,* ed. Ernest LePore (Oxford: Blackwell, 1986), pp. 477–494.

In my picture, Davidson stands to Wittgenstein as Derrida stands to Heidegger: both of these more recent writers are trying to purify the doctrines of the earlier writer, trying to divest them of the last traces of the tradition which they had tried to overcome. Derrida's suspicion of what he calls "Heideggerian nostalgia" is the counterpart to Davidson's suspicion of the later Wittgenstein's distinction between "grammar" and "fact." Davidson and Derrida are both protesting against vestiges of what Derrida calls "logocentrism" – trying to free their respective predecessors from their last remaining attachments to the idea that philosophy can shield itself from natural science, art, and history by isolating what Derrida calls "a full presence which is beyond play." (Derrida, *Writing and Difference,* trans. Alan Bass [Chicago: University of Chicago Press, 1978], p. 279.) Texts for Derrida, and human behavior for Davidson, are both centerless networks of relations, networks which can always be redescribed and recontextualized by themselves being placed within some larger network. For both writers, there is no such thing as "the largest network" – no bounded whole which can be the object of specifically philosophical inquiry.

form of the world," something which underlies the available or lies at the edges of the available, something which is a condition of the possibility of availability. When in the *Investigations* he is criticizing the Tractarian desire for "something like a final analysis of our forms of language," he says that it is as if we had in mind "a state of complete exactness" as opposed to whatever relative degree of exactness may be required for some particular purpose. This notion impels us, Wittgenstein continues, to ask "questions as to the *essence* of language, of propositions, of thought." He diagnoses the urge to ask such questions as due to the idea that "the essence is hidden from us." Obsession with this image of something deeply hidden makes one want to ask questions whose answers would be, as he says, "given once for all; and independently of any future experience."[22]

This last phrase sums up the idea that there is a nonempirical discipline which can tell us about the conditions of "all possible experience," or of all possible languages and forms of life. This is the idea which *Being and Time* rejected by insisting on the primordiality of the *Zuhanden,* on the fact that everything was always already related. The early Heidegger saw as clearly as the later Wittgenstein that the present-at-hand was only available in the context of pre-existent relations with the ready-to-hand, that social practice was the presupposition of the demand for exactness and for answers that could be given once and for all. Both saw that the only way in which the present-at-hand could explain the ready-to-hand was in the familiar unphilosophical way in which evolutionary biology, sociology, and history combine to give a causal explanation of the actuality of one particular social practice rather than another. Early Heidegger and late Wittgenstein set aside the assumption (common to their respective predecessors, Husserl and Frege) that social practice – and in particular the use of language – can receive a noncausal, specifically philosophical explanation in terms of conditions of possibility. More generally, both set aside the assumption that philosophy might explain the unhidden on the basis of the hidden, and might explain availability and relationality on the basis of something intrinsically unavailable and nonrelational.

One can imagine a possible Heidegger who, after formulating the Dewey-like social-practice pragmatism of the early sections of *Being and Time,* would have felt that his job was pretty well done.[23] But the early Heidegger was driven by the

22 All the passages cited in this paragraph are from *Philosophical Investigations*, I, secs. 91–92. Norman Malcolm's admirable account of the relation of the *Tractatus* to Wittgenstein's later thought is entitled *Nothing is Hidden,* a reference to *Investigations,* I, sec. 126: "Philosophy simply puts everything before us, and neither explains nor deduces anything. Since everything lies open to view there is nothing to explain. For what is hidden, for example, is of no interest to us."

23 I am following Robert Brandom ("Heidegger's Categories in *Being and Time," The Monist* 66 [1983]) and Mark Okrent (*Heidegger's Pragmatism* [Ithaca, N.Y.: Cornell University Press, 1988]) in taking Heidegger's attack on Cartesianism as central to the achievement of *Being and Time.* See also Charles Guignon, *Heidegger and the Theory of Knowledge* (Indianapolis: Hackett, 1983), chapter 1, "Heidegger's Problem and the Cartesian Model." These writers agree in thinking that what Brandom describes as the recognition that social practice is determinative of what is and is

same urge to *purity* which drove the early Wittgenstein. The same drives which led Heidegger to develop the notions of "authenticity" and "being-toward-death" in the later portions of *Sein und Zeit* led Wittgenstein to write the final sections of the *Tractatus* — the sections in which the doctrine of showing is extended from logic to ethics. These are the so-called "Schopenhauerian" sections in which we are told such things as

It is clear that ethics cannot be put into words. . . . It is impossible to speak about the will in so far it is the subject of ethical attributes. . . . Death is not an event in life. . . . *How* things are in the world is a matter of complete indifference for what is higher. . . . It is not *how* things are in the world that is mystical, but *that* it exists. . . . Feeling the world as a limited whole — it is this that is the mystical.[24]

What is common to early Heidegger on authenticity and to the early Wittgenstein on the sense of the world as a limited whole is the urge to see social practice as *merely* social practice, thereby rising above it. This is the urge to *distance* the social practice to which one has been accustomed (though not necessarily to cease to participate in it) by seeing it as contingent — as something into which one has been thrown. So seen, it is something which one can only make authentic, only properly appropriate, by being able to say, with Nietzsche, "thus I willed it," thereby "becoming what one is."

To become authentic in this way is to see the requirement of mere accuracy (Heidegger's *Richtigkeit*) — the requirement to say what "one" (*das Man*) says, to give the right answers to "scientific" and "empirical" questions — as the requirement only of a "*limited* whole," of one possible ontic situation among others. This attempt to distance mere accuracy, to find something more important than giving the correct answers to intelligible questions, something more important than anything empirical science might offer, was encouraged by Kant's project of denying reason in order to make room for faith, and developed further by Schopenhauer, from whose hands both Nietzsche and the young Wittgenstein received it. It was also encouraged by Kierkegaard's and Nietzsche's sneers at Hegel's pretensions to scientificity and rigor.

But whereas the attempt to find what Habermas calls (following Adorno) "an Other to Reason" was common to the young Heidegger and the young Wittgenstein, Heidegger pressed it further as he grew older, whereas Wittgenstein gradually abandoned it. The crucial difference between their later selves is in

not up to social practice is Heidegger's crucial insight in this work. See especially Brandom's interpretation of the claim that the analytic of Dasein is fundamental ontology as an expression of this recognition (Brandom, p. 389). I take the criticism of Husserl at *Prolegomena der Geschichte des Zeitbegriffs* (Heidegger, *Gesamtausgabe*, vol. 20 [Frankfurt: Klostermann, 1979], p. 62), and Heidegger's claim on the following page that what is needed to get beyond Husserl is to clear up "the togetherness of *intentum* and *intentio*" as prefiguring the claim of *Being and Time* that, in Brandom's words, "Dasein-in-the-world-of-the-ready-to-hand is ontologically self-adjudicating."

24 These passages are extracted from *Tractatus* 6.421–6.52.

their attitude toward the projects of their earlier selves. Whereas Heidegger came to feel that *Being and Time* was insufficiently radical, because "not yet thought through in terms of the history of Being,"[25] Wittgenstein came to feel that the *Tractatus* was just a last outbreak of a disease from which he had been almost, but not quite, cured. Whereas Heidegger continued his own quest for authenticity by attempting to win himself a place in the history of Being as the first postmetaphysical Thinker, Wittgenstein's attitude toward philosophy became steadily more casual. Whereas the young Wittgenstein had had large quasi-Schopenhauerian things to say about such subjects as "the whole modern Weltanschauung,"[26] that sort of topic no longer surfaces in his later work. Heidegger becomes more and more interested in his own relation to history, and Wittgenstein less and less.

This is particularly clear in their respective attitudes toward metaphors of *depth* and *antiquity*. As Heidegger goes along, he worries more and more about whether he is being sufficiently *primordial*. Although Wittgenstein expressed sympathy with what he had heard of early Heidegger, one imagines that he would have mocked the later Heidegger's search for ever greater primordiality. That search would have seemed an instance of the process he described as "In order to find the true artichoke, we divested it of its leaves."[27]

The same opposition turns up if one looks at the way in which the two men change their attitudes toward language as a topic of study. The *Tractatus* starts out by telling us that the problems of philosophy are posed "because the logic of our language is misunderstood," but by the time we get to the *Philosophical Investigations* Wittgenstein is mocking the idea that there is any such logic to study. He mocks his younger self for believing that logic is "the incomparable essence of language," something "of purest crystal," something deeply hidden and graspable only after strenuous philosophizing. In the *Investigations* philosophy does not study a subject called "language," nor does it offer a theory of how meaning is possible – it offers only what Wittgenstein calls "reminders for a particular purpose."[28]

By contrast, the term "language" (*Sprache*) plays a very small role in *Being and Time,* and when it does occur, in section 34, it is subordinated to "talk" (*Rede*) and thus to Dasein. But by the time we get to the "Letter on Humanism," we find Heidegger saying "If the truth of Being has become thought-provoking for thinking, then reflection on the essence of language must also attain a different rank."[29] The stock of language rises as that of Dasein falls, as Heidegger worries more and more about the possibility that his earlier work has been infected with the "human-

25 See the citation of this passage in "Philosophy as Science, as Metaphor, and as Politics" above, fn. 20.
26 See *Tractatus* 6.371–6.372. Compare *Philosophical Remarks*, p. 7.
27 *Philosophical Investigations*, I, sec. 164.
28 Ibid., I, sec. 127.
29 *Basic Writings*, p. 198 (*Wegmarken*, 2nd ed., p. 315). Heidegger goes on to suggest that he already knew this when he wrote section 34 of *Sein und Zeit*, but I think this claim to prescience should be taken with a grain of salt.

ism" characteristic of the age of the world picture, about the possibility that Sartre had not misread him, and that Husserl had had a point when he said that *Being and Time* was merely anthropology.[30] More generally, Heidegger's turn from the earlier question "What are the roots of the traditional ontotheological problematic?" to the later question "Where do we stand in the history of Being?" is accompanied by a desperate anxiety that he be offering something *more* than, as he puts it, "simply a history of the alterations in human beings' self-conceptions."[31] So, at the same time as Wittgenstein was coming to see "language" as referring simply to the exchange of marks and noises among human beings for particular purposes, as no more denoting a real essence than does "game," Heidegger is trying desperately to think of the various houses of Being in which human beings have dwelt as "gifts of Being" rather than "human self-conceptions."

In order to justify my obvious preference for the later Wittgenstein over the later Heidegger, and my view that Heidegger's "turn" was a failure of nerve, I need to offer an account of the motives which dictated the trajectories of the two philosophers' careers. As I see it, they both started from a need to escape from what they both called "chatter" (*Geschwätz*),[32] a need for purity, a need to become authentic by ceasing to speak the language of the philosophical tribe within which they had been raised. The early Wittgenstein was convinced that this meant getting beyond language altogether. In his "Lecture on Ethics" Wittgenstein says that "the tendency of all men who ever tried to talk about Ethics or Religion was to run against the boundaries of language."[33] Elsewhere he said that "Man has the urge to thrust against the limits of language. . . . This thrust against the limits of language is *ethics*. . . ."[34] In a much-quoted letter he said that the point of the *Tractatus* was "an ethical one."[35] The *Tractatus* was supposed to help us get beyond

30 See Heidegger, *Nietzsche* II, p. 194, for a grudging admission on this point.
31 *Nietzsche* IV (trans. Frank Capuzzi), p. 138. The original is at *Nietzsche* II, p. 192: *eine Geschichte des Wandels der Selbstauffasung der Menschen.*
32 See McGuiness, ed., *Wittgenstein und der Wiener Kreis* (Frankfurt: Suhrkamp, 1984), p. 69: "I think it obviously important that we put an end to all the chatter about ethics [*Geschwätz über Ethik*] – whether it is cognitive, whether values exist, whether "good" is definable, and so on." The context is his famous remark that he could understand what Heidegger meant by "Being" and "Angst." Compare Heidegger, *Was heisst Denken?* (Tübingen, 1954), p. 19: *Was einmal Schrei war: 'Die Wüste wächst . . .' droht zum Geschwätz zu werden* ([Nietzsche's words] 'The wasteland grows' were once a shout, but now threaten to become merely chatter).
33 Wittgenstein, "Lecture on Ethics," *Philosophical Review* 74 (1965), p. 13. For a detailed account of the connection between the *Tractatus*'s doctrine of showing and Wittgenstein's ideas about spiritual perfection, see James Edwards, *Ethics Without Philosophy: Wittgenstein and the Moral Life* (Tampa: University Presses of Florida, 1982) – a book to which I am much indebted for my understanding of Wittgenstein. Unfortunately, I read Edwards's *The Authority of Language: Heidegger, Wittgenstein and the Threat of Philosophical Nihilism* (Tampa: University of South Florida Press, 1990) too late to use it when composing this paper. That book now seems to me the most illuminating of the many attempts to bring Heidegger and Wittgenstein together.
34 *Wittgenstein und der Wiener Kreis*, p. 68.
35 Englemann, *Letters from Wittgenstein*, ed. McGuiness, p. 143.

chatter, help eliminate the temptation to try to say what could only be shown, to talk of type A entities in terms appropriate only to type B entities.

As Wittgenstein grew older, however, he became reconciled to the fact that the difference between chatter and nonchatter is one of degree. As he gradually became reconciled to the fact that he would never see the world as a limited whole, he gradually dropped the notion of the "limits of language." So he turned the *Tractatus* distinction between saying and showing into the distinction between assertions and the social practices which gave meaning to assertions. He thereby reinvented Heidegger's doctrine that assertion is a derivative mode of interpretation. The later Wittgenstein would have heartily agreed with the claim in *Being and Time* that

The pointing-out which assertion does is performed on the basis of what has already been disclosed in understanding or discovered circumspectively. Assertion is not a free-floating kind of behavior which, in its own right, might be capable of disclosing entities in general in a primary way: on the contrary it always maintains itself on the basis of Being-in-the-world.[36]

This claim is the one developed in detail in Quine's and Davidson's holism – a holism deplored by Nagel and Dummett because, as Nagel puts it, it shows a lack of humility, an "attempt to cut the universe down to size."

Anyone who, like Nagel and the later Heidegger, wants to retain a sense of humility, or a sense of gratitude, toward something which transcends humanity must insist that there are some uses of language which *are* cases of free-floating behavior. Such a philosopher must insist that the presentation of a succession of worlds revealed by social practices – world pictures – does not exhaust the function of language. So anyone who wants to escape from what Heidegger calls our "age of the world picture" must either resurrect the early Wittgenstein's doctrine of ineffability, as Nagel does, or else hypostatize language in the way in which the older Heidegger does in the following passage:

Man acts as though he were the shaper and master of language, while in fact language remains the mistress of man. . . . For strictly, it is language that speaks. Man first speaks when, and only when, he responds to language by listening to its appeal.[37]

But the reification of language in the later Heidegger is simply a stage in the hypostatization of Heidegger himself – in the transfiguration of Martin Heidegger from one more creature of his time, one more self constituted by the social practices of his day, one more reactor to the work of others, into a world-historical figure, the first postmetaphysical thinker. The hope for such transfiguration is the hope that

---

36 *Being and Time*, p. 199 (*Sein und Zeit*, 156).
37 Heidegger, "Poetically man dwells . . . ," in *Poetry, Language, Thought*, trans. Albert Hofstadter (New York: Harper & Row, 1971), pp. 215–216. (I have changed Hofstadter's "master" [for *Herrin*] to "mistress.") The original is at *Vorträge und Aufsätze*, p. 190.

there is still the possibility of something called "thinking" after the end of philosophy. It is the hope that the thinker can avoid immersion in the "always already disclosed," avoid relationality, by following a single star, thinking a single thought. To break free of metaphysics, free of the world which metaphysics has made, would require that Heidegger himself be capable of rising above his time. It would mean that his work was not simply one more *Selbstauffassung,* one more human self-conception, for he would have escaped oneself by escaping his time.

This hope is not to be mocked. It is the same hope which led Plato, Kant, and Russell to invent regress-stopping type A entities, and which led the young Wittgenstein to seek for the limits of language. But, from the point of view of the older Wittgenstein, it is a vain hope: the hope that one may, by coming to look down upon language, or the world, or the West, as a limited whole, become a type A entity oneself. Such an entity would be one which *imposes* limits. Without such an entity, the old Heidegger thought, language, or the world, or the West, is doomed to remain shapeless, a mere tohubohu. This attempt to avoid relatedness, to think a single thought which is not simply a node in a web of other thoughts, to speak a word which has meaning even though it has no place in a social practice, is the urge to find a place which, if not above the heavens, is at least beyond chatter, beyond *Geschwätz.*

But I think that the later Wittgenstein had concluded that there was no such place. He summed up the reason for the failure of the *Tractatus* when he said, in the *Investigations:*

So in the end when one is doing philosophy one gets to the point where one would like just to emit an inarticulate sound. – But such a sound is an expression only if it occurs in a particular language-game, which should now be described.[38]

The later Wittgenstein saw all philosophical attempts to grasp type A entities, all attempts to express the ineffability of such entities, as succeeding only in creating one more language-game.

From the later Wittgenstein's naturalistic and pragmatic point of view, we can be grateful to Heidegger for having given us a new language-game. But we should not see that language-game as Heidegger did – as a way of distancing and summing up the West. It was, instead, simply one more in a long series of self-conceptions. Heideggerese is only Heidegger's gift to us, not Being's gift to Heidegger.

38 *Philosophical Investigations* I, sec. 261.

Heidegger, Kundera, and Dickens

Imagine that the nations which make up what we call "the West" vanish tomorrow, wiped out by thermonuclear bombs. Only Eastern Asia and sub-Saharan Africa remain inhabitable, and in these regions the reaction to the catastrophe is a ruthless campaign of de-Westernization – a fairly successful attempt to obliterate the memory of the last three hundred years. But imagine also that, in the midst of this de-Westernizing campaign, a few people, mostly in the universities, squirrel away as many souvenirs of the West as they can – as many books, magazines, small artifacts, reproductions of works of art, movie films, videotapes, and so on, as they can conceal.

Now imagine that, around the year 2500, memory of the catastrophe fades, the sealed-off cellars are uncovered, and artists and scholars begin to tell stories about the West. There will be many different stories, with many different morals. One such story might center around increasing technological mastery, another around the development of artistic forms, another around changes in sociopolitical institutions, and another around the lifting of sexual taboos. There would be dozens of other guiding threads which story tellers might seize upon. The relative interest and usefulness of each story will depend upon the particular needs of the various African and Asian societies within which they are disseminated.

If, however, there are *philosophers* among the people who write such stories, we can imagine controversies arising about what was "paradigmatically" Western, about the *essence* of the West. We can imagine attempts to tie all these stories together, and to reduce them to one – the one true account of the West, pointing the one true moral of its career. We think of *philosophers* as prone to make such attempts because we tend to identify an area of a culture as "philosophy" when we note an attempt to substitute theory for narrative, a tendency toward essentialism. Essentialism has been fruitful in many areas – most notably in helping us see elegant mathematical relationships behind complex motions, and perspicuous microstructures behind confusing macrostructures. But we have gradually become suspicious of essentialism as applied to human affairs, in areas such as history, sociology, and anthropology. The attempt to find laws of history or essences of cultures – to substitute theory for narrative as an aid to understanding ourselves, others, and the options which we present to one another – has been notoriously unfruitful. Writings as diverse as Karl Popper's on Hegel and Marx,

Charles Taylor's on reductionist social science, and Alasdair MacIntyre's on the role of tradition, have helped us realize this unfruitfulness.

Despite growing recognition that the essentialistic habits of thought which pay off in the natural sciences do not assist moral and political reflection, we Western philosophers still show a distressing tendency to essentialism when we offer intercultural comparisons. This comes out most clearly in our recent willingness to talk about "the West" not as an ongoing, suspenseful adventure in which we are participating but rather as a structure from which we can step back in order to inspect it from a distance. This willingness is partly the cause and partly the effect of the profound influence of Nietzsche and Heidegger on contemporary Western intellectual life. It reflects the sociopolitical pessimism which has afflicted European and American intellectuals ever since we tacitly gave up on socialism without becoming any fonder of capitalism – ever since Marx ceased to present an alternative to Nietzsche and Heidegger. This pessimism, which sometimes calls itself "postmodernism," has produced a conviction that the hopes for greater freedom and equality which mark the recent history of the West were somehow deeply self-deceptive. "Postmodernist" attempts to encapsulate and sum up the West have made it increasingly tempting to contrast the West as a whole with the rest of the world as a whole. Such attempts make it easy to start using "the East" or "non-Western modes of thought" as the names of a mysterious redemptive force, as something which may still offer hope.

I am dubious about such attempts to encapsulate the West, to treat it as a finished-off object which we are now in a position to subject to structural analysis. In particular, I want to protest the tendency to take Heidegger's account of the West for granted. There is, it seems to me, a growing willingness to read Heidegger as the West's final message to the world. This message consists largely of the claim that the West has, to use one of Heidegger's favorite phrases, "exhausted its possibilities." Heidegger was one of the great synoptic imaginations of our century, but his extraordinary gifts make his message sound more plausible than I think it is. We need to remember that the scope of Heidegger's imagination, great as it was, was largely restricted to philosophy and lyric poetry, to the writings of those to whom he awarded the title of "Thinker" or that of "Poet." Heidegger thought that the essence of an historical epoch could be discovered by reading the works of the characteristic philosopher of that epoch and identifying his "Understanding of Being." He thought that the history of the West could best be understood by finding a dialectical progression connecting the works of successive great philosophical thinkers. Those of us who teach philosophy are especially susceptible to the persuasive power of Heidegger's account of the West's history and prospects. But this susceptibility is a professional deformation which we should struggle to overcome.

As a way of counteracting Heidegger and, more generally, the kind of post-Heideggerian thinking which refuses to see the West as a continuing adventure, I want to put forward Charles Dickens as a sort of anti-Heidegger. If my imaginary Asians and Africans were, for some reason, unable to preserve the works of both men, I should much prefer that they preserve Dickens's. For Dickens could help them grasp a complex of attitudes which was important to the West, and perhaps unique to the West, in a way that neither Heidegger nor any other philosopher could. The example of Dickens could help them think of the novel, and particularly the novel of moral protest, rather than the philosophical treatise, as the genre in which the West excelled. Focusing on this genre would help them to see not technology, but rather the hope of freedom and equality as the West's most important legacy. From this point of view, the interaction of West and East is better exemplified by the playing of Beethoven's Ninth Symphony by the students in Tienanmen Square than by the steel mills of Korea or the influence of Japanese prints on European painters of the nineteenth century.[1]

I shall do three things in the remainder of this paper. First, I shall offer an account of Heidegger as one more example of what Nietzsche called "the ascetic priest." Second, I shall summarize and gloss Milan Kundera's account of the novel as the vehicle of a revolt against the ontotheological treatise, of an anticlerical reaction against the cultural dominance of the ascetic priests. Third, I shall use the example of Dickens to illustrate Kundera's suggestion that the novel is the characteristic genre of democracy, the genre most closely associated with the struggle for freedom and equality.

Heidegger's later work was an attempt to provide the one right answer to the question asked by my imaginary African and Asian philosophers of the future. Heidegger would advise these philosophers to start thinking about the West by thinking about what killed it – technology – and to work backward from there. With a bit of luck, they could then re-create the story which Heidegger himself told, the story he called "the history of Being." For Heidegger, the West begins with the pre-Socratics, with what he calls the separation between the "what" and the "that." This separation between what a thing is in itself and the relations which it has to other things engenders distinctions between essence and accident, reality and appearance, objective and subjective, rational and irrational, scientific and unscientific, and the like – all the dualisms which mark off epochs in the history of an increasing lust for power, and increased inability to do what Heidegger called "letting beings be." This is the history which Heidegger summarizes in Nietzsche's phrase *die Wüste wächst* (the desert grows, the wasteland spreads).[2] As Heidegger tells this story, it culminates in what he calls the "age of

---

1 The students were reported to have played a recording of this symphony as the troops were being held up by masses of people jamming the highways leading into the square. The same point about the impact of the West could be made by reference to the students' repeated invocations of Thoreau and of Martin Luther King, Jr.

2 See Heidegger, *What Is Called Thinking?*, trans. J. Glenn Gray (New York: Harper and Row, 1972) pp. 29ff. The original is at *Was Heisst Denken?* (Tübingen: Niemayer, 1954), pp. 11ff.

the world picture," the age in which everything is enframed, made into material either for manipulation or for aesthetic delectation. It is an age of giantism, of aesthetico-technological frenzy. It is the age in which people build 100-megaton bombs, slash down rain forests, try to create art more thoroughly postmodern than last year's, and bring hundreds of philosophers together to compare their respective world pictures. Heidegger sees all these activities as aspects of a single phenomenon: the age of the world picture is the age in which human beings become entirely forgetful of Being, entirely oblivious to the possibility that anything can stand outside of a means-end relationship.

Seeing matters in this way is an instance of what Habermas describes as Heidegger's characteristic "abstraction by essentialization." In 1935 Heidegger saw Stalin's Russia and Roosevelt's America as "metaphysically speaking, the same." In 1945 he saw the Holocaust and the expulsion of ethnic Germans from Eastern Europe as two instances of the same phenomenon. As Habermas puts it, "under the levelling gaze of the philosopher of Being even the extermination of the Jews seems merely an event equivalent to many others."[3] Heidegger specializes in rising above the need to calculate relative quantities of human happiness, in taking a larger view. For him, successful and unsuccessful adventures – Gandhi's success and Dubček's failure, for example – are just surface perturbations, distractions from essence by accidents, hinderances to an understanding of what is *really* going on.

Heidegger's refusal to take much interest in the Holocaust typifies the urge to look beneath or behind the narrative of the West for the *essence* of the West, the urge which separates the philosophers from the novelists. Someone dominated by this urge will tell a story only as part of the process of clearing away appearance in order to reveal reality. Narrative is, for Heidegger, always a second-rate genre – a tempting but dangerous one. At the beginning of *Being and Time,* Heidegger warned against the temptation to confuse ontology with a story which relates beings to other beings.[4] At the end of his career he takes back his earlier suggestion that what he called "the task of thinking" might be accomplished by narrating the History of Being, by telling a story about how metaphysics and the West exhausted their possibilities. In 1962 he cautions himself that he must cease to tell stories about metaphysics, must leave metaphysics to itself, if he is ever to undertake this task.[5]

Despite this suspicion of epic and preference for lyric, the ability to spin a dramatic tale was Heidegger's greatest gift. What is most memorable and origi-

3 Habermas, "Work and Weltanschauung: The Heidegger Controversy from a German Perspective," *Critical Inquiry* 15 (Winter 1989): 453.

4 *Being and Time,* trans. John Macquarrie and Edward Robinson (New York: Harper and Row, 1962), p. 26. (*Sein und Zeit,* 10th edn. [Tübingen: Niemeyer, 1963], p. 6.)

5 See Heidegger, *On Time and Being,* trans. Joan Stambaugh (New York: Harper and Row, 1972), pp. 24, 41. (*Zur Sache des Denkens* (Tübingen: Niemeyer, 1969), pp. 25, 44.)

nal in his writings, it seems to me, is the new dialectical pattern he finds in the canonical sequence of Western philosophical texts. I think that his clue to this pattern was Nietzsche's interpretation of the attempts at wisdom, contemplation, and imperturbability by the people whom he called "the ascetic priests" as furtive and resentful expressions of those priests' will to power.[6]

Heidegger, however, tried to out-Nietzsche Nietzsche by reading Nietzsche himself as the last of the metaphysicians. He hoped thereby to free himself from the resentment which, despite himself, Nietzsche displayed so conspicuously. Heidegger thought that if he could free himself from this resentment, and from the urge to dominate, he could free himself from the West and so, as he said, quoting Hölderlin, "sing a new song." He thought that he could become free of the will to power as a result of having seen through its last disguise. He thought that by leaving metaphysics to itself, turning from narrating the History of Being to what he called "thinking from the *Ereignis*" (the event, the happening, the appropriation), he could accomplish the transition from epic to lyric, turn from the West to something Wholly Other than the West.

But on my reading, Heidegger himself was just one more of the people whom Nietzsche called "ascetic priests." His attempt to encapsulate the West, to sum it up and distance himself from it, was one more power play. Heidegger was intensely aware of the danger that he was making such a play. But to be intensely aware of a danger is not necessarily to escape it. On my reading, Heidegger is still doing the same sort of thing which Plato tried to do when he created a supersensible world from which to look down on Athens, or Augustine when he imagined a City of God from which to look down on the Dark Ages. He is opting out of the struggles of his fellow humans by making his mind its own place, his own story the only story that counts, making himself the redeemer of his time precisely by his abstention from action. Like Hegel, Heidegger historicizes the Platonic divided line, tipping it over on its side. The Heideggerian counterpart of Plato's world of appearance seen from above is the West seen from beyond metaphysics. Whereas Plato looks down, Heidegger looks back. But both are hoping to distance themselves from, cleanse themselves of, what they are looking at.

This hope leads both men to the thought that there must be some purificatory

---

6 Here is a sample of Nietzsche on the subject of ascetic priests: "The moot point is the value which the ascetic priest places on existence. He confronts existence (comprising all of 'nature,' our whole transitory terrestrial world) with a different constituted kind of Being, which it must oppose and exclude – unless it wishes to turn against itself; in which case our earthly existence may be viewed as a bridge to transcendence. The ascetic treats life as a maze in which we must retrace our steps to the point at which we entered or as an error which only a resolute act can correct, and he further *insists* that we conduct our lives conformably to his ideal. This appalling code of ethics is by no means a curious, isolated incident in the history of mankind; rather it is one of its broadest and longest traditions." *Genealogy of Morals* III, 11, trans. Francis Golffing (New York: Doubleday, 1956), p. 253.

askesis which can render them fit for intercourse with something Wholly Other — for impregnation by the Form of the Good, for example, or for Openness to Being. This thought is obviously an important part of the Western tradition, and it has obvious analogues (and perhaps sources) in the East. That is why Heidegger is the twentieth-century Western thinker most frequently "put into dialogue" with Eastern philosophy.[7] Such Heideggerian themes as the need to put aside the relations between beings and beings, to escape from busyness, to become receptive to the splendor of the simple, are easy to find in the East.

But there are other elements in Western thought, the elements which Heidegger despised, which may be much harder to put into dialogue with anything in the East. In particular, as I shall be saying in more detail shortly, there is the novel — the Rabelaisian response to the ascetic priests. So, insofar as we philosophers become content either with a dialogue between Plato and the East or with one between Heidegger and the East, we may be taking the easy way out of the problems of intercultural comparison. Insofar as we concentrate on philosophy, we may find ourselves concentrating on a certain specific human type which can be counted upon to appear in *any* culture — the ascetic priest, the person who wants to set himself apart from his fellow humans by making contact with what he calls his "true self" or "Being" or "Brahma" or "Nothingness."

All we philosophers have at least a bit of the ascetic priest in us. We all hanker after essence and share a taste for theory as opposed to narrative. If we did not, we should probably have gone into some other line of work. So we have to be careful not to let this taste seduce us into the presumption that, when it comes to other cultures, only our counterparts, those with tastes similar to our own, are reliable sources of information. We should stay alert to the possibility that comparative philosophy not only is not a royal road to intercultural comparison, but may even be a distraction from such comparison. For it may turn out that we are really comparing nothing more than the adaptations of a single transcultural character type to different environments.

Those who embody this character type are always trying to wash the language of their respective tribes off their tongues. The ascetic priest finds this language *viscous,* in Sartre's sense. His ambition is to get above, or past, or out of, what can be said in language. His goal is always the ineffable. Insofar as he is forced to use language, he wants a language which either gives a purer sense to the words of the tribe or, better yet, a language entirely disengaged from the business of the tribe, irrelevant to the mere pursuit of pleasure and avoidance of pain. Only such a person

7 See, for example, Graham Parkes, ed., *Heidegger and Asian Thought* (Honolulu: University of Hawaii Press, 1987). As what I say below makes clear, I have doubts about Parkes's claim (p. 2) that "Heidegger's claim to be the first Western thinker to have overcome the tradition should be taken more seriously if his thought can be brought to resonate deeply with ideas that arose in totally foreign cultural milieux, couched in more or less alien languages, over two millenia ago." This resonance can also be taken as a sign of regression rather than of transcendence — as an indication of a return to the womb.

can share Nietzsche's and Heidegger's contempt for the people whom Nietzsche called "the last men." Only he can see the point of Heidegger's disdainful remark that the greatest disaster — the spread of the wasteland, understood as the forgetfulness of Being — may "easily go hand in hand with a guaranteed living standard for all men, and with a uniform state of happiness for all men."[8] Ascetic priests have no patience with people who think that mere happiness or mere decrease of suffering might compensate for *Seinsvergessenheit,* forgetfulness of Being.

My adaptation of Nietzsche's notion of "the ascetic priest" is deliberately pejorative and gendered. I have been sketching a portrait of a phallocentric obsessive, someone whose attitude toward women typically resembles Socrates' attitude of dismissive irritation when he was asked whether there are Forms of hair and mud. Such a person shares Nietzsche's endlessly repeated desire for, above all else, cleanliness. He also shares Heidegger's endlessly repeated desire for simplicity. He is likely to have the same attitude toward sexual as to economic commerce: he finds it *messy.* So he is inclined both to keep women in their traditional subordinate place, out of sight and mind, and to favor a caste system which ranks the manly warriors, who bathe frequently, above the smelly traders in the bazaar. But the warrior is, of course, outranked by the priest — who bathes even more frequently and is still manlier. The priest is manlier because what is important is not the fleshly phallus but the immaterial one — the one which penetrates through the veil of appearances and makes contact with true reality, reaches the light at the end of the tunnel in a way that the warrior never can.

It is easy, with the help of people like Rabelais, Nietzsche, Freud, and Derrida, to make fun of these seekers after ineffability, immateriality, and purity. But to do them justice, we should remind ourselves that ascetic priests are very *useful* people. As Nietzsche himself admitted, "Until the advent of the ascetic ideal, man, the animal *man,* had no meaning at all on this earth."[9] It is unlikely that there would have been much high culture in either West or East if there had not been a lot of ascetic priests in each place. For the result of trying to find a language different from the tribe's is to enrich the language of later generations of that tribe. The more ascetic priests a society can afford to support, the more surplus value is available to provide these priests with the leisure to fantasize, the richer and more diverse the language and projects of that society are likely to become. The spin-offs from private projects of purification turn out to have enormous social utility. Ascetic priests are often not much fun to be around, and usually are useless if what you are interested in is happiness, but they have been

8 See Heidegger, *What Is Called Thinking?,* p. 30 (*Was Heisst Denken?,* p. 11). Heidegger goes on to say that Nietzsche's words *die Wüste wächst* "come from another realm than the appraisals of our age [*aus einem anderen Ort als die gängigen Beurteilungen unserer Zeit*]." For another passage which brushes aside happiness as beneath the Thinker's consideration, see the passage from "The Word of Nietzsche" discussed above at p. 20.

9 *Genealogy of Morals* III, 28 (Golffing translation, p. 298).

the traditional vehicles of linguistic novelty, the means by which a culture is able to have a future interestingly different from its past. They have enabled cultures to change themselves, to break out of a tradition into a previously unimagined future.

My purpose in this paper, however, is not to arrive at a final, just evaluation either of Heidegger in particular or of ascetic priests in general. Instead it is to develop an opposition between the ascetic priest's taste for theory, simplicity, structure, abstraction, and essence and the novelist's taste for narrative, detail, diversity, and accident. From now on, I shall be preaching a sermon on the following text from Kundera's *The Art of the Novel:*

The novel's wisdom is different from that of philosophy. The novel is born not of the theoretical spirit but of the spirit of humor. One of Europe's major failures is that it never understood the most European of the arts – the novel; neither its spirit, nor its great knowledge and discoveries, nor the autonomy of its history. The art inspired by God's laughter does not by nature serve ideological certitudes, it contradicts them. Like Penelope, it undoes each night the tapestry that the theologians, philosophers and learned men have woven the day before. . . . I do not feel qualified to debate those who blame Voltaire for the gulag. But I do feel qualified to say: The eighteenth century is not only the century of Rousseau, of Voltaire, of Holbach; it is also (perhaps above all!) the age of Fielding, Sterne, Goethe, Laclos.[10]

The first moral I draw from this passage is that we should stay on the lookout, when we survey other cultures, for the rise of new genres – genres which arise in reaction to, and as an alternative to, the attempt to *theorize* about human affairs. We are likely to get more interesting and more practically useful East–West comparisons if we supplement dialogues between our respective theoretical traditions with dialogues between our respective traditions of antitheory. In particular, it would help us Western philosophers get our bearings in the East if we could identify some Eastern cultural traditions which made fun of Eastern philosophy. The kind of fun I have in mind is not the in-house kind which we philosophers make of one another (e.g., the kind of fun which Plato makes of Protagoras, Hume of natural theology, Kierkegaard of Hegel, or Derrida of Heidegger). It is rather the kind made by people who either could not follow a philosophical argument if they tried, or by people who have no wish to try. We need to be on the lookout not just for Japanese Heideggers, Indian Platos, and Chinese Humes, but for Chinese Sternes and Indonesian Rabelaises. I am too ignorant to know whether there *are* any people of the latter sort, but I hope and trust that there are. Somewhere in the East there *must* have been people who enjoyed unweaving the tapestries which the saints and sages had woven.

The need to unweave these tapestries can be thought of as the revenge of the

10　Milan Kundera, *The Art of the Novel,* trans. Linda Asher (New York: Grove Press, 1986), p. 160.

vulgar upon the priests' indifference to the greatest happiness of the greatest number. This indifference is illustrated by the way in which Horkheimer and Adorno look for a dialectic of Enlightenment which will permit them to weave *Candide* into the same pattern as Auschwitz, the way in which they allow contemplation of that pattern to convince them that Enlightenment hopes were vain. It is also illustrated by the way in which Heidegger blurs the distinction between automobile factories and death camps. We philosophers not only want to see dialectical patterns invisible to the vulgar, we want these patterns to be clues to the outcomes of world-historical dramas. For all our ascetism, we want to see ourselves, and people like ourselves, as engaged in something more than merely private projects. We want to relate our private obsessions, our private fantasies of purity, novelty, and autonomy, to something larger than ourselves, something with causal power, something hidden and underlying which secretly determines the course of human affairs.[11]

From Kundera's point of view, the philosopher's essentialistic approach to human affairs, his attempt to substitute contemplation, dialectic, and destiny for adventure, narrative, and chance, is a disingenuous way of saying: what matters for me takes precedence over what matters for you, entitles me to ignore what matters to you, because I am in touch with something – reality – with which you are not. The novelist's rejoinder to this is: it is comical to believe that one human being is more in touch with something nonhuman than another human being. It is comical to use one's quest for the ineffable Other as an excuse for ignoring other people's quite different quests. It is comical to think that *anyone* could transcend the quest for happiness, to think that any theory could be more than a means to happiness, that there is something called Truth which transcends pleasure and pain. The novelist sees us as Voltaire saw Leibniz, as Swift saw the scientists of Laputa, and as Orwell saw the Marxist theoreticians – as comic figures. What is comic about us is that we are making ourselves unable to see things which everybody else can see – things like increased or decreased suffering – by convincing ourselves that these things are "mere appearances."

The novelist's substitute for the appearance–reality distinction is a display of diversity of viewpoints, a plurality of descriptions of the same events. What the novelist finds especially comic is the attempt to privilege one of these descriptions, to take it as an excuse for ignoring all the others. What he finds most heroic is not the ability sternly to reject all descriptions save one, but rather the ability to move back and forth between them. I take this to be the point Kundera is making when he says

it is precisely in losing the certainty of truth and the unanimous agreement of others that man becomes an individual. The novel is the imaginary paradise of individuals. It is the

11 I discuss this urge, with reference to Heidegger, at pp. 107f. and 119f. of my *Contingency, Irony, and Solidarity* (Cambridge: Cambridge University Press, 1989).

territory where no one possesses the truth, neither Anna nor Karenin, but where everyone has the right to be understood, both Anna and Karenin.[12]

Kundera is here making the term "the novel" roughly synonymous with "the democratic utopia" – with an imaginary future society in which nobody dreams of thinking that God, or the Truth, or the Nature of Things, is on their side. In such a utopia nobody would dream of thinking that there is something realer than pleasure or pain, or that there is a duty laid upon us which transcends the search for happiness. A democratic utopia would be a community in which tolerance and curiosity, rather than truth-seeking, are the chief intellectual virtues. It would be one in which there is nothing remotely approximating a state religion or a state philosophy. In such a community, all that is left of philosophy is the maxim of Mill's *On Liberty,* or of a Rabelaisian carnival: everybody can do what they want if they don't hurt anybody else while doing it. As Kundera says, "The world of one single Truth and the relative ambiguous world of the novel are molded of entirely different substances."

One can, if one likes, see Kundera and Heidegger as trying to overcome a common enemy: the tradition of Western metaphysics, the tradition which hints at One True Description which exhibits the underlying pattern behind apparent diversity. But there is a big difference between what the two men propose as an alternative to this tradition. For Heidegger the opposite of metaphysics is Openness to Being, something most easily achieved in a pretechnological peasant community with unchanging customs. Heidegger's utopia is pastoral, a sparsely populated valley in the mountains, a valley in which life is given shape by its relationship to the primordial Fourfold – earth, sky, man, and gods. Kundera's utopia is carnivalesque, Dickensian, a crowd of eccentrics rejoicing in each other's idiosyncrasies, curious for novelty rather than nostalgic for primordiality. The bigger, more varied, and more boisterous the crowd the better. For Heidegger, the way to overcome the urge to domination is to take a step back and to see the West and its history of power plays from afar, as the Hindu sage sees the Wheel of Life from afar. For Kundera the way to overcome the urge to domination is to realize that everybody has and always will have this urge, but to insist that nobody is more or less justified in having it than anybody else. Nobody stands for the truth, or for Being, or for Thinking. Nobody stands for *anything* Other or Higher. We all just stand for ourselves, equal inhabitants of a paradise of individuals in which everybody has the right to be understood but nobody has the right to rule.

Kundera summarizes his attitude toward the ascetic priest when he says

Man desires a world where good and evil can be clearly distinguished, for he has an innate and irrepressible desire to judge before he understands. Religions and ideologies are founded on this desire. . . . They require that somebody be right: either Anna Karenina is

12 Kundera, *Art of the Novel,* p. 159.

the victim of a narrow-minded tyrant, or Karenin is the victim of an immoral woman; either K. is an innocent man crushed by an unjust Court, or the Court represents divine justice and K. is guilty.

This "either–or" encapsulates an inability to tolerate the essential relativity of things human, an inability to look squarely at the absence of the Supreme Judge.[13]

In a brief allusion to Heidegger, Kundera politely interprets his term "forgetfulness of Being" as meaning forgetfulness of this essential relativity.[14] But this is too polite. Heidegger never, even in his early "pragmatist" phase,[15] believed in essential relativity in Kundera's sense of the term. Heidegger's genre, as I have said, is the lyric: his hero is Hölderlin, not Rabelais or Cervantes. For Heidegger the other human beings exist for the sake of the Thinker and the Poet. Where there is a Thinker or a Poet, there human life is justified, for there something Wholly Other touches and is touched. Where there is not, the wasteland spreads.

Whereas for Heidegger there are certain moments in certain lives which both redeem history and permit the past to be encapsulated, for Kundera the thing to do with history is to keep it going, to throw oneself into it. But this throwing oneself into history is not the sort which is recommended by the ideological revolutionary. It is not a matter of replacing Tradition with Reason or Error with Truth. Kundera thinks that if we want to know what went wrong with the expectations of the Enlightenment we should read Flaubert rather than Horkheimer and Adorno. As he says:

Flaubert discovered stupidity. I daresay that is the greatest discovery of a century so proud of its scientific thought. Of course, even before Flaubert, people knew stupidity existed, but they understood it somewhat differently: it was considered a simple absence of knowledge, a defect correctable by education. . . . Flaubert's vision of stupidity is this: Stupidity does not give way to science, technology, modernity, progress; on the contrary, it progresses right along with progress![16]

I take Kundera to be saying that the Enlightenment was wrong in hoping for an age without stupidity. The thing to hope for is, instead, an age in which the prevalent varieties of stupidity will cause less unnecessary pain than is caused in our age by our varieties of stupidity. To every age, its own glory and its own

---

13 Ibid., p. 7.

14 Ibid., p. 5. Here, at the beginning of his book, Kundera thinks of Husserl's *Lebenswelt* and Heidegger's *In-der-Welt-Sein* as standing over against "the one-sided nature of the European sciences, which reduced the world to a mere object of technical and mathematical investigation," and casually assimilates both to his own notion of "the essential relativity of human affairs." But this assimilation is misleading. Husserl and early Heidegger were insistent on getting down to the basic, permanent structure of the *Lebenswelt*, or of *In-der-Welt-Sein*. For Kundera, we make up this structure as we go along.

15 See Mark Okrent, *Heidegger's Pragmatism* (Ithaca, N.Y.: Cornell University Press, 1988) for an account of Heidegger's career which distinguishes the early pragmatism from the later antipragmatism.

16 Kundera, *Art of the Novel*, p. 162.

stupidity. The job of the novelist is to keep us up to date on both. Because there is no Supreme Judge and no One Right Description, because there is no escape to Wholly Other, this is the most important possible job. But it is a job which can only be undertaken with a whole heart by someone untroubled by dreams of an ahistorical framework within which human history is enacted, a universal human nature by reference to which history can be explained, or a far-off divine event toward which history necessarily moves. To appreciate the essential relativity of human affairs, in Kundera's sense, is to give up the last traces of the ascetic priest's attempt to escape from time and chance, the last traces of the attempt to see us as actors in a drama already written before we came on the scene. Heidegger thought that he could escape from metaphysics, from the idea of a Single Truth, by historicizing Being and Truth. He thought that he could escape Platonic escapism by telling a story about the event, the *Ereignis,* which was the West, rather than about *Being.* But from Kundera's point of view Heidegger's project was just one more attempt to escape from time and chance, though this time an escape into historicity rather than into eternity. For Kundera, eternity and historicity are equally comic, equally essentialist notions.

The difference between Kundera's and Heidegger's reaction to the Western metaphysical tradition comes out best in their attitude toward closure. It is as important for Kundera to see the Western adventure as open-ended – to envisage forever new sorts of novels, recording strange new joys and ingenious new stupidities – as it is for Heidegger to insist that the West has exhausted its possibilities. This comes out in Kundera's insistence that the novel does not have a *nature,* but *only* a history, that the novel is a "sequence of discoveries."[17] There is no Platonic Form for the novel as a genre to live up to, no essential structure which some novels exhibit better than others, any more than there is such a Form or such a structure for human beings. The novel can no more exhaust its possibilities than human beings can exhaust their hope for happiness. As Kundera says, "The only context for grasping the novel's worth is the history of the European novel. The novelist need answer to no one but Cervantes."[18]

The same point emerges when Kundera insists that the history of the novel and of Europe cannot be judged by the actual political future of Europe – or by the actual fate, whatever it may be, of the West. In particular, the West blowing itself up with its own bombs should not be read as a judgment on the novel, or on Europe – nor should the coming of an endless totalitarian night. Doing so would be like judging a human life by some ludicrous accident which ends it violently, or like judging Western technology by Auschwitz. As Kundera says,

Once upon a time I too thought that the future was the only competent judge of our works and actions. Later on I understood that chasing after the future is the worst conformism of

17   Ibid., p. 14.
18   Ibid., p. 144.

all, a craven flattery of the mighty. For the future is always mightier than the present. It will pass judgment upon us, of course. But without any competence.

He continues:

But if the future is not a value for me, then to what am I attached? To God? Country? The people? The individual?

My answer is as ridiculous as it is sincere. I am attached to nothing but the depreciated legacy of Cervantes.[19]

Kundera's phrase "paradise of individuals" has an obvious application to Dickens, because the most celebrated and memorable feature of his novels is the unsubsumable, uncategorizable idiosyncrasy of the characters. Dickens's characters resist being subsumed under moral typologies, being described as exhibiting these virtues and those vices. Instead, the names of Dickens's characters *take the place* of moral principles and of lists of virtues and vices. They do so by permitting us to describe each other as "a Skimpole," "a Mr. Pickwick," "a Gradgrind," "a Mrs. Jellyby," "a Florence Dombey." In a moral world based on what Kundera calls "the wisdom of the novel," moral comparisons and judgments would be made with the help of proper names rather than general terms or general principles. A society which took its moral vocabulary from novels rather than from ontotheological or ontico-moral treatises would not ask itself questions about human nature, the point of human existence, or the meaning of human life. Rather, it would ask itself what we can do so as to get along with each other, how we can arrange things so as to be comfortable with one another, how institutions can be changed so that everyone's right to be understood has a better chance of being gratified.

To those who share Nietzsche's sense that the "last men" give off a bad smell, it will be ludicrous to suggest that *comfort* is the goal of human social organization and moral reflection. But this suggestion would not have seemed ludicrous to Dickens. That is why Dickens has been anathematized by Marxists and other ascetic priests as a "bourgeois reformer." The term "bourgeois" is the Marxist equivalent of Nietzsche's term "last man" – it stands for everything which the ascetic priest wants to wash off. For Marxism, like Platonism and Heideggerianism, wants more for human beings than comfort. It wants transformation, transformation according to a single universal plan; Marxists are continually envisaging what they call "new socialist man." Dickens did not want anybody to be transformed, except in one respect: he wanted them to notice and understand the people they passed on the street. He wanted people not to make each other uncomfortable by applying moral labels, but to recognize that all their fellow humans – Dombey and Mrs. Dombey, Anna and Karenin, K. and the Lord Chancellor – had a right to be understood.

19 Ibid., p. 20. I am not sure why Kundera says "depreciated" here, and wish that he had not.

Despite having no higher goal than comfortableness of human association, Dickens did an enormous amount for equality and freedom. The last line of Swift's self-written epitaph — "Imitate him if you dare: he served human liberty"[20] — would do for Dickens's tablet as well. But Dickens performed his services to human liberty not with the help of the "savage indignation" which Swift rightly ascribed to himself but with something more bourgeois — sentimental tears and what Orwell called "generous anger." Dickens strikes us as a more bourgeois writer than the man who described the Yahoos because he is more comfortable with, and hopeful for, human beings. One indication of this comfortableness is the fact which Orwell remarked in the following passage:

In *Oliver Twist, Hard Times, Bleak House, Little Dorrit,* Dickens attacked English institutions with a ferocity that has never since been approached. Yet he managed to do it without making himself hated, and, more than this, the very people he attacked have swallowed him so completely that he has become a national institution himself.[21]

The important point is that Dickens did not make himself hated. I take it that this was partly because he did not attack anything as abstract as "humanity as such," or the age or the society in which he lived, but rather concrete cases of particular people ignoring the suffering of other particular people. He was thus able to speak as "one of us" — as the voice of one who happened to notice something to which the rest of us could be counted upon to react with similar indignation as soon as we notice it.[22]

Dickens was, as Orwell says, "a good-tempered antinomian," a phrase which would apply equally to Rabelais, Montaigne, or Cervantes, but hardly to Luther

20 Yeats's translation of Swift's ". . . imitare si poteris, strenuum pro virili libertatis vindicem."
21 George Orwell, *Collected Essays, Journalism and Letters* (Harmondsworth: Penguin, 1968), vol. 1, pp. 414–415. In his illuminating *The Politics of Literary Reputation: The Making and Claiming of 'St. George' Orwell* (Oxford: Oxford University Press, 1989), John Rodden has noted both that Orwell in this essay "directly identified himself with Dickens" (p. 181) and that the identification worked, in the sense that "What Orwell wrote of Dickens [in the last sentence of the passage I have quoted] soon applied to himself" (p. 22). One facet of the identification was the patriotism common to the two men — a sense of identification with England and its history which trumped any theory about the place of England in universal history. From the theorist's point of view, patriotism is invariably suspicious, as is any loyalty to a mere sector of space-time. But for people like Orwell, Dickens, and Kundera, the only substitute for patriotism is attachment to some other spatiotemporal sector, to the history of something which is not a country – e.g., the history of the European novel, "the depreciated legacy of Cervantes."
22 Orwell (*Collected Essays* I:460) says that "Even the millionaire suffers from a vague sense of guilt, like a dog eating a stolen leg of mutton. Nearly everyone, regardless of what his conduct may be, responds emotionally to the idea of human brotherhood. Dickens voiced a code which was and on the whole still is believed in, even by people who violate it. It is difficult otherwise to explain why he could be both read by working people (a thing that has happened to no other novelist of his stature) and buried in Westminster Abbey." If one had asked Dickens whether he thought that ideal and that code inherent in human nature, or rather an historically contingent development, he would presumably have replied that he neither knew nor cared. That is the kind of question which "the wisdom of the novel" rejects as without interest or point.

or Voltaire or Marx. So I take Orwell's term "generous anger" to mean something like "anger which is without malignity because it assumes that the fault is ignorance rather than malice, assumes that the evil has merely to be noticed to be remedied." This was the kind of anger later found in Martin Luther King, Jr., but not the kind of anger found in the ascetic priests. For the latter believe that social change is not a matter of mutual adjustment but of re-creation – that to make things better we must create a new kind of human being, one who is aware of reality rather than appearance. Their anger is *ungenerous* in the sense that it is aimed not at a lack of understanding of particular people by other particular people but rather at an ontological deficit common either to people in general or, at least, all those of the present age. The generosity of Dickens's, Stowe's, and King's anger comes out in their assumption that people merely need to turn their eyes toward the people who are getting hurt, notice the *details* of the pain being suffered, rather than needing to have their entire cognitive apparatus restructured.

As an empirical claim, this assumption is often falsified. As a moral attitude, it marks the difference between people who tell stories and people who construct theories about that which lies beyond our present imagination, because beyond our present language. I think that when Orwell identified a capacity for generous anger as the mark of "a free intelligence," he was adumbrating the same sort of opposition between the theorist and the novelist which I am trying to develop in this essay. Earlier I said that theorists like Heidegger saw narrative as always a second-best, a propaedeutic to a grasp of something deeper than the visible detail. Novelists like Orwell and Dickens are inclined to see theory as always a second-best, never more than a reminder for a particular purpose, the purpose of telling a story better. I suggest that the history of social change in the modern West shows that the latter conception of the relation between narrative and theory is the more fruitful.

To say that it is more fruitful is just to say that, when you weigh the good and the bad the social novelists have done against the good and the bad the social theorists have done, you find yourself wishing that there had been more novels and fewer theories. You wish that the leaders of successful revolutions had read fewer books which gave them general ideas and more books which gave them an ability to identify imaginatively with those whom they were to rule. When you read books like Kolakowski's history of Marxism, you understand why the Party theoretician, the man responsible for the "correct ideological line," has always been, apart from the maximum leader himself, the most feared and hated member of the Central Committee. This may remind you that Guzmán, the leader of the quasi-Maoist Sendero Luminoso movement in Peru, wrote his dissertation on Kant. It may also remind you that Heidegger's response to the imprisonment of his Social Democratic colleagues in 1933 came down to "Don't bother me with petty details."

The important thing about novelists as compared with theorists is that they are good at details. This is another reason why Dickens is a useful paradigm of the novel. To quote Orwell again, "The outstanding, unmistakable mark of Dickens's writing is the *unnecessary detail*"; "He is all fragments, all details – rotten architecture, but wonderful gargoyles – and never better than when he is building up some character who will later on be forced to act inconsistently."[23] If we make Dickens paradigmatic of the West, as I hope my fantasized Africans and Asians would, then we shall see what was most instructive about the recent history of the West as its increased ability to tolerate diversity. Viewed another way, this is an increased ability to treat apparent inconsistency not as something to be rejected as unreal or as evil, but as a mark of the inadequacy of our current vocabularies of explanation and adjudication.[24] This change in our treatment of apparent inconsistency is correlated with an increasing ability to be comfortable with a variety of different sorts of people, and therefore with an increasing willingness to leave people alone to follow their own lights. This willingness is reflected in the rise of pluralistic bourgeois democracies, societies in which politics becomes a matter of sentimental calls for alleviation of suffering rather than of moral calls to greatness.

It may seem strange to attribute this sort of willingness to the recent West – a culture often said, with excellent reason, to be racist, sexist, and imperialist. But it is of course also a culture which is very *worried* about being racist, sexist, and imperialist, as well as about being Eurocentric, parochial, and intellectually intolerant. It is a culture which has become very conscious of its capacity for murderous intolerance and thereby perhaps more wary of intolerance, more sensitive to the desirability of diversity, than any other of which we have record. I have been suggesting that we Westerners owe this consciousness and this sensitivity more to our novelists than to our philosophers or to our poets.

When tolerance and comfortable togetherness become the watchwords of a society, one should no longer hope for world-historical greatness. If such greatness – radical difference from the past, a dazzlingly unimaginable future – is what one wants, ascetic priests like Plato, Heidegger, and Suslov will fill the bill. But if it is not, novelists like Cervantes, Dickens, and Kundera may suffice.[25] The fact that philosophy as a genre is closely associated with the quest for such greatness – with the attempt to focus all one's thoughts into a single narrow beam and send them out beyond the bounds of all that has been previously thought – may help explain why it is among the philosophers of the West that

23 See Orwell, *Collected Essays*, I:450, 454, for the passages quoted.
24 I argue in "Freud and Moral Reflection" (below) that the increasing popularity of Freudian explanations of untoward actions is an example of this changed attitude toward apparent inconsistency.
25 Byron is a good example of someone who saw the rising stock of tolerance and comfortableness as endangering the possibility of greatness. I learned from my colleague Jerome McGann that he took out his exasperation on, among other people, Cervantes: "Cervantes smiled Spain's chivalry away;/A single laugh demolished the right arm/Of his own country; – seldom since that day/Has Spain had heroes" (*Don Juan*, XIII, 11.)

contemporary Western self-hatred is most prevalent. It must be tempting for Africans and Asians – the principal victims of Western imperialism and racism – to see this self-hatred as about what the West deserves. But I would suggest that we take this self-hatred as just one more symptom of the old familiar quest for purity which runs through the annals of the ascetic priesthood in both East and West. If we set these annals to one side, we may have a better chance of finding something distinctive in the West which the East can use, and conversely.

PART II

Deconstruction and circumvention

1. The literature–philosophy distinction

Jonathan Culler has recently argued that we should not think of deconstruction as "an attempt to abolish all distinctions, leaving neither literature nor philosophy, but only a general, undifferentiated textuality." He explains that

> a distinction between literature and philosophy is essential to deconstruction's power of intervention: to the demonstration, for example, that the most truly philosophical reading of a philosophical work – a reading that puts in question its concepts and the foundations of its discourse – is one that treats the work as literature, as a fictive rhetorical construct whose elements and order are determined by various textual exigencies. Conversely, the most powerful and apposite readings of literary works may be those that treat them as philosophical gestures by teasing out the implications of their dealings with the philosophical oppositions that support them.[1]

I think this passage shows that we ought to distinguish two senses of "deconstruction." In one sense the word refers to the philosophical projects of Jacques Derrida. Taken this way, breaking down the distinction between philosophy and literature is *essential* to deconstruction. Derrida's initiative in philosophy continues along a line laid down by Nietzsche and Heidegger. He rejects, however, Heidegger's distinctions between "thinkers" and "poets" and between the few thinkers and the many scribblers. So Derrida rejects the sort of philosophical professionalism which Nietzsche despised and which Heidegger recovered. This does indeed lead Derrida in the direction of "a general, undifferentiated textuality." In his work, the philosophy-literature distinction is, at most, part of a ladder which we can let go of once we have climbed up it.

In a second sense of "deconstruction," however, the term refers to a method of reading texts. Neither this method, nor any other, should be attributed to Derrida – who shares Heidegger's contempt for the very idea of method.[2] But the method exists, and the passage I have quoted from Culler describes one of its central

---

1 Jonathan Culler, *On Deconstruction: Theory and Criticism after Structuralism* (Ithaca, N.Y., 1982), pp. 149–50.
2 See, e.g., Martin Heidegger, "The Age of the World Picture," *The Question Concerning Technology and Other Essays,* trans. William Lovitt (New York, 1977), p. 118, for a discussion of method as a variety of "procedure," which in turn requires "a fixed ground plan." Heidegger takes this requirement to be "the essence of technology."

features. Culler is quite right to say that deconstruction, in the second sense, needs a clear distinction between philosophy and literature. For the kind of reading which has come to be called "deconstructionist" requires two different straight persons: a macho professional philosopher who is insulted by the suggestion that he has submitted to a textual exigency, and a naive producer of literature whose jaw drops when she learns that her work has been supported by philosophical oppositions. The philosopher had thought of himself as speaking a sparse, pure, transparent language. The poetess shyly hoped that her unmediated woodnotes might please. Both reel back in horror when the deconstructionist reveals that each has been making use of complex idioms to which the other has contributed. Both go all to pieces at this news. A wild disorder overtakes their words. Their whimpers blend into interminable androgynous keening. Once again, deconstructionist intervention has produced a splendidly diffuse irresolution.

There is something suspiciously old-fashioned about this way of setting up one's subjects. It is a long time since we have had writers who considered themselves in the business of providing pleasure. It is also considerably more difficult than it used to be to locate a real live metaphysical prig.[3] Still, the quest for philosophical machismo is not nearly so hopeless as that for literary naiveté. You can still find philosophy professors who will solemnly tell you that they are seeking *the truth,* not just a story or a consensus but an honest-to-God, down-home, accurate representation of the way the world is. A few of them will even claim to write in a clear, precise, transparent way, priding themselves on manly straightforwardness, on abjuring "literary" devices.

Lovably old-fashioned prigs of this sort may provide the only excuses which either Culler or I have for staying in business. Still, *pace* Culler, I think that all of us – Derrideans and pragmatists alike – should try to work ourselves out of our jobs by conscientiously blurring the literature–philosophy distinction and pro-

---

3   Derrida was, for example, overhasty in picking J. L. Austin as an example of someone who accepted the traditional idea of meaning being communicated "within a homogenous element across which the unity and integrity of meaning is not affected in an essential way" (*Margins of Philosophy,* trans. Alan Bass [Chicago, 1982], p. 311; all further references to this work, abbreviated *MP,* will be included parenthetically in the text). Derrida says that this idea has been held throughout the entire history of philosophy. When he comes to Austin, he blithely attributes to him all sorts of traditional motives and attitudes which Austin prided himself on having avoided. John Searle's criticism of Derrida on this point seems to me (*pace* Culler and Christopher Norris) largely right (see "Reiterating the Differences: A Reply to Derrida," *Glyph* 1 (1977): 198–208. I cannot see that in his reply to Searle (see "Limited Inc abc . . . ," *Glyph* 2 [1977]: 162–254) Derrida laid a glove on Searle, as far as Searle's charges of misreading Austin are concerned – though Derrida did formulate an effective criticism of various metaphilosophical assumptions common to Austin and Searle. (See n. 19 below.) Stanley Fish seems to me right in reading *How to Do Things with Words* as saying (about language, if not about philosophy) pretty much what Derrida himself wants to say (see Fish, "With the Compliments of the Author: Reflections on Austin and Derrida," *Critical Inquiry* 8 [Summer 1982]: 693–721, esp. the concluding pages).

moting the idea of a seamless, undifferentiated "general text." In what follows, I shall be urging the following points:

(1) The only form of the philosophy–literature distinction which we need is one drawn in terms of the (transitory and relative) contrast between the familiar and the unfamiliar, rather than in terms of a deeper and more exciting contrast between the representational and the nonrepresentational, or the literal and the metaphorical.

(2) The fact that language is a play of differences, as well as an instrument useful in acquiring knowledge, gives us no reason to think that words like *différance* and *trace* can do to, or for, philosophy what Heidegger failed to accomplish with his own magic words – *Sein, Ereignis,* and so forth.

(3) When Derrida says that philosophy has a "blind spot" (*MP,* p. 228) in regard to its own "metaphorics," he is right only in the familiar Hegelian sense that each philosophical generation points out some unconscious presuppositions built into the vocabulary of its predecessors, thereby enlarging the relevant metaphorics (and providing work for the next generation).

(4) The claim, shared by Heidegger and Derrida, that the "ontotheological" tradition has permeated science, literature, and politics – that it is central to our culture – is a self-deceptive attempt to magnify the importance of an academic speciality.

(5) Derrida's importance, despite his own occasional hints and the insistence of some of his fans, does not include showing us how to see the philosophical as literary or the literary as philosophical. We know how to do both things well enough already.[4] Rather, it consists in pursuing a certain academic speciality (or, equivalently, a certain literary tradition) – the re-reading of the texts of Western philosophy which was begun by Nietzsche and continued by Heidegger.

(6) The big esoteric problem common to Heidegger and Derrida of how to "overcome" or escape from the ontotheological tradition is an artificial one and needs to be replaced by lots of little pragmatic questions about which bits of that tradition might be used for some current purpose.

4 One reason why it may seem that it took Derrida to enable us to do the sorts of readings which Culler describes in the passage I quoted earlier is that for several decades, in Anglo-Saxon countries, students of literature tended to avoid philosophy, and conversely. The problem has not been that we lacked a method but simply that practically nobody read both literary and philosophical texts, and so practically nobody was able to play the two genres off each other in the way Culler recommends. The influence of the New Critics and of F. R. Leavis was, on the whole, antiphilosophical. Before the appearance of books like M. H. Abrams' *The Mirror and the Lamp,* it often did not occur to students of English literature to read Hegel. During the same period, students of analytic philosophy were encouraged to keep their reading in literature well clear of their philosophical work and to avoid reading German philosophy between Kant and Frege. It was widely believed that reading Hegel rotted the brain. (Reading Nietzsche and Heidegger was thought to have even worse effects – doing so might cause hair to sprout in unwonted places, turning one into a snarling fascist beast.)

2. Philosophical closure

I shall start with a definition of literature suggested by Geoffrey Hartman. He asks:

> Is not literary language the name we give to a diction whose frame of reference is such that the words stand out as words (even as sounds) rather than being, at once, assimilable meanings?[5]

This contrast between "assimilable meanings" conveyed by words which we don't notice as words and "words [which] stand out as words" seems to me on the right track. But rather than contrasting two sorts of diction, or a frame of reference in which words are expected to stand out as words with another frame in which they are expected not to, I would contrast two sorts of conversational situations. One is the sort of situation encountered when people pretty much agree on what is wanted and are talking about how best to get it. In such a situation there is no need to say anything terribly unfamiliar, for argument is typically about the truth of assertions rather than about the utility of vocabularies. The contrasting situation is one in which everything is up for grabs at once, where the motives and the terms of discussion are a central subject of argument.

This way of drawing the contrast permits us to think of a "literary" or a "poetic" moment as occurring periodically in many different areas of culture – science, philosophy, painting, and politics, as well as the lyric and the drama. It is the moment when things are not going well, when a new generation is dissatisfied, when the young have come to look at what is being done in a given genre as hackwork, or as so overburdened with what Thomas Kuhn calls "anomalies" that a new start is needed.[6] In such periods, people begin to toss around old words in new senses, to throw in the occasional neologism, and thus to hammer out a new idiom which initially attracts attention to itself and only later gets put to work. In this initial stage, words stand out as words, colors as encrusted pigments, chords as dissonances. Half-formed materiality becomes the mark of the avant-garde. The jargon or style that wins – the one that exhibits staying power, that becomes the bearer of assimilable meanings and provides the tools with which to resume normal operations – ceases to stand out. It is not noticed again until the next dissatisfied generation comes along and "problematizes" it by contrasting that jargon or style invidiously with recent novelties.[7]

5 Geoffrey H. Hartman, *Saving the Text: Literature, Derrida, Philosophy* (Baltimore, 1981), p. xxi.
6 See Thomas S. Kuhn, *The Structure of Scientific Revolutions*, 2d ed., enl. (Chicago, 1970) for an account of the tendency of scientists to begin sounding philosophical when anomalies have been piling up and a state of "crisis" is reached.
7 Another way of putting the point I am making is to say that philosophical problems are not "out there" waiting to be found, but rather made. Philosophical problems come into existence when people think up alternatives which have not been envisaged before and thereby question a commonsensical belief which there had previously been no reason to doubt. On the metaphilosophical view I take to be common to John Dewey and Derrida, it is a mistake to think that Derrida, or anybody else, "recognized" problems about the nature of textuality or writing which had been

If philosophy always were what Derrida accurately says it has sometimes dreamed of being, then this "literary" moment would be unnecessary — not only within philosophy but everywhere else. That is why there is a prima facie opposition between the dreams of literature and the dreams of philosophy. Derrida describes the "dream at the heart of philosophy" as follows:

If one could reduce their [the metaphors'] play to the circle of a family or a group of metaphors, that is, to one "central," "fundamental," "principial" metaphor, there would be no more true metaphor, but only, through the one true metaphor, the assured legibility of the proper. [*MP*, p. 268]

"Metaphor" in this passage can be replaced, without changing the force of the remark, by "language" or "vocabulary" or "description." To say that philosophers dream of there being only one true metaphor is to say that they dream of eradicating not only the distinction between the literal and the metaphorical but the distinction between the language of error and the language of truth, the language of appearance and the language of reality — that is, their opponents' language and their own language. They would like to show that there is really only one language and that all the other (pseudo) languages lack some property which is necessary to be "meaningful" or "intelligible" or "complete" or "adequate." It is essential to philosophy, as defined by this dream, to aim at some statement of the form "No linguistic expression is intelligible unless . . ." (Unless, for example, it is translatable into the language of unified science, or cuts reality at the joints, or bears its logical form on its sleeve, or satisfies the verifiability criterion, or is the language in which Adam named the beasts, or whatever.)

This may seem a narrow definition of the "dream at the heart of philosophy," but it brings into focus an ancient hope: the hope for a language which can receive no gloss, requires no interpretation, cannot be distanced, cannot be sneered at by later generations. It is the hope for a vocabulary which is intrinsically and self-evidently final, not merely the most comprehensive and fruitful vocabulary we have come up with so far.[8] Such a vocabulary would have to be adequate to "place" all of history and all of contemporary culture. For if it did not, there would always be the danger of the vocabulary itself being put in a subordinate place — either by the wisdom of the ancients or by whatever competing contemporary discipline was feeling its oats (for example, psychoanalysis, economic history, microbiology, cybernetics). Isolating the single central metaphor at the heart of language, making possible the assured legibility of the proper, would put the vocabularies of all such disciplines in their places. That is, it would reveal them to be only

ignored by the tradition. What he did was to think up ways of speaking which made old ways of speaking optional, and thus more or less dubious.

8 I have discussed this desire in *Consequences of Pragmatism* (*Essays: 1972–1980*) (Minneapolis, 1982), pp. 130–37.

pseudolanguages, standing to the true way of speaking as the babblings of children stand to adult speech.

Any proposal for such a language has to face a familiar problem, one as old as the archetypal patriarchal prig, Father Parmenides: when you make an invidious contrast between the Way of Truth and the Way of Opinion, between the one proper vocabulary and the many pseudovocabularies, you have to explain the relation between the two. You have to have a theory about the origin and nature of error, about the possibility of progress from error to truth. You have to understand a bad language in terms of the good one while not permitting the bad one to be either a proper part of the good one or "intertranslatable" with it.

To make this dilemma more concrete, consider some examples. The clearest is the metaphysical monism common to Parmenides and Spinoza. Monism has always had difficulty explaining the appearance of plurality. Appearance, after all, is as unreal as plurality. But monists like Spinoza would like to find some way of describing the relation of the finite modes to the one infinite substance, something more than Parmenides' stiff and off-putting insistence that non-Being is not. Spinoza would like to say that he knows all about finite modes and can describe what they are in a vocabulary which gets them right. But it is hard to see how one can get the unreal right. Further, getting something right, representing it accurately, seems to be a relation between two things. Yet the whole point of monism is that there is only one thing.

This sort of difficulty, the one created by error, finitude, and temporality for metaphysical monists and orthodox theologians of transcendence, is also found in Aristotle's use of "matter." Form is, for Aristotle, the principle of intelligibility just as, in Spinoza, the clear and distinct idea of infinite substance is the means by which the confused ideas of finite modes are to be clarified. But how are we to understand matter qua matter, as unformed? This is as perplexing as the question of how, in Spinoza, we are to understand confusion qua confusion, as unclarified. Worse yet, most of what we think we know about form seems to consist in invidious contrasts between it and matter, just as most of what we know about the infinite seems to consist in invidious contrasts with the finite. So the less intelligible "matter" or "finitude" becomes, the less sure we are of our grip on "form" and "infinite." Once it becomes clear that most of what we know about the upper and privileged member of such an opposition is a matter of contrast-effects with the lower and despised member, we begin to wonder if we can *ever* do better than Parmenides did. Mysticism, or the *via negativa,* or sacred Wittgensteinian silence seem the only options.

Still another hackneyed example of this sort of problem is Kant's contrast between the phenomenal and the noumenal. He needed noumena, things-in-themselves, to give sense to his claim that the spatiotemporal world was phenomenal, merely apparent. There cannot, as he said, be appearance without something that appears. But we have no idea what it would be like for the nonspatiotemporal to appear (or to do anything else, for that matter). So Kant needs a way of conceptualizing the unconceivable, just as Aristotle needed a form of the form-less[9] and Spinoza needed a distinct idea of the indistinct.

An equally hackneyed example is the logical positivist's attempt to distinguish the "cognitively meaningful" from the "cognitively meaningless," not simply (as Wittgenstein had in the *Tractatus*) by the Parmenidean distinction between speech and silence but by articulating a principle that will demarcate, for exam-ple, science from metaphysics. This attempt gave rise to two problems for positiv-ists. First, "meaningless" seemed the wrong word, since one had to know a lot about what a metaphysician meant before deciding that his utterances were meaningless. Second, and more serious, the verifiability principle itself seemed to be unverifiable. The vocabulary which was to subsume all the other vocabularies did not fit into its own specifications for being a good vocabulary. So an attempt to give a sense to the notion of nonsense, in a proposition stating the conditions for being a proposition, wound up by not having sense itself, not being a proposi-tion itself – just as attempts to give intelligibility to the officially unintelligible wound up making themselves unintelligible.

What is common to the various impasses I have sketched? At a first approxima-tion, the problem is that one cannot say that only x's are intelligible if the only way to explain what an x is is by assuming that one's auditor knows what a non-x is. But this formulation is unsatisfactory because the notion of intelligibility is obscure when it is applied to *things* (for example, a noumenon, an infinite sub-stance). One knows the difference between an intelligible and an unintelligible *sentence,* but it is hard to explain what it means to say that, for example, tables and chairs are intelligible but God is not (or vice versa). The positivist idiom, the so-called formal mode of speech, is more satisfactory because it treats intelligibility as a property of linguistic expressions rather than things. It thereby converts metaphysics into philosophy of language, bringing it into accord with Derrida's description of the dream at the heart of philosophy.

Using this idiom, one can say that the problem common to all the philosophers I have mentioned, from Parmenides to A. J. Ayer, is that they are continually tempted to say, "The conditions making an expression intelligible are . . . ," despite the fact that that proposition itself does not fulfill the conditions it lists. Thus Aristotle should not say that no term is intelligible unless the potential intellect can become identical with its referent, for that will make the term "matter" unintelligible. Aristotle needs to use that term in order to explain, among other things, what the potential intellect is. Kant should not say that no term is meaningful unless it stands for a mental content which is the synthesis of

---

9 Derrida likes to quote Plotinus' *"to gar ichnos tou amorphou morphē"* ("the trace is the form of the formless") (*MP*, p. 66 n.41, and see pp. 157 and 172 n.16). If one regards this as a definition of the sense in which Derrida himself uses *trace,* then *trace* can be taken as meaning "the sort of thing philosophers need but cannot have." But I am not sure that it should be taken so.

sensory intuitions by a concept, for that will make the term "noumenon" unintelligible. Positivists should not say that no statement is meaningful except under certain conditions, unless that remark fulfills those conditions.

I have run through these examples in order to flesh out Derrida's description of the dream at the heart of philosophy. Philosophy, defined by the dream of finding the one true metaphor, has to aim at some statement of the form "No linguistic expression is intelligible unless . . ." Further, this statement must be part of a vocabulary which is *closed,* in the sense that the statement is applicable to iself without paradox. Not only must a philosophical vocabulary be *total,* in the sense that anything literally or metaphorically sayable in any other vocabulary can be literally said in it, but it must speak of *itself* with the same "assured legibility" as it does of everything else.

3. Literary openness

Given this more detailed account of the dream of philosophy, I can now turn back to Derrida and say that his great theme is the impossibility of closure. He loves to show that whenever a philosopher lovingly shapes a new model of Parmenides' well-rounded sphere, something will always stick, or leak, out. There is always a supplement, a margin, a space within which the text of philosophy is written, a space which forms the conditions of the intelligibility and the possibility of philosophy. "Beyond the philosophical text there is not a blank, virgin, empty margin, but another text, a weave of differences of forces without any present center of reference." Derrida wants to make us conscious of that text by letting us "think a writing without presence and without absence, without history, without cause, without *archia* [*sic*], without *telos,* a writing that absolutely upsets all dialectics, all theology, all teleology, all ontology" (*MP,* pp. xxiii, 67).

Only if we get such a writing would we be able to do what Derrida wants to do to philosophy, namely "to think – in the most faithful, interior way – the structured genealogy of philosophy's concepts, but at the same time to determine – from a certain exterior that is unqualifiable or unnameable by philosophy – what this history has been able to dissimulate or forbid."[10]

Such a writing would be literature which was no longer opposed to philosophy, literature which subsumed and included philosophy, literature crowned king of an infinite undifferentiated textuality. Derrida says that "the history of the literary arts [has been linked with] the history of metaphysics" (*Pos,* p. 11) – linked, presumably, as the dependent to the independent variable. He thinks that the history of metaphysics, the ontotheological tradition, has imprisoned all the rest

10 Derrida, *Positions,* trans. Bass (Chicago, 1981), p. 6; all further references to this work, abbreviated *Pos,* will be included parenthetically in the text.

of culture, even science.[11] So what lies on the other side of what he envisages as a "total transformation" of our culture will be a writing marked by self-conscious interminability, self-conscious openness, self-conscious lack of philosophical closure (see *Pos,* p. 20).

Derrida would like to write in this new way, but he is caught in a dilemma. He can either forget about philosophy as the liberated slave forgets his master, demonstrating his forgetfulness by his own uncaring spontaneous activity, or he can insist on his rights over the master, on the dialectical dependence of the text of philosophy on its margins. When he grasps the first horn and forgets about philosophy, his writing loses focus and point. If there were ever a writer whose *subject* was philosophy, it is Derrida. His central theme is the way in which the dream of philosophy turns into nightmare just at its climax: just when everything is sewn up, when every way of speaking other than the philosopher's own has been revealed to be unintelligible, when the sphere is rounding itself off nicely, when the Aristophanic halves are coming together, interpenetrating and ecstatically merging, something goes horribly wrong. Self-referential paradox appears; the unintelligible repressed returns as the condition of the intelligible. Derrida is at his best when recounting such tragicomedies. But this second horn has a disadvantage: to remember philosophy, to tell this story over and over again, is to verge on doing what the philosophers do – to propound some generalization of the form "The attempt to formulate a unique, total, closed vocabulary will necessarily . . ."

Derrida is obviously in danger of doing this when he produces a new metalinguistic jargon, full of words like *trace* and *différance,* and uses it to say Heideggerian-sounding things like "it is only on the basis of *différance* and its 'history' that we can allegedly know who and where 'we' are" (*MP,* p. 7). Just insofar as Derrida tries to give arguments for such theses as "Writing is prior to speech" or "Texts deconstruct themselves" – all those slogans which his followers are tempted to regard as "results of philosophical inquiry" and as providing the basis for a method of reading – he betrays his own project. The worst bits of Derrida are the ones where he begins to imitate the thing he hates and starts claiming to offer "rigorous analyses." Arguments work only if a vocabulary in which to state premises is shared by speaker and audience. Philosophers as original and important as Nietzsche, Heidegger, and Derrida are forging new ways of speaking, not making surprising philosophical discoveries about old ones. As a result, they are not likely to be good at argumentation.[12]

11 See *Pos,* p. 35, where Derrida speaks of "freeing [science] of the metaphysical bonds that have borne on its definition and its movement since its beginnings."

12 Culler, in his book referred to above, attempts to preserve some of Derrida's arguments (and, alas, one of Nietzsche's very worst arguments) and has been attacked by Searle for doing so (see "The Word Turned Upside Down," *New York Review of Books,* 27 Oct. 1983, pp. 74–79). Searle is, I think, right in saying that a lot of Derrida's arguments (not to mention some of Nietzsche's)

One horn of the dilemma I have been sketching consists in not saying anything about philosophy but instead showing what literature looks like once it is freed from philosophy. The other horn of the dilemma consists in outdoing the philosophers at their own game by finding a general criticism of their activity — something comparable to Parmenides' criticism of the Way of Opinion, or Spinoza's of confused ideas, or Kant's of the search for the unconditioned, or Ayer's of cognitive meaninglessness. The dilemma can be summed up by saying that any new sort of writing which is without *archai* and without a *telos* will also be without *hypokeimenon,* without a subject. So, a fortiori, it will not tell us anything about philosophy. Or else, if it does tell us about philosophy, it will have *archai,* namely, the new metaphilosophical jargon, in terms of which we describe and diagnose the text of philosophy. It will also have a *telos,* encapsulating and distancing that text. So grasping the second horn will produce one more philosophical closure, one more metavocabulary which claims superior status, whereas grasping the former horn will give us openness, but more openness than we really want. Literature which does not connect with anything, which has no subject and no theme, which does not have a moral tucked up its sleeve, which lacks a dialectical context, is just babble. You can't have a ground without a figure, a margin without a page of text.

are just awful. He is very acute in remarking that many of them depend upon the assumption "that unless a distinction can be made rigorous and precise it isn't really a distinction at all." But I think that Searle oversimplifies the dialectical situation and, so, misunderstands and underestimates both Culler's book and Derrida's project. He says that Derrida shares with Edmund Husserl the assumption that unless philosophical "foundations [of knowledge]" are provided, "something is lost or threatened or undermined or put in question" (p. 78). But Derrida is not interested in the quest for foundations of knowledge, except as one local example of the idea of philosophy as a sort of universal science which can "place" all other cultural activities by describing them in a peculiarly clear and transparent vocabulary — a vocabulary which gets a firm grip on the world by making possible an intrinsic precision and rigor (as opposed to simply making it possible to solve particular problems raised at a contingent historical juncture; see n. 7 above).

It is just this conception of philosophy which is presupposed by Searle's very Husserlian praise of the "clarity, rigor, precision, theoretical comprehensiveness, and above all, intellectual content" which he takes to characterize the present "golden age in the philosophy of language," highlighted by the work of "Chomsky and Quine, of Austin, Tarski, Grice, Dummett, Davidson, Putnam, Kripke, Strawson, Montague, and a dozen other first-rate writers." When Searle says that this work is "written at a level that is vastly superior to that at which deconstructive philosophy is written," (p. 78) he is attempting exactly the sort of apotheosis of currently familiar textbook problems, and of the styles prevalent within a local disciplinary matrix, which Nietzsche and Derrida are right to mock. He is making just the kind of assumption that Derrida made in his discussion of Austin (see n. 3 above), namely, that an author working in an unfamiliar tradition must necessarily be trying (and failing) to do the sort of thing which authors with whom one is more familiar are doing. The idea that there is something called "intellectual content," measurable by universal and ahistorical standards, links Searle with Plato and Husserl, and separates him from Derrida. The weakness of Searle's treatment of Derrida is that he thinks of him as doing amateurish philosophy of language rather than as asking metaphilosophical questions about the value of such philosophy.

4. Derrida and Heidegger

Derrida is fully conscious of this dilemma. The best way to see how he confronts it is to watch him struggle to differentiate himself from Heidegger. Derrida thinks Heidegger is the best example of somebody who tried and failed to do what Derrida himself wants to do — write about philosophy unphilosophically, get at it from the outside, be a postphilosophical thinker. Heidegger, in the end, decided that "a regard for metaphysics still prevails even in the intention to overcome metaphysics. Therefore our task is to cease all overcoming, and leave metaphysics to itself."[13] But Heidegger was never able to take his own advice. For he had only one theme: the need to overcome metaphysics. Once that theme came to seem self-deceptive, he was left speechless. Heidegger was so obsessed by the need to awake from the dream of philosophy that his work turned into a monotonous insistence that everybody, even Nietzsche, had dreamt it.

Derrida would, I think, agree with this line of criticism of Heidegger but would want to take it further. In his view, Heidegger's magic words, words like *Sein* and *Ereignis* and *Alētheia,* are attempts to carry the climactic ecstasy of the dream into waking life, to obtain the satisfaction of philosophical closure by retreating to the sheer sound of words, words which are not given sense by use but possess force precisely by lack of use. Thus Derrida quotes Heidegger as saying, " 'In order to name the essential nature of Being . . . , language would have to find a single word, the unique word.' "[14] Derrida rejoins by saying, "There will be no unique name, even if it were the name of Being. And we must think this without *nostalgia.*" He goes on to add that we must do so without "the other side of nostalgia, what I will call Heideggerian *hope*" (*MP,* p. 27).

In this passage and elsewhere, Derrida thinks of himself as standing on Heidegger's shoulders, and seeing farther:

What I have attempted to do would not have been possible without the opening of Heidegger's questions . . . would not have been possible without the attention to what Heidegger calls the difference between Being and beings, the ontico-ontological difference such as, in a way, it remains unthought by philosophy. But despite this debt to Heidegger's thought, or rather because of it, I attempt to locate in Heidegger's text . . . the signs of a belonging to metaphysics, or to what he calls onto-theology. [*Pos,* pp. 9–10]

Derrida thinks that Heidegger never got beyond a cluster of metaphors which he shared with Husserl, the cluster which suggests that we are all in possession of the "truth of Being" deep down inside, that we simply need to be reminded of what we have forgotten, reminded by those *"most elemental"* words which have been

---

13   Heidegger, *On Time and Being,* trans. Joan Stambaugh (New York, 1972), p. 24.
14   See Heidegger, *Early Greek Thinking,* trans. David Farrell Krell and Frank A. Capuzzi (New York, 1975), p. 52.

rescued for thought from metaphysics.[15] This notion that there is something called "the truth of Being" seems to Derrida the hidden link between the traditional philosophical quest for a total, unique, and closed vocabulary and Heidegger's own quest for magic, unique words.[16]

Derrida diagnoses in Heidegger "the dominance of an entire metaphorics of proximity, of simple and immediate presence, a metaphorics associating the proximity of Being with the values of neighboring, shelter, house, service, guard, voice, and listening" (*MP*, p. 130). Heidegger may have renounced the usual Platonic metaphors of vision in favor of auditory metaphors of calling and listening, but this shift does not, Derrida thinks, escape the circle of inter-explicable notions which binds the ontotheological tradition together with its insufficiently radical critic. "The valorization of spoken language," he says, "is constant and massive in Heidegger" (*MP*, p. 132 n.36). So Derrida sometimes tries to describe his own contribution in terms of the difference between the metaphors common to seeing and hearing and those which can be built up around *writing*.[17]

Derrida's account of Heidegger suggests the following picture: the early Heidegger spots the fatal similarities between Plato and Hegel (despite Hegel's historicism); the later Heidegger spots the fatal similarities between both of these, Nietzsche, and Heidegger's earlier self. Derrida sees the fatal similarities between all four and Heidegger's later self. So we find Hegel, Nietzsche, Heidegger, Derrida, and pragmatical commentators on Derrida like myself jostling for the position of history's first really *radical* anti-Platonist. This somewhat farcical attempt to be ever more un-Platonic has produced the suspicion that, like so many windup dolls, the philosophers of this century are still performing the same tedious dialectical inversions which Hegel did to death in the *Phenomenology*, the inversions which Kierkegaard liked to call "dog-tricks." The only difference may be that everybody is now trying to back farther and farther away from absolute knowledge and philosophical closure, rather than moving ever closer to them.

Derrida is well aware of the danger that, despite this difference, we may (as Foucault put it) be doomed to find Hegel waiting patiently at the end of whatever road we travel (even if we walk backward). But he thinks that he has a way of stepping off the path. He distinguishes between Heidegger's way of dealing with

---

15 Heidegger, *Being and Time*, trans. John Macquarrie and Edward Robinson (New York, 1962), p. 262.

16 Derrida recognizes, however, that Husserl was wrong to interpret *Being and Time* "as an anthropologistic deviation from transcendental phenomenology" and that Heidegger, in his later work, implicitly renounced his earlier quasi-phenomenological claim to be explicating a universal human "vague average understanding of Being" (*MP*, pp. 118, 124).

17 This is, I think, a vagary on his part. As is clear in "Limited Inc," all that "the primacy of writing" comes to is the claim that certain universal features of all discourse are more clearly seen in the case of writing than in the case of speech. I now think that I took the speech–writing contrast too seriously in an essay on Derrida which I wrote some years ago (see "Philosophy as a Kind of Writing: An Essay on Derrida," included in *Consequences of Pragmatism*).

the tradition, which he describes as "using against the edifice the instruments or stones available in the house," and the attempt to "change terrain, in a discontinuous and irruptive fashion, by brutally placing oneself outside, and by affirming an absolute break and difference" (*MP*, p. 135).

Neither of these, he thinks, will do by itself. My previous account of the dilemma Derrida faces may help us see why not. On the first alternative, you cannot avoid continuing an old conversation, with pretty much the same *archai, telos,* and so on. On the second alternative, you cannot say anything about philosophy, because you have lost touch with your subject. You cannot claim to be talking about the philosophical tradition if none of the words you use stand in any inferential relationships to any of the words used by that tradition. Either you gloss what the tradition has said, and thus continue down the page, or you don't, and thus are out at the margins, ignoring philosophy and being ignored by it.

Derrida proposes not to go between the horns of this dilemma but rather to twine the horns together into an interminably elongated double helix. He says that "a new writing must weave and interlace these two motifs of deconstruction. Which amounts to saying that one must speak several languages and produce several texts at once" (*MP*, p. 135). It is hardly clear why this would help. The best guess I have about why Derrida *thinks* it might help is that he wants to invoke the distinction between *inferential connections* between *sentences,* the connections which give the words used in those sentences their meaning, and *noninferential associations* between *words,* associations which are not dependent upon their use in sentences.[18] Like Heidegger, he seems to think that if we attend only to the former, we will be trapped in our current, ontotheological form of life. So, he may infer, we must break away from meaning, thought of in the Wittgenstein-Saussure way as a play of *inferential* differences, to something like what Heidegger called "force," the result of a play of *non*inferential differences, the play of *sounds* – or, concomitantly with the shift from the phonic to the written, the play of inscriptional features, of chirography and typography.

The distinction between these two sorts of play of difference is the distinction between the sort of abilities you need to write a grammar and a lexicon for a language and the sort you would need to make jokes in that language, to construct metaphors in it, or to write in it in a distinguished and original style rather

---

18 Let me try to clarify the distinction by an example. You will not be able to use the word "angle" correctly, to know the meaning of that word, unless you can also use a lot of words such as "line," "square," "circle," etc. Specifically, your knowledge of the meaning of "angle" consists largely in your ability to leap rapidly from the premise "It lies at an angle" to the conclusions "It lies where several lines meet," "It lies at a corner," etc. Again, you have to be able to leap from "It is a circle" to "It has no angles." You would, however, count as having grasped both use and meaning even if your ear were too dull to notice the noninferential associations of "angle," "England," "angel," "Anglican," etc. You can make rapid inferences in both English and Latin and still fail to get the joke when, in 1066 *and All That,* the Pope's remark to the British schoolboys ("Non Angli, sed angeli") is translated as "Not angels, but Anglicans."

than simply writing *clearly*. The clarity and transparency sought after by argumentative macho metaphysicians can be thought of as a way of implying that only inferential connections matter, because only those are relevant to argumentation. In this view, words matter only because one makes propositions, and thus *arguments,* out of them. Conversely, within Hartman's "frame of reference . . . such that the words stand out as words (even as sounds)," they matter even if they are never used in an indicative sentence.

The distinction between inferential connections and noninferential associations is, however, as blurry as the distinction between a word and a proposition, or as that between the metaphorical and the literal. There is a continuum between metaphors so dead they might as well be included in a dictionary as alternative "literal" senses and metaphors so fervid as to be merely inscrutable private jokes. But Derrida needs to make something of all these distinctions. He has to keep them looking sharp enough so that it will seem shocking to ignore them. If his tactic of speaking several languages at once, producing several texts at once, is to seem effective, he will have to claim that it is something his predecessors have not done themselves. He will have to claim that their practice as well as their theory has eschewed metaphor, has depended only on knowledge of inferential connections, and that he is doing something original in weaving together such connections with noninferential associations. He will have to think that whereas Heidegger, and everybody else in the tradition, simply rearranged the inferential connections between sentences and thus has simply rebuilt the same edifice on the same terrain, he is succeeding in shifting the terrain by, for the first time, relying on noninferential associations. Or, at least, he will have to say that he is the first to have done this in full self-consciousness.

5. Reading several texts at once

Given this interpretation of how Derrida thinks he can do what Heidegger failed to do, how he hopes to move outside the tradition instead of being mired within it as Heidegger was, I want to make two criticisms of his attempt. First, it is just not true that the sequence of texts which make up the canon of the ontotheological tradition has been imprisoned within a metaphorics which have remained unchanged since the Greeks. That sequence of texts, like that which makes up the history of astronomical treatises, or of the epic, or of political discourse, has been marked by the usual alternation between "revolutionary," "literary," "poetic" moments and normal, banal, constructive interludes. Speaking several languages and writing several texts at once is just what all important, revolutionary, original thinkers have done. Revolutionary physicists, politicians, and philosophers have always taken words and beaten them into new shapes. They have thereby given their angry conservative opponents reason to charge them with introducing strange new senses of familiar expressions, frivolously punning, no longer playing by the rules, using rhetoric rather than logic, imagery rather than argument. The stages "in the history of Being" which Heidegger recounts are marked, as Heidegger himself says, by people (sometimes ironically and sometimes self-deceptively) pretending to say the same old thing while subversively putting a new spin on the old words. Consider, in this connection, Aristotle's use of *ousia*, Descartes' of *res*, Hume's of "impression," Wittgenstein's of "game," Einstein's of "simultaneous," and Bohr's of "atom."

If science were as literal and methodical as philosophy of science has liked to pretend, and if philosophy were as much a matter of solving problems, analyzing concepts, and contemplating ideas as it has sometimes dreamed of being, then it might be possible to draw a philosophy—literature or a science—literature distinction which paralleled the distinction between the universal and literal, on the one hand, and the idiosyncratic and metaphorical, on the other. Then one might, like Derrida, try to shift the terrain by replacing these with the distinction between inferential connections and noninferential associations. But just as the history of science is not much like what either empiricism or rationalism has described it as being, so the history of philosophy is not much like what the dream at the heart of philosophy hoped it might be. It is one thing to say that the metaphorical—literal distinction has traditionally been exploited to distinguish philosophy from literature, if this means that two ideal types have been constructed with the aid of that distinction. It is another to say that the areas of culture which are demarcated by the usual bibliographical criteria as "literature" and "philosophy" have anything much to do with these ideal types.

Important, revolutionary physics, and metaphysics, has always been "literary" in the sense that it has faced the problem of introducing new jargon and nudging aside the language-games currently in place. If it has not always been "violent" and "brutal," this is because it has sometimes been civil and conversational, not because it has stayed trapped within an unyielding metaphoric. The Derridean contrasts between rebuilding the edifice and shifting the terrain, between inferential connections and noninferential associations, cannot be made sharp enough to serve Derrida's purposes. Once one turns away from dreams and ideal types to narratives which trace the history of genres, all these distinctions blur.

I cannot prove this point without actually producing such narratives, but let me put forward one argument which may help buttress my claim. Consider the abstract problem of how one can ever "escape" from a vocabulary or a set of assumptions, how one avoids being "trapped" within a language or a culture. Suppose that there is universal agreement within a community on "the conditions of intelligible linguistic expression" or "the only vocabulary in which it is permissible to speak." Then suppose somebody in that community wishes to say that we made a mistake — that actually these conditions or criteria, or that vocabulary, were the wrong ones. This revolutionary suggestion would be easily disposed of.

For either it would be made in obedience to the old conditions or criteria, within the old vocabulary, or it would not be. If it were, then it would be self-referentially inconsistent. If it were not, it would be unintelligible, or irrational, or both. Derrida talks as if this neat textbook dilemma were a real one, as if there were a terrible, oppressive force called "the metaphorics of philosophy" or the "history of metaphysics" which is making life impossible not only for playful punsters like himself but for society as a whole. But things are just not that bad, except in special circumstances, circumstances of the sort which once produced the Inquisition and, more recently, the KGB. The discourse of physics, metaphysics, and politics is considerably more pliant than this. Not only is there no universal agreement on the conditions of intelligibility or the criteria of rationality, but nobody even tries to pretend there is, except as an occasional and rather ineffective rhetorical device. The discourse of high culture has, particularly in the last two hundred years, been considerably more fluid and chatty and playful than one would guess from reading either Heidegger or Derrida.

To sum up this first criticism of Derrida, I think that he effectively invokes two dreams, two ideal types, and plays them off each other to good effect. But this ideal and dreamlike world, with its contrasts between text and margin, the insiders and the outsiders, the same terrain and the new terrain, has not got much to do with present-day forms of intellectual life. This leads me to my second criticism: if one wants to twist the horns of the artificial dilemma Derrida constructs into a corkscrew, one might do so simply by *reading* several texts at once as opposed to *writing* several texts at once. Indeed, one might claim to have been doing just that for quite some time. That genre of writing which does exemplify the dream of philosophy, which culminates in claims like "All intelligible linguistic expression must . . ." or "All rational discourse must . . . ," forms only a small part of the history of philosophy. That particular genre has been read with more and more irony and distance in recent centuries. For it is being read by people who have read not only other genres of philosophy but also many of the various other genres of writing shelved under "literature." A typical contemporary reader of Parmenides, Spinoza, Kant, Hegel, and Ayer will also be a reader of Heraclitus, Hume, Kierkegaard, Austin, Freud, Borges, Joyce, Nabokov, and Wallace Stevens – and, for that matter, Jean Genet. In *Glas* Derrida has, to be sure, spoken several languages at once, written several texts at once, produced a kind of writing which has no *archai*, no *telos*, and so on. But he is doing brilliantly and at length something most of his readers have been doing spasmodically and awkwardly in their heads. It is no small feat to get this sort of thing down on paper, but what we find in *Glas* is not a new terrain. It is a realistic account of a terrain upon which we have been camping for some time.

I can put this second criticism in more general terms by saying that most contemporary intellectuals live in a culture which is self-consciously without *archai*, without *telos*, without theology, teleology, or ontology. So it is not clear that we need a "new sort of writing" in order to think what "the structured genealogy of philosophy's concepts . . . has been able to dissimulate or forbid." Much of Derrida's account of what he is up to depends, as I have already said, on the idea that literature, science, and politics have been forbidden to do various things by "the history of metaphysics." This idea repeats Heidegger's claim that the history of the genre which has sought a total, unique, and closed language is central to the entire range of human possibilities in the contemporary West. This claim seems very implausible.

The only justification it seems to have is that the West still goes in for a lot of talk about the need to be *wissenschaftlich* or "rigorous" or "objective." But, apart from a few philosophy professors who (like Searle) enjoy insisting on "plain facts" and a few others (like myself) who enjoy debunking this notion of factuality, nobody connects these terms with the dream of a total, unique, closed vocabulary. Both Searle's and my efforts may by now be irrelevant to contemporary high culture – just as the professional wowsers and professional atheists, suing and countersuing over the issue of morning prayer in public schools, are irrelevant to American politics. By now, words like "scientific" or "objective" have been worn down to the point where most people are content to let them mean "the way we do things around here." Certain subcultures use words like "radical" or "subversive" to mean the same thing. Both sets of terms are conventional expressions of approbation, given specificity and meaning by their sociological context of use rather than by their links with a project of totalization.

6. *Writing about interminability*

I said previously that Derrida sometimes illustrated what it is like to escape the iron cage of tradition by invoking noninferential associates and that at other times he did so by writing argumentatively. My criticisms so far have concentrated on his explanation of why he does the former. I now want to turn briefly to the latter tactic and to develop my previous point that Derrida cannot *argue* without turning himself into a metaphysician, one more claimant to the title of the discoverer of the primal, deepest vocabulary.

This danger looms in such passages as the following, in which Derrida is explaining why Heidegger's word "Being" won't do to distance the tradition and suggesting that words like *différance* and *trace* might succeed:

Since Being has never had a "meaning," has never been thought or said as such, except by dissimulating itself in beings, then *différance,* in a certain and very strange way, (is) "older" than the ontological difference or than the truth of Being. When it has this age it can be called the play of the trace. The play of a trace which no longer belongs to the horizon of Being, but whose play transports and encloses the meaning of Being. . . . There is no maintaining, and no depth to, this bottomless chessboard on which Being is put into play. [*MP*, p. 22]

Such passages are exciting in a good old-fashioned, dialectical, Hegelian way. They suggest that we have finally managed to look beyond the familiar horizon, beneath the familiar surface, back behind the putative origin, and thus have finally managed to close the last circle, overcome the last dialectical tension, and so on. They attract, therefore, the following sort of objection:

"The Derridean grammatic is 'modeled,' in its major lines, on Heideggerean metaphysics, which it attempts to 'deconstruct' by substituting the anteriority of a trace for the 'presence of the logos'; it constitutes itself as an onto-theology based on the trace as 'ground,' 'foundation' or 'origin.' " (*Pos,* p. 52]

To this objection Derrida replies indignantly:

How does one model oneself after what one deconstructs? Can one speak so simply of Heideggerean *metaphysics?* But above all (because these first two eventualities are not absurd in themselves, even if they are so here) have I not indefatigably repeated – and I would dare say demonstrated – that the trace is neither a ground . . . nor an origin, and that in no case can it provide for a manifest or disguised onto-theology? . . . This confusion . . . consists in turning against my texts criticisms one forgets one has found in them first and borrowed from them. [*Pos,* p. 52]

This reply is very puzzling. It would be more Derridean to ask how one could possibly *avoid* modeling oneself after what one deconstructs. In the case of a metaphorics as large and sprawling as that of philosophy, it seems very unlikely that one will manage to talk about one's predecessors while using no term which is inter-explicable with the terms they used. In particular, it is puzzling how Derrida can speak of having *demonstrated* that "the trace is neither a ground . . . nor an origin" or how he can tell which is " 'older,' " *différance* or the truth of Being. Those who wish to sidestep the metaphysics of presence should not speak of *demonstrating.* Those who are trying to back out of the metaphorics of the tradition should not worry about what is older than what.

Consider, in this connection, Derrida's claim that "the movement of *différance* . . . is the common root of all the oppositional concepts that mark our language, such as, to take only a few examples, sensible/intelligible, intuition/ signification, nature/culture, etc." (*Pos,* p. 9). Notice that "common root" here does not mean either "cause of" or "primitive form of." For the movement of *différance,* like the *trace,* can be neither a ground nor an origin. Nor should it mean "common feature of." If it meant that, then *différance* would be a perfectly ordinary word which stood to the various oppositions constituting the metaphorics of philosophy as the word "bird" stands to the eagle, the ostrich, and the sparrow. But Derrida tells us, over and over, that *différance* is "neither a word nor a concept."

This is, however, not true. The first time Derrida used that collocation of letters, it was, indeed, not a word, but only a misspelling. But around the third or fourth time he used it, it had *become* a word. All that it takes for a vocable or an inscription to become a word, after all, is a place in a language game. By now it is a very familiar word indeed. Any literary theorist who confused *différance* with *différence* would be out on his ear, just like a theology student in the fifth century who confused *homoousion* and *homoiousion*. As to concepthood, we Wittgensteinian nominalists think that to have a concept is to be able to use a word. Any word that has a use automatically signifies a concept. It can't *help* doing so. It is no use Derrida telling us that since *différance* "cannot be elevated into a master-word or a master-concept, since it blocks every relationship to theology, [it] finds itself enmeshed in the work that pulls it through a chain of other 'concepts,' other 'words,' other textual configurations" (*Pos*, p. 40). For us Wittgensteinians, *every* word finds itself enmeshed in this way, and such enmeshment is no safeguard against elevation. Derrida cannot simultaneously adopt the language-game account of meaning for all words and try to privilege a few selected magic words as incapable of theological use.

If we are to find some point in all this sidestepping of Hegel, out-magicking Heidegger, escaping to the margins, and so on, it had better be something more than a repeat of Austin's and Quine's criticisms of Locke's and Condillac's "idea idea."[19] Again, if Derrida wants "a general strategy of deconstruction," he must formulate one which is something more than "avoiding both simply neutralizing the binary oppositions of metaphysics and simply residing with the closed field of oppositions, thereby confirming it." Such dual avoidance can be achieved simply by pointing out that the oppositions are there, and then not taking them very seriously. That is what most of our culture has been doing for a long time now. Our culture has not only been carried upward by a bubbling fountain of puns and metaphors; it has been increasingly conscious of itself as resting on nothing more solid than such a geyser.[20] If all Derrida is saying is that we should take the dead

19 One of the barriers to Derrida's understanding of Austin was that he did not realize how thoroughly this idea had been extirpated from Oxford in the 1950s, thanks to Gilbert Ryle. One of the barriers to Anglo-Saxon understanding of Derrida is the assumption that all he can possibly be doing is to discover belatedly what Austin and Quine already knew.

20 For an example of this attitude in respect to scientific progress, see Mary Hesse, *Revolutions and Reconstructions in the Philosophy of Science* (Bloomington, Ind., 1980). Hesse makes the crucial point that the analysis of progress in terms of "convergence" may work for propositions but that "there is no obvious sense in which convergence of *concepts* can be maintained" (p. x). The replacement of one set of theoretical concepts by another, concepts which cannot themselves be defined in terms of an overarching observation language, is essential to the attainment of greater predictive success, but there is no way to see such replacement as "getting closer to the way things really are" unless this means simply "getting more predictive power." If that is all that it means, then one cannot explain the success of science in terms of the notion of corresponding better to reality. In chap. 4 of her book, "The Explanatory Function of Metaphor," Hesse suggests that we view scientific theories as metaphors and concludes, "Rationality consists just in the continuous adaptation of our language to our continually expanding world, and metaphor is one of the chief means by which this is accomplished" (p. 123). I have argued that Hesse's view can be expanded along Deweyan lines in such a way as to leave no epistemological difference between science and the rest of culture. See my "Reply to Dreyfus and Taylor" (and the ensuing discussion), *Review of Metaphysics* 24 (Sept. 1980): 39–56.

metaphors of the philosophical tradition less seriously than Heidegger took them, it is fair to reply that his own early writing takes them rather more seriously than the later Heidegger himself took them.

7. *Conclusion*

Summing up, I think that one can make better use both of Derrida's puns and of his magic words if one shrugs off the idea that there is something called "philosophy" or "metaphysics" which is central to our culture and which has been radiating evil influences outward. This is not to say that the puns are not funny, or that the words are not powerful, but only that the tone of urgency which surrounds them is out of place. One would only adopt this Heideggerian tone if one thought that the various de-centerings of which Freud spoke – that effected by Copernicus, by Darwin, and by himself – had still left us stuck on the same terrain, the place where all those bad old binary oppositions hold sway. But such a view makes a bogeyman of oppositions which, fortunately, have long since been "level[ed] off to that unintelligibility which functions in turn as a source of pseudo-problems."[21] Heidegger mistakenly thought that this was a *mis*fortune. He thought that the "most elementary words" needed to have force restored to them. I agree with Derrida that Heidegger is here indulging in pointless nostalgia. We need to create our own elementary words, not spruce up Greek ones. But I disagree with his assumption that there is more to be done with the leveled-off remnants of the old words than to make fun of attempts to build them up again, attempts to make the pseudoproblems they produce look real. In Derrida's earlier, more argumentative work, alas, his effects depend on making them look both real and urgent.

Without attributing to Derrida himself the beliefs and practices of his more incautious followers, one can nevertheless say that the idea that philosophy is central to culture, an idea implicit in his earlier work, has encouraged literary critics to believe that Derrida has discovered the key to unlocking the mystery of any and every text. In its extreme form, this belief leads critics to treat every text as "about" the same old philosophical oppositions: time and space, sensible and intelligible, subject and object, being and becoming, identity and difference, and so on. Just when we pragmatic Wittgensteinian therapists were congratulating ourselves on having disabused the learned world of the idea that these oppositions were "deep," just when we thought we had got this terminology nicely leveled off and trivialized, we found all the dear old textbook "problems of philosophy" being heralded as the hidden agenda of our favorite poems and novels. This has created an awkward social situation: we therapeutic philosophers who try to dissolve the textbook problems now find that our old professional opponents (for example, Searle) are in agreement with our new interdisciplinary friends (for

21 Heidegger, *Being and Time,* p. 262 (also cited above in n. 15).

example, Culler). They both think that the textbook distinctions are terribly important. The former want to reconstruct them and the latter want to deconstruct them, but neither is content to take them lightly, to "de-thematize" them, to view them as just a few extra tropes. It is as important for the deconstructors as for the realists to think that metaphysics – that genre of literature which attempted to create unique, total, closed vocabularies – is very important. Neither can afford to admit that, like the epic, it is a genre which had a distinguished career and an important historical function but which now survives largely in the form of self-parody.

Only if one takes this genre to be more than an intriguing historical artifact will the contrast between philosophical closure and literary openness seem important. I have been urging that the latter contrast, between the classic attempt to close off language and the Romantic insistence on breaking out of any proposed closure, is the only basis for making more than routine bibliographical and genealogical contrasts between "philosophy" and "literature." So, to return to the point with which I began, I think we would do well to see philosophy as just one more literary genre within which the classic–Romantic opposition is prominent. We should not use "philosophy" as the name of the classic pole of this ubiquitous opposition. We should see the classic–Romantic, scientific–literary, and order–freedom oppositions as emblematic of an internal rhythm which pervades every discipline and every sector of culture.

My suggestion that we return to the ironic eclecticism of the *Phenomenology of Mind* and the second part of *Faust* may seem reactionary. Yet it will only seem that way if we are so fervently Romantic as to discount the classic altogether, the moment in which intellectual history looks like a story of eternal recurrence. We are never going to stop swinging back and forth between that moment and the Romantic one, the moment in which it seems as if (in Robinson Jeffers' words) "the river of the ages turns round the rock of this year." To hope for a standpoint from which we shall escape this oscillation would be to hope for just the sort of unique, total, closed vocabulary which Heidegger and Derrida rightly say we are not going to get.

From this point of view, there is not an urgent task called "deconstructing metaphysics" which needs to be performed before we can get to work on the rest of culture. Despite himself, what Heidegger did to the history of philosophy was not to deconstruct it but to further encapsulate and isolate it, thus enabling us to *circumvent* it. What Derrida has done, also despite himself, is to show us how to take Heidegger with Nietzschean gaiety, how to see his handling of the metaphysical tradition as a brilliantly original narrative rather than as an epochal transformation. This reading of Derrida gives us no reason to think that, as some North American Derrideans have suggested, he has shown us how to do to something called "literature" what Heidegger did to something else called "philosophy." It is one thing to circumvent a particular literary genre – philosophy –

by encapsulating it. It is another thing to show that that genre is the armature, or the template, for all the others. Nothing in either Heidegger or Derrida gives plausibility to this latter claim, which is an unquestioned premise in much of the work of both. But this claim is essential to the attempt of Anglo-Saxon Derrideans to take philosophical oppositions as the implicit topic of any, arbitrarily chosen, literary text. The attempt to find a closed and total vocabulary produced lots of great big binary oppositions which poets and essayists and novelists then proceeded to use as tropes. But one can use a trope perfectly well without taking seriously its claim to be part of such a vocabulary. One does not need to see it as deconstructing itself, as committing suicide, in order to escape its baleful totalizing influence. Concepts like causality, originality, intelligibility, literalness, and the like are no more dangerous, and no more suicidal, than sunsets or blackbirds. It is not their fault that in another country, long ago, they were believed to have magical powers.

Two meanings of "logocentrism": A reply to Norris

"The discourse of philosophy" is to early Derrida as "Being" is to late Heidegger. Both terms refer to something we can never simply walk away from, but instead must constantly struggle with. As Christians think God inescapable and Heidegger thinks Being inescapable, so Derrida thinks "the discourse of philosophy" inescapable. All our attempts to do without it are relations to it. It follows us down the nights and down the days. It waits at the end of every road that seems to lead away from it. Just as Freud thought that we never cease from erotic struggle with images of our parents, no matter how long we live or how little we consciously think about them, so the early Derrida thinks that we cannot escape from logocentric discourse. For him, as Norris says, "philosophy's influence on our language and habits of thought is utterly pervasive."[1] Just as Freud thought that we might be able to replace neurotic misery with ordinary human unhappiness by *realizing* that our struggle with those figures of infantile fantasy is interminable, so may we replace self-deception with the endless labor of deconstruction by *realizing* that there will never be a *last* philosophical discourse.

If (but only if) philosophy's influence *is* that pervasive, we have no choice but to use, as Norris says, "the language that comes to hand (along with its inescapable logocentric residues) . . . in precisely such a way as to bring out its inherent strains and contradictions." Just as the abstract knowledge gained from psychoanalysis is useful only insofar as it is artfully applied to particular events in our lives, so the abstract knowledge that the discourse of philosophy is self-contradictory is no help unless we artfully bring it to bear on particular texts. If the premise about philosophy's pervasiveness is true, then American deconstructive criticism — with its dreary and repetitious discovery of tiresomely familiar "inherent strains and contradictions" — may be the best we can hope for.

My own view, as I said in "Deconstruction and Circumvention," is that that crucial premise is false. The "discourse of philosophy" does function as an inescapable parent figure for some people. But for other people it is only an aging great-uncle, briefly glimpsed in childhood at the occasional family celebration. The idea of God is, in part, the idea of the Father of Us All — the parent we all have in

---

1 This and all other quotations from Christopher Norris in this paper are from the paper to which this is a reply: "Philosophy as *Not* Just a 'Kind of Writing': Derrida and the Claim of Reason," in *Redrawing the Lines: Analytic Philosophy, Deconstruction and Literary Theory*, ed. Reed Way Dasenbrock (Minneapolis: University of Minnesota Press, 1989), pp. 189–203.

common. The idea of Being, or of "the discourse of philosophy," as something we purport to forget only to find ourselves bonded to it anew, is pretty much the same idea. Prophets who claim a personal, quasi-filial relationship with God tell us that he is as inescapable for us as for them. But, Freud suggested, such prophets may simply be trying to excuse their own idiosyncratic difficulties by taking them to be universal: imagining that their own tiresome and embarrassing parents are also the parents of everyone else. Late Heidegger and early Derrida are, to my mind, this sort of prophet.

My view has, at least, the virtue of explaining why the writings of both men are so important for some of us — those of us for whom the discourse of philosophy actually *has* been important — while looking so absurd, so little worth reading, to many other people. Having myself cathected the discourse of philosophy when young, I find Heidegger and Derrida among the most powerful and fascinating writers of my time. They speak to my condition. But I doubt very much that they speak to a universal human, or even a universal Western, condition. My own imagination is filled with the same images as fill theirs: Socrates and Phaedo, shifty Matter and stalwart Form, dubious mind-dependent redness and reliable mind-independent squareness, the starry a priori above and the grimy a posteriori below, Hegel's rose, Nietzsche's tarantulas, and Quine's rabbit stages. These are powerful, but not universally compelling, images. Their power over me, I take it, comes from the way I happened to acquire them, the way they happened to interlock with, and eventually to symbolize, my own idiosyncratic hopes and fears. Their power over Heidegger and Derrida, I assume, is a result of similarly idiosyncratic interlockings.

Consider, from this point of view, Norris's claim that one cannot "escape philosophy simply by determining no longer to have any truck with it." This is certainly true for those of us who have had a lot of truck with it in the past; nobody escapes his past, his parents, or his Bloomian precursors just by turning his back on them. But, as I suggested in "Deconstruction and Circumvention," a lot of people never have had much truck with philosophy. Even the intellectuals, in recent centuries, have been having less and less truck with it. As science, scholarship, and (especially) literature have ramified, the number of people who cathected philosophy in their youth has steadily decreased. So, to evaluate Norris's argument, we have to look at the premise I have already isolated: the premise about philosophy being "utterly pervasive."

I think this premise seems plausible only if one identifies the "discourse of philosophy" with any and all binary oppositions. Few pieces of writing will not invoke, implicitly or explicitly, some such oppositions as good–evil, noble–base, cause–effect, free–necessary, original–derivative, eternity–time, positive–negative, male–female, and white–black. But it is not plausible to think of *all* these oppositions as equally "philosophical." Their casual ubiquity suggests that they swing free of whatever logocentric assumptions might have been associated with their use, just as the word "atom" has come to swing free of Democritean assumptions. As Barbara Herrnstein Smith has said, if one identifies the whole list of familiar oppositions with "logocentrism" then

> there is no reason to believe that the metaphysics of Western thought is distinct from that of Eastern thought, or tribal thought, or the thought of illiterates or of preverbal or as yet unacculturated children. On the contrary, I would suggest here that "the metaphysics of Western thought" *is* thought, all of it, root and branch, everywhere and always.[2]

Smith's point suggests that we distinguish a narrow from a wide sense of the term "logocentric metaphysics of presence." In the *narrow* sense, this metaphysics consists of something like the doctrines that, toward the beginning of his essay, Norris identifies as "the three main assumptions that underpin the discourse of philosophy as a quest for ultimate, self-validating truth." The notions invoked in aid of this project of self-validation – notions like "self-evident," "intuitive," "directly present to consciousness," "conditions of the possibility of experience," and so on – are not commonsensical, but obviously philosophical.

But in the *wide* sense, the metaphysics of presence and "the discourse of philosophy" include *all* the invidious binary oppositions listed earlier, and thousands more. These are distinctions some philosophers have been tempted to explicate with reference to the idea of self-validation, but that explication is no more essential to their use than astrophysics is to our casual references to heavenly bodies. It is one thing to say that the quest for ultimate, self-validating truth has "inherent strains and contradictions." It is another to say that "the language of the West" or "the discourse of philosophy" has such strains. The former strains are quite specific, and are the kind Derrida finds in Husserl and other authors who are driven by the quest for certainty, the need for direct, immediate confrontation, and the like. The latter strains are merely the ordinary strains that appear in any and every vocabulary (scientific, political, technical, or whatever) when it meets an anomaly – something with which it was not designed to cope. To develop a new vocabulary that will handle the new, perplexing cases is not a matter of escaping from philosophy, or from "the structure of previous thought," but simply of reweaving our web of linguistic usage – our habits of responding to marks and noises with other marks and noises. Some such reweavings are relatively easy and painless (e.g., those involved in Kuhnian "normal science" and in reformist politics); others are dramatic and disturbing (e.g., those involved in intellectual and political revolutions).

Although they may appear dramatic to hindsight, revolutions in philosophy,

---

2 Smith, *Contingencies of Value* (Cambridge, Mass.: Harvard University Press, 1988), p. 118. Smith goes on to note that "the cheapest way for any system to process an array of information is by binary classification, which is, of course, the minimal classification. Moreover, because, in an organic system, classification, like any other activity, is economically energized – energized, that is, by self-interest or, if you like, the profit-motive – any classification that is produced is likely to be an *evaluative hierarchy*" (p. 122).

like the Copernican Revolution in science and unlike violent political revolutions, take quite a long time: sometimes a century or two. During the last hundred and fifty years, there has been continually increasing dissatisfaction among philosophers with ideas like "self-validating truth," "intuition," "transcendental argument," and "principles of the ultimate foundation of all possible knowledge." So, as Searle remarked in his review of Culler's *On Deconstruction*, if deconstruction is no more than another version of antifoundationalism, it is not very exciting. Most philosophers nowadays *are* antifoundationalists. If Derrida were simply telling us that ideas like "self-validation" and "intuition" contain "inherent strains and contradictions," he would be telling us little that we might not have learned from Peirce's criticism of Descartes, T. H. Green's of Locke, Sellars's and Quine's of the various dogmas of empiricism, and Wittgenstein's and Davidson's of "building-block" theories of language learning. Norris is quite right that Derrida does a first-class, highly professional job on Husserl. But, *mutatis mutandis*, it is pretty much the same job the philosophers I just mentioned did on their respective targets.[3] The basic anti-intuitionist and antifoundationalist point common to Derrida and these others is that knowledge is a matter of asserting sentences, and that you cannot validate an assertion by confronting an object (e.g., a table, the concept "tablehood," or the Platonic Idea of Table), but only by asserting other sentences. This point is linked to lots of other holist and antiessentialist doctrines, doctrines that make it possible to set aside the subject–object, representationalist notions of knowledge we inherited from the Greeks.[4]

---

3   See Samuel Wheeler, "Indeterminacy of French Translation," in *Perspectives on Truth and Interpretation: The Philosophy of Donald Davidson*, ed. Ernest LePore (Oxford: Blackwell, 1986). Wheeler draws parallels between Derrida's arguments and those of Quine and Davidson. The great difference between such writers and Derrida, of course, is that the former do not share Heidegger's sense of "Western metaphysics" as pervasive and all-encompassing. So their polemics lack the apocalyptic tone common to late Heidegger and early Derrida.
        Notice, in particular, Wheeler's point that "the core-problem which drives the analyses of both Derrida and Davidson . . . is that allegedly non-Aristotelian and nonessentialist accounts of the world (e.g., Kantian and 'linguistic' ones) still seem to rest on essentialism about conceptual or linguistic items. . . . The radical break which both Davidson and Derrida make is to work out the consequences of denying essentialism and objective necessities across the board" ("Indeterminacy," p. 484). Whereas Davidson thinks these consequences can be worked out naturalistically, early Derrida and Gasché think that a nonnaturalistic theory involving notions such as "trace," "différance," etc., is required. My agreement with Davidson on this point amounts to saying that these latter notions are dispensable, and that there is no need for "transcendental deductions" in this area.

4   One consequence of getting rid of this picture is that it is no longer a criticism of philosophy to say, with Norris, that "its concepts most often come down to metaphors at root." In order to have a polemically useful contrast between "concept" and "metaphor" one would have to assume that concepts necessarily have literal meaning, and then construe such meaning as possible only by virtue of ostension (exhibiting a sensible or intelligible object to consciousness, bringing that which the concept signified before the mind and naming it). It would be hard to find an important twentieth-century philosopher (other than Husserl, Russell, and a few of their more ardent followers) who held any such view. Russell-bashing and Husserl-bashing remain good sport, but bashing their doctrines is not bashing anything central to recent philosophical thought. Husserl's "Philosophy as Strict Science" (which did indeed call for, in Norris's words, "the ultimate ground-

I think Norris is wrong when he says that my view requires me to "politely ignore all the passages of hard-pressed textual analysis where Derrida shows deconstruction actually at work on the grounding assumptions of logocentric discourse." The passages I assume Norris would pick out as fulfilling this description seem to me to divide into two sets. The first set offers the standard anti-intuitionist, antiessentialist arguments Derrida shares with many of his contemporaries. The second set is made up of all those passages in which Derrida refuses to allow his opponents to invoke some innocuous, commonsensical distinction by pointing out that this distinction can be "brought into question." Bringing it into question often involves no more, as Searle rightly remarks, than pointing out that there are difficult borderline cases, or that some philosopher might attempt to construe the distinction at hand as one more instance of the distinction between self-validating plenitude and non-self-validating deficiency.

The latter set includes, for example, the much-discussed passages in which Derrida questioned Austin's use of the distinction between serious and nonserious uses of a given sentence. Here Derrida seemed either to invoke what Searle calls the "positivistic" assumption that a distinction cannot be used if it cannot adjudicate all borderline cases, or else simply to assume that *all* distinctions (except, for some reason, his own) are somehow "complicit" with "the discourse of philosophy." The positivistic assumption is as bad as Searle says it is, and the notion of "complicity" is too vague to have any argumentative force; its use would be defensible only if any binary opposition were dubious just because it is binary, or just because one side of the opposition has traditionally been taken as superior to the other. But such an opposition becomes dubious only when the purpose it is serving is dubious.[5] In itself, it is just a tool that can be used for good or for ill.

I confess that I find the knee-jerk suspicion of binary oppositions among deconstructionists baffling. To say, as they often do, that the "preferred" term of such an opposition "presupposes" the other term is true enough, if all it means is that you will not understand the meaning of, for example, "white" unless you understand that of "black," of "noble" unless you understand that of "base," and so on. But the fact that two contrasting terms get their meaning by reciprocal definability, and in that sense "presuppose" each other, does nothing to cast doubt on their utility.[6] Nor would such doubt be cast by showing, as deconstructionists

ing of reason in a sense of those constitutive structures of knowledge and perception which *cannot be doubted*") proved to be a swan song, not a new beginning. The same fate has now overtaken Russell's "Logic as the Essence of Philosophy."

5 This pragmatic point is made by Derrida himself: "If words and concepts receive meaning only in sequences of differences, one can justify one's language, and one's choice of terms, only within a topic and an historical strategy. The justification can therefore never be absolute and definitive. It corresponds to a condition of forces and translates an historical calculation" (*Of Grammatology*, trans. Gayatn Chakravorty Spivak [Chicago: University of Chicago Press, 1976], p. 70). Dewey would have happily agreed, as would Wittgenstein.

6 It would cast such doubt only if one held that the "upper" term of an opposition must be definable by ostension – by direct confrontation with an object – whereas the "lower" can be defined only

often do, that the "upper" term can be seen as a "special case" of the "lower" term. Practically anything can be seen, with a bit of imagination and contrivance, as a special case of practically anything else; dialectical and linguistic ingenuity will always suffice to recontextualize anything so as to cast doubt on its importance, or its previous role. But such ingenuity is in vain if it has no purpose more specific than "escaping from logocentrism."[7]

I am also baffled by Norris's (and Gasché's) invocation of the notion of "transcendental argument" as a description of what Derrida is up to. A transcendental argument is an argument to the effect that something is a condition of the *possibility* of something else – a *noncausal* condition. Kant's argument that a nonconscious synthesis of a manifold of intuition is a condition of the possibility of conscious experience should be viewed as a *reductio ad absurdum* of the very idea of such conditions. Taken at face value, arguments such as Kant's amount to positing an unverifiable I-know-not-what to explain a fact – a fact that only seems in need of explanation because one has previously posited that ordinary, scientific, causal explanations of it will not do. The most charitable construal of such arguments is that they are misleading ways of making the point that a certain set of terms cannot be used by people who are incapable of using another set – as in Strawson's construal of the conclusion of Kant's "Transcendental Deduction of the Categories" as the claim that people who could not talk about things could not talk about sense impressions either.

Insofar as Derrida remains faithful to the nominalism he shares with Strawson, transcendental arguments will not permit him to infer the existence of such quasi entities as "différance," "trace" and "archi-writing." Insofar as he does not remain faithful to it, he is just one more metaphysician. A philosopher cannot, as Derrida does, set his face against totalization, insist that the possibilities of recontextualization are boundless, and nonetheless offer transcendental arguments. For how

indirectly, parasitically, on the basis of an antecedent knowledge of the meaning of the "upper" term. But, as I said earlier, it is getting pretty hard to find anybody who takes the notion of ostensive definition seriously. Aristotle, to be sure, can be interpreted as holding that we grasp some terms by *nous* and others by secondary and derivative means, but there are not many Aristotelians around anymore. Even Husserl and Russell, who do take ostension seriously, can hardly be saddled with this view of any and every binary opposition. Culler says that in binary oppositions "the first term has been conceived as prior, a plenitude of which the second is a negation or complication" (*On Deconstruction: Theory and Criticism After Structuralism* (Ithaca, N.Y.: Cornell University Press, 1982], p. 160). I think he would be hard-pressed to find recent philosophers who so conceive the matter.

7 Derrida's example has inspired a good deal of ingenious, and sometimes effective, recontextualization on behalf of less fuzzy purposes, e.g., overcoming patriarchy, and other forms of sociopolitical oppression. But such efforts are, I think, weakened rather than strengthened by attempts to associate such oppression with "logocentrism." In the narrow sense of that term, the association is hardly evident. In the wide sense, it is like associating something with Satan, or the Forces of Darkness. Like "capitalism" as used by some Marxists, "logocentrism" has become less and less useful as a scare-word as it has been stretched to cover more and more territory. It becomes vaguer and less scary with each stretch.

could he hope to grasp *the conditions of possibility of all possible contexts?* What context would he be putting the potential infinity of contexts in when he did so? How can Derrida's "trace," "différance," and the rest of what Gasché calls "infra-structures" be *more* than the vacuous nonexplanations characteristic of a negative theology?[8]

To sum up, I think it as important to insist that Derrida is *not* giving rigorous arguments against logocentrism, in the wide and vacuous sense of that term, as to say that he is indeed (like most other important twentieth-century philosophers) giving such arguments against what Norris calls "a quest for ultimate, self-validating truth." That these assumptions are pretty well moribund by now does not make Derrida's arguments less worthy, but it does mean that we have to seek elsewhere for an explanation of the attention he has received and the extent of his influence.

My own explanation of these phenomena goes like this. I think Derrida appeals to at least three different audiences. The first audience admires the way in which he continues a dialectical sequence that runs through Hegel, Nietzsche, and Heidegger. In his variations on the themes found in these writers – notably the theme of overcoming the tradition, of making a new beginning – he is splendidly original. His stature as a reader of Heidegger is on a level with Heidegger's as a reader of Nietzsche, and with Nietzsche's as a reader of Plato. A second audience admires him simply as a writer. However else Derrida may look to history, he will be viewed as one of the great French writers of his time – a writer who happened, like Sartre, to have started off as a philosophy professor, but who quickly transcended his humble origins. Apart from his incredible, almost Nabokovian, polylingual linguistic facility, he is a great *comic* writer – perhaps the funniest writer on philosophical topics since Kierkegaard.

I am an enthusiastic member of both of these first two audiences. But I see them as distinct from a third, and much larger, audience, to which I do not belong. This one contains most of the people who write deconstructive literary criticism. These people assimilate early Derrida to the thought of Paul de Man.

8 Norris is quite right in saying that, on my view, early Derrida is "falling back into a kind of negative theology that merely replaces one set of absolutes (truth, meaning, clear and distinct ideas) with another (trace, *différance,* and other such deconstructive key-terms)." But the main justification for distinguishing between an earlier and a later Derrida is that he *stops* doing this. Just as Heidegger stopped using terms like "phenomenological ontology," "Dasein" and "*existen-tial*" about five years after *Being and Time,* so Derrida has pretty well given up using notions like "grammatology," "archi-writing," and the rest. This seems to me very sensible on his part. The Derrida of *The Post Card* is no longer warning us that the "discourse of philosophy" will get us if we don't watch out. Instead, he alternately plays and struggles with concrete, particular thinkers – e.g., Freud and Heidegger – rather than with a protean, putatively inescapable quasi-divinity called "the discourse of philosophy." As Michael Ryan says, Derrida's work since 1975 "has become increasingly difficult, self-referential and esoteric" (*Marxism and Deconstruction* [Baltimore: Johns Hopkins University Press, 1982], p. xiv).

They tend to accept de Man's explanation of what it is that readers of literature do: namely, continually rediscover, by close reading, the impossibility of reading. Even when they do not, they agree with de Man that philosophical reflection can teach literary critics something important, and useful in their work, about the nature of "language," "reading," or "literature." They think these words name distinctive natural kinds. For they believe, with Husserl, Dilthey, and de Man, that a great gulf separates "natural objects" and "intentional objects."[9] They accept de Man's claim that those who "resist theory," who do not read closely, assimilate texts to natural objects. They think philosophy can help us see why they are wrong to do so. This third audience, committed in advance to literary criticism as a pursuit, welcomes philosophical guarantees that close reading is indeed as important as critics take it to be.

De Man offered such guarantees much more explicitly than does Derrida. Far more than Derrida, de Man is responsible for the tone of the Anglo-American movement called "deconstruction" — a tone that mixes elegy with polemic. Consider such passages from de Man as the following:

The distinctive character of literature [is] an inability to escape from a condition that is felt to be unbearable.[10]

Literature is fiction not because it somehow refuses to acknowledge "reality," but because it is not *a priori* certain that language functions according to principles which are those, or which are *like* those, of the phenomenal world. It is therefore not *a priori* certain that literature is a reliable source of information about anything but its own language. . . . Resistance to theory is in fact a resistance to reading.[11]

Poetic language names this void ["the presence of a nothingness"] with ever-renewed understanding. . . . This persistent naming is what we call literature.[12]

The systematic avoidance of reading, of the interpretive or hermeneutic moment, is a general symptom shared by all methods of literary analysis.[13]

Reading or writing "literary language" or "poetic language" — the sort of language that makes *evident* that "language" as such functions differently from "the phenomenal world," the realm of "natural objects" whose "meaning is equal to the totality of [their] sensory appearances"[14] — is, for de Man and his followers, a way of mourning a *Deus absconditus,* of participating in a divine absence. To have to do with poetic language in that special way in which those who do *not* "systematically avoid reading" have to do with it is an ascetic practice that confronts one ever and again with "the presence of a nothingness." For de Manians, the analogue of

9 See de Man, *Blindness and Insight,* 2nd edn. (Minneapolis: University of Minnesota Press, 1983), p. 24.
10 Ibid., p. 162.
11 De Man, *The Resistance to Theory* (Minneapolis: University of Minnesota Press, 1986), pp. 11, 15.
12 De Man, *Blindness and Insight,* p. 18.
13 Ibid., p. 282.
14 Ibid., p. 24.

bad, *positive* theology is attachment to a "method of literary analysis" and the analogue of good, negative theology is success in overcoming that "resistance to reading" that is also a "resistance to theory." The positive theologians are the people who think literature *is* a "reliable source of information about something other than its own language." The initiates, the negative theologians, the worshippers of the Dark God whose Voice is in the Literariness of Language, are those who no longer believe that "language functions according to principles which are those, or which are *like* those, of the phenomenal world."

Many readers of de Man, searching for reasons *why* poetic language – the most linguistic sort of language, as it were – names the presence of a nothingness, thought they had found the answer in such Derridean claims as the following:

The sign represents the present in its absence. . . . The sign, in this sense, is deferred presence.[15]

From the moment there is meaning there are nothing but signs. *We think only in signs.* Which amounts to ruining the notion of the sign at the very moment when, as in Nietzsche, its exigency is recognized in the absoluteness of its right. One could call *play*, the absence of the transcendental signified as limitlessness of play, that is to say as the destruction of ontotheology and the metaphysics of presence.[16]

But on my own nominalist and pragmatic reading of them, the only relevance of these Derridean claims to poetic language – with its familiar "untranslatability" and "interpenetration of sound and sense" – is that such language is an especially good *example* of what is wrong with the Lockean idea that linguistic signs are sensible vehicles of intelligible meanings. This idea is equally wrong for flat-footed nonpoetic language. The right idea, according to us nominalists, is that "recognition of meaning" is simply ability to substitute sensible signs (i.e., marks and noises) for other signs, and still other signs for the latter, and so on indefinitely. This latter doctrine is found, for example, in Peirce, Wittgenstein, and Davidson as well as in Derrida. On this reading, Derrida is simply restating Peirce's attack on the idea that a regress of interpretation of a sign can be stopped by a self-validating Cartesian intuition – an attack he says "goes very far in the direction that I have called the deconstruction of the transcendental signified, which, at one time or another, would place a reassuring end to the reference from sign to sign."[17]

The third audience I have described takes Derrida's revival of Peirce's anti-Cartesian point as the "philosophical basis" for de Manian readings of texts. The problem with putting de Man and Derrida together in this way, however, is that Derrida does *not* contrast the way language works with the way "the phenomenal

15 Derrida, *Margins of Philosophy*, trans. Alan Bass (Chicago: University of Chicago Press, 1982), p. 9.
16 Derrida, *Of Grammatology*, p. 50.
17 Ibid., p. 49. On the analogies between Peirce's and Wittgenstein's insistence on the endlessness of interpretation, see my "Pragmatism, Categories and Language," *Philosophical Review* 70 (1961): 197–223.

world" works. He is not, as Michael Ryan has pointed out, "privileging language, rhetoric, or 'literary texts.' "[18] He does not distinguish between placid scientific or legal texts on the one hand and restless, self-deconstructing, literary texts on the other. The Diltheyan dualism that de Man takes for granted is not to be found in Derrida. Indeed, Derrida follows up his reference to Peirce by saying that "the thing itself is a sign" – *any* thing, a rock as much as a text.[19] For all the anti-Husserlian reasons given in Derrida's *Speech and Phenomenona* and all those given in Sellars's attack on "the Myth of the Given," we cannot preserve de Man's notion of "natural objects" as having a meaning exhausted by the "totality of their sensory appearances." *Pace* de Man, "the phenomenal world" – the world of nonlinguistic *things* – works just the way language does.

I take this difference between de Man and Derrida to be a mark of their divergent concerns, concerns that diverge more and more as one moves from earlier to later Derrida. To my mind, Derrida's best statement of his own project is the following:

> To make enigmatic what one thinks one understands by the words "proximity," "immediacy," "presence" (the proximate [*proche*], the own [*propre*], and the pre- of presence) is my final intention in this book.[20]

Notice the difference between "making enigmatic what one means by" certain words and reacting to the absence of what one takes to be denoted by them. De Man is doing the latter. He *needs* the discourse of Cartesian philosophy – with its talk of immediate knowledge, self-validating intuitions, and all the rest of it – to remain intelligible and *non*enigmatic. He needs it to remain intelligible in order to contrast the way language works with the way "the phenomenal world" works (and, indeed, to make sense of the notion of "phenomenal" – what appears to the

18 *Marxism and Deconstruction*, p. 24. I am sympathetic to Ryan's point that "Derrida's emphasis on repetition and difference is lopsided. As Anglo-American literary critics prove, it can itself become a metaphysics" (p. 36). But I should prefer to say a "theology" rather than a "metaphysics" – the worship of a Dark God, the celebration of perpetual absence. A distinctively theological tone emerges in the chapter on de Man in J. Hillis Miller's recent *The Ethics of Reading* (New York: Columbia University Press, 1987). Miller says that "the failure to read takes place inexorably within the text itself. The reader must reenact this failure in his or her own reading" (p. 53) – an update of the Christian's duty continually to reenact the Passion.

19 On the general point that redescription can decompose anything – a piece of rock or a piece of writing – into a chain of relations to other things, see my "Texts and Lumps," in vol. 1 of these papers.

20 *Of Grammatology*, p. 70. The passage continues as follows: "This deconstruction of presence accomplishes itself through the deconstruction of consciousness, and therefore through the irreducible notion of the trace [*Spur*] as it appears in both Nietzschean and Freudian discourse. And finally, in all scientific fields, notably in biology, this notion seems currently to be dominant and irreducible." For light on this last sentence, see *Of Grammatology*, p. 9. There it is clear that Derrida has in mind the notion of a "genetic code" in biology and of "program" in computer science. I doubt that either notion is at all relevant to Derrida's project. But his *belief* that they are relevant does help confirm the claim that he is *not* saying that "Language is the realm of trace and difference; outside of language there is the realm of presence, phenomenality, structure, etc."

senses, what is present to consciousness, etc.). He needs "the discourse of philosophy" as a medium in which to write his elegiac readings of literature. He needs a clear vision of the dead, but luminous, God of Presence in order to display (by the contrast of darkness to light) his living but invisible Dark God of Absence.

By contrast, as the passage about "making enigmatic" suggests, Derrida is torn between the negative theologian's urge to find a new pantheon – "trace," "différance," and the rest of what Gasché calls "infrastructures" – and the comic writer's urge to make something once held sacred look funny. In his later work, it seems to me, he is less torn. He is content simply to have fun rather than to feel haunted. De Man needs the "discourse of philosophy" in the way a negative theologian needs positive theology – as an exhibition of what we must forgo. De Man's analogue of negative theology is a way of "reading" that eschews "methods of literary analysis" – eschews the idea that structures of historical, scientific, psychoanalytic, or sociopolitical thought can be used to filter out what is essential from what is accidental in a literary text (in the way in which such structures *are* legitimately used in dealing with "the phenomenal world"). But, at his best, Derrida offers not a way of reading but a kind of writing – comic writing that does not presuppose "the discourse of philosophy" as anything more than a butt.

On my account, de Man (and the constructive and argumentative strain in early Derrida – the strain that produces notions like "trace") represents merely one more *inversion* of a traditional philosophical position – one more "transvaluation of all values" that nevertheless remains within the range of alternatives specified by "the discourse of philosophy." The great Greek logocentrists told us that reality is divided into two realms, one of which is the unwobbling pivot about which the other revolves. Their preferred realm is, as Derrida says, the one that gives a center to structures, which "limits what we might call the *play* of the structure."[21] If Derrida is read as confirming or explaining or arguing for the sort of thing de Man says about the difference between "language" and "the phenomenal world," he would have to be read as saying that the former is the realm of nonlimit, of play, of the unbearable absence of the present and fixed. He would have to say that whereas in "the phenomenal world" the flux is an epiphenomenon of the stable, in "language" the stable is an epiphenomenon of the flux, and that the latter realm is somehow more "basic" than the former.

If Derrida *were* saying that, he would indeed be just what he most fears to be – one more example of the inversion of traditional philosophical oppositions. Heidegger thought that Nietzsche's exaltation of Becoming over Being was an example of the fruitlessness of such an inversion – fruitless because it retained the overall form of ontotheological systems, merely changing God's name to that of

21 Derrida, *Writing and Difference,* trans. Alan Bass (Chicago: University of Chicago Press, 1978), p. 278.

the Devil, and conversely.[22] Derrida agrees with Heidegger that inverted logocentrism is still logocentrism, and that some movement more complex and powerful than inversion is needed. Furthermore, he thinks Heidegger himself did not succeed in becoming sufficiently different from what he was trying to evade.[23] I think he was on the right track when he suggested that the only strategy of evasion that is going to work will be to write in a way that makes the discourse of philosophy enigmatic rather than ubiquitous. At his best, Derrida realizes that one good way to make something look enigmatic is to treat it as a joke.

If Derrida does indeed want to make the discourse of philosophy enigmatic, then he should not try to do what Gasché and Norris say he tries to do: discover the conditions of possibility of language, and in particular of the discourse of philosophy. There must be something wrong with Gasché's claim that "Derrida's inquiry into the limits of philosophy is an investigation into the conditions of possibility and impossibility of a type of discourse and questioning which he recognizes as absolutely indispensable."[24] Specifically, there must be some sense in which Derrida regards this discourse not as "absolutely indispensable" but as the sort of thing we can make so enigmatic as to be no longer tempted to put it to argumentative use.

22 Such inversion was popular around the turn of the century. It is the least common denominator of Nietzsche, James, and Bergson. The later Heidegger tries desperately to distance himself from this exaltation of flux over permanence, an exaltation some readers had detected in *Being and Time*.

23 Referring to Heidegger, Derrida says "one risks ceaselessly confirming, consolidating, *relifting* (*relever* [Derrida's translation of *Aufhebung*]), at an always more certain depth, that which one allegedly deconstructs" ("The Ends of Man," *Margins of Philosophy*, p. 135). In this same passage, and elsewhere, Derrida says that what is needed to avoid repeating Heidegger's failure is a "double" movement — one that "must speak several languages and produce several texts at once." This latter technique is, I think, what we find in later Derrida, in the writings that look less and less like one more "discourse of philosophy" and are less and less susceptible to the sort of reading Gasché offers.

24 Rodolphe Gasché, *The Tain of the Mirror* (Cambridge, Mass.: Harvard University Press, 1986), p. 2.

Is Derrida a transcendental philosopher?

For years a quarrel has been simmering among Derrida's American admirers. On the one side there are the people who admire Derrida for having invented a new, splendidly ironic way of writing about the philosophical tradition. On the other side are those who admire him for having given us rigorous arguments for surprising philosophical conclusions. The former emphasize the playful, distancing, oblique way in which Derrida handles traditional philosophical figures and topics. The second emphasize what they take to be his results, his philosophical discoveries. Roughly speaking, the first are content to admire his manner, whereas the second want to say that the important thing is his matter − the truths that he has set forth.

Geoffrey Hartman's *Saving the Text* set the tone for the first way of appropriating Derrida. At the same time that I was picking up this tone from Hartman, and imitating it, Jonathan Culler was criticizing Hartman for light-mindedness. The term "Derridadaism," Culler said, was "a witty gesture by which Geoffrey Hartman blots out Derridean argument."[1] I weighed in on Hartman's side, claiming that Culler was too heavy-handed in his treatment of Derrida, too anxious to treat him as having demonstrated theorems which literary critics might now proceed to apply.[2] I thought it too much to ask of "deconstruction" that it be, in Culler's words, *both* "rigorous argument within philosophy and displacement of philosophical categories and philosophical attempts at mastery."[3] Something, I claimed, had to go. I suggested we jettison the "rigorous argument" part.

This suggestion was contested by Christopher Norris.[4] Norris was concerned to show that Derrida has arguments, good solid arguments, and is not just playing around. Like Culler, he was also concerned to block my attempt to assimilate deconstruction to pragmatism. Whereas a pragmatist view of truth, Culler said, treats conventionally accepted norms as foundations, deconstruction goes on to point out that "norms are produced by acts of exclusion." "Objectivity," Culler quite justly pointed out, "is constituted by excluding the views of those who do

---

1   Jonathan Culler, *On Deconstruction* (Ithaca: Cornell Univ. Press, 1982) p. 28.
2   See my "Deconstruction and Circumvention" above.
3   Culler, p. 85.
4   See Norris' "Philosophy as *not* just a 'kind of writing': Derrida and the claim of reason," in *Redrawing the Lines*, ed. R. W. Dasenbrock (Minneapolis: Univ. of Minnesota Press, 1989); and my "Two meanings of 'logocentrism,' " above.

not count as sane and rational men: women, children, poets, prophets, mad-men."[5] Culler was the first to make the suggestion, later taken up and developed in considerable detail by others,[6] that pragmatism (or at least my version of it) and deconstruction differ in that the one tends toward political conservatism and the other toward political radicalism.

In his recent book on Derrida, Norris repeats this suggestion, and reaffirms that to read Derrida in Hartman's and my way is

> to ignore the awkward fact that Derrida has devoted the bulk of his writings to a patient working-through (albeit on his own, very different terms) of precisely those problems that have occupied philosophers in the "mainstream" tradition, from Kant to Husserl and Frege. And this because those problems are indubitably *there*, installed within philosophy and reaching beyond it into every department of modern institutionalized knowledge.[7]

The quarrel about whether Derrida has arguments thus gets linked to a quarrel about whether he is a private writer — writing for the delight of us insiders who share his background, who find the same rather esoteric things as funny or beautiful or moving as he does — or rather a writer with a public mission, someone who gives us weapons with which to subvert "institutionalized knowledge" and thus social institutions. I have urged that Derrida be treated as the first sort of writer,[8] whereas most of his American admirers have treated him as, at least in part, the second. Lumping both quarrels together, one can say that there is a quarrel between those of us who read Derrida on Plato, Hegel and Heidegger in the same way as we read Bloom or Cavell on Emerson or Freud — in order to see these authors transfigured, beaten into fascinating new shapes — and those who read Derrida to get ammunition, and a strategy, for the struggle to bring about social change.

Norris thinks that Derrida should be read as a transcendental philosopher in the Kantian tradition — somebody who digs out hitherto unsuspected presuppositions. "Derrida," he says, "is broaching something like a Kantian transcendental deduction, an argument to demonstrate ('perversely' enough) that *a priori* notions of logical truth are *a priori* ruled out of court by rigorous reflection on the powers and limits of textual critique."[9] By contrast, my view of Derrida is that he nudges

5 Culler, p. 153.
6 For a partial list of those who make this sort of charge, and my attempt to reply to it, see my "Thugs and Theorists: A Reply to Bernstein," *Political Theory* 15 (Nov. 1987): 564–80. A fuller reply can be found in my *Contingency, Irony, and Solidarity* (Cambridge: Cambridge Univ. Press, 1989). In that book I claim that "theory" cannot do much to bring the excluded in from the margins — to enlarge the community whose consensus sets the standards of objectivity — but that other kinds of writing (notably novels and newspaper stories) can do quite a lot.
7 Christopher Norris, *Derrida* (Cambridge: Harvard Univ. Press, 1987), p. 156.
8 See, especially, chapter 6 ("From Ironist Theory to Private Allusions: Derrida") of *Contingency, Irony, and Solidarity*. The original title of this chapter, which I sometimes wish I had retained, was "From Ironist Theory to Private Jokes."
9 Norris, p. 183. Also: "[D]econstruction is a Kantian enterprise in ways that few of its commentators have so far been inclined to acknowledge" (p. 94).

us into a world in which "rigorous reflection on the powers and limits . . ." has as little place as do *a priori* notions of logical truth." This world has as little room for transcendental deductions, or for rigor, as for self-authenticating moments of immediate presence to consciousness.

On my view, the only thing that can displace an intellectual world is another intellectual world – a new alternative, rather than an argument against an old alternative. The idea that there is some neutral ground on which to mount an argument against something as big as "logocentrism" strikes me as one more logocentric hallucination. I do not think that demonstrations of "internal incoherence" or of "presuppositional relationships" ever do much to disabuse us of bad old ideas or institutions. Disabusing gets done, instead, by offering us sparkling new ideas, or utopian visions of glorious new institutions. The result of genuinely original thought, on my view, is not so much to refute or subvert our previous beliefs as to help us forget them by giving us a substitute for them. I take refutation to be a mark of unoriginality, and I value Derrida's originality too much to praise him in those terms. So I find little use, in reading or discussing him, for the notion of "rigorous argumentation."

Culler and Norris have now been joined, on their side of the quarrel I have been describing, by Rodolphe Gasché. Gasché's *The Tain of the Mirror* is by far the most ambitious and detailed attempt to treat Derrida as a rigorous transcendental philosopher. Gasché says that

[i]n this book I hope that I have found a middle ground between the structural plurality of Derrida's philosophy – a plurality that makes it impossible to elevate any final essence of his book into its true meaning – and the strict criteria to which any interpretation of his work must yield, if it is to be about that work and not merely a private fantasy. These criteria, at center stage in this book, are, as I shall show, philosophical and not literary in nature.[10]

Just as in the case of Culler I doubted that one could displace philosophical concepts while still having rigorous philosophical arguments, so in Gasché's case I doubt that one can eschew the project of stating Derrida's "true meaning" while still judging him by "strict criteria." I do not think that one should try to pay good old logocentric compliments to enemies of logocentrism.

In what follows, I shall try to spell out why the compliments Gasché offers Derrida seem to me misapplied. To my mind, "private fantasy" is, if not entirely adequate, at least a somewhat better compliment. Many responsibilities begin in dreams, and many transfigurations of the tradition begin in private fantasies. Think, for example, of Plato's or St. Paul's private fantasies – fantasies so original and utopian that they became the common sense of later times. Someday, for all I

10   Rodolphe Gasché, *The Tain of the Mirror* (Cambridge, Mass.: Harvard Univ. Press, 1986), p. 8.

know, there may be some social changes (perhaps even changes for the better) which retrospection will see as having originated in Derrida's fantasies. But the *arguments* which Derrida can be read as offering on behalf of his fantasies seem to me no better than the ones Plato offered for his. Anybody who reads through Plato in search of rigorous arguments is in for a disappointment. I think that the same goes for Derrida.

I can begin quarreling with Gasché by taking up his distinction between philosophy and literature. On my view, "philosophy" is either a term defined by choosing a list of writers (e.g., Parmenides, Plato, Aristotle, Kant, Hegel, Heidegger) and then specifying what they all have in common, or else just the name of an academic department. The first sense of the term is hard to apply to a writer who, like Derrida, is trying to extricate himself from the tradition defined by such a list. But the second sense of the term is not much help either, for in this sense "philosophy" is just an omnium gatherum of disparate activities united by nothing more than a complicated tangle of genealogical connections – connections so tenuous that one can no longer detect even a family resemblance between the activities.[11] Only if one buys in on the logocentric idea that there just *must* be an autonomous discipline which adjudicates ultimate questions would "philosophy" have a third sense, one appropriate for Gasché's purposes. It is only by reference to some such idea that it makes sense to worry, as he does, about the lines between philosophy and literature.

For my purposes, the important place to draw a line is not between philosophy and non-philosophy but rather between topics which we know how to argue about and those we do not. It is the line between the attempt to be objective – to get a consensus on what we should believe – and a willingness to abandon consensus in the hope of transfiguration. Gasché, by contrast, thinks that we can separate the philosophical books (or, at least, the important philosophical books of recent centuries) from other books by a fairly straightforward test. The former are the books in which we find a specifically *transcendental* project – a project of answering some question of the form "what are the conditions of the possibility of . . . ?" – of, for example, experience, self-consciousness, language or philosophy itself.

I have to admit that asking and answering that question is, indeed, the mark of a distinct genre. But unlike Gasché I think that it is a thoroughly self-deceptive question. The habit of posing it – asking for noncausal, nonempirical, nonhistorical conditions – is the distinctive feature of a tradition which stretches from the *Critique of Pure Reason* through Hegel's *Science of Logic* to *Being and Time* (and, if Gasché is right about the early Derrida's intentions, through *Of Grammatology*). The trouble with the question is that it looks like a "scientific" one, as if we knew

11 There is no interesting least common denominator of, for example, Rawls, Croce, Frege, Nietzsche and Gödel – no feature which makes them all representative of the same natural kind. One can only explain why all five are studied within a single academic department by developing a complicated historico-sociological story.

how to debate the relative merits of alternative answers, just as we know how to debate alternative answers to questions about the conditions for the *actuality* of various things (e.g., political changes, quasars, psychoses). But it is not. Since that for which the conditions of possibility are sought is always *everything* that any previous philosopher has envisaged – the whole range of what has been discussed up to now – anybody is at liberty to identify any ingenious gimmick that he dreams up as a "condition of possibility."

The sort of gimmick in question is exemplified by Kantian "transcendental synthesis," Hegelian "self-diremption of the concept," Heideggerian *Sorge,* and (on Gasché's interpretation) Derridean *différance.* These suggestions about transcendental conditions are so many leaps into the darkness which surrounds the totality of everything previously illuminated. In the nature of the case, there can be no pre-existent logical space, no "strict criteria" for choosing among these alternatives. If there were, the question about "conditions of possibility" would automatically become merely "positive" and not properly "transcendental" or "reflective."[12] Once again, I would want to insist that you cannot have it both ways. You cannot see these leaps in the dark as the magnificent poetic acts they are and still talk about "philosophical rigor." Rigor just does not come into it.

This insusceptibility to argument is what makes "the philosophy of reflection" – the tradition of transcendental inquiry within which Gasché wishes to embed Derrida – the *bête noire* of philosophers who take public discussability as the essence of rationality. Habermas's polemic against the late Heidegger and against Derrida has the same motives as Carnap's attack on the early Heidegger.[13] Like Carnap, Habermas thinks that philosophy ought to be argumentative. He thinks that Heidegger and Derrida are merely oracular. My own view is that we should avoid slogans like "philosophy ought to be argumentative" (or any other slogan that begins "philosophy ought to be . . .") and recognize that the writers usually identified as "philosophers" include both argumentative problem-solvers like Aristotle and Russell and oracular world-disclosers like Plato and Hegel – both people good at rendering public accounts and people good at leaping in the dark.

But this conciliatory ecumenicism still leaves me hostile to those who, like Gasché, think that one can synthesize world-disclosing and problem-solving into

12 Another way of putting this point is to note that each important figure in the tradition in question has had to invent his own "central problem of philosophy" rather than work on some issue previously agreed to be problematic. Consider, in this light, Gasché's claim that "Archewriting is a construct aimed at resolving the philosophical problem of the very possibility (not primarily the empirical fact, which always suffers exceptions) of the usurpation, parasitism and contamination of an ideality, a generality, a universal by what is considered its other, its exterior, its incarnation, its appearance, and so on" (p. 274). Nobody knew *that* was a "philosophical problem" before Derrida came along, any more than we knew that "the conditions of the possibility of synthetic a priori judgments" was a problem before Kant came along.

13 See Jürgen Habermas, *The Philosophical Discourse of Modernity* (Cambridge: MIT Press, 1987); Rudolf Carnap, "The Overcoming of Metaphysics through the Logical Analysis of Language" in *Logical Positivism,* edited by A. J. Ayer (Glencoe: The Free Press, 1963).

a single activity called "reflection." In particular, I object to the idea that one can be "rigorous" if one's procedure consists in inventing new words for what one is pleased to call "conditions of possibility" rather than playing sentences using old words off against each other. The latter activity is what I take to constitute argumentation. Poetic world-disclosers like Hegel, Heidegger and Derrida have to pay a price, and part of that price is the inappropriateness to their work of notions like "argumentation" and "rigor."[14]

Habermas differs with me and agrees with Gasché in thinking that philosophy ought to be argumentative, but he agrees with me and differs from Gasché in refusing to see the transitions in Hegel's *Logic,* or the successive "discoveries" of new "conditions of possibility" which fill the pages of *Being and Time,* as *arguments.* Habermas and I are both in sympathy with Ernst Tugendhat's nominalist, Wittgensteinian rejection of the idea that one can be nonpropositional and still be argumentative. Tugendhat sees the attempt of a German tradition stemming from Hegel to work at a subpropositional level, while nevertheless claiming the "cognitive status" which people like Carnap want to deny them, as doomed to failure.[15] By contrast, Gasché explicitly rejects Tugendhat's "theoretical ascetism," his self-confinement to "linguistic and propositional truth."[16] Gasché thinks that such

---

14   Consider Gasché's claim that Derrida has "demonstrated" that "the source of all being beyond being is *generalized,* or rather *general,* writing" (p. 176). This is just the sort of claim which inspired the logical positivists to say that metaphysics lacked "cognitive status." Their point was that such a claim cannot be "demonstrated," unless "demonstration" means something very different from "can be argued for on the basis of generally shared beliefs."

15   For Tugendhat's Wittgensteinian working-through of Frege's holistic dictum ("only in the context of a sentence does a word have meaning") see his *Traditional and Analytic Philosophy* (Cambridge: MIT Press, 1984) and my review of that book in *Journal of Philosophy* 82 (1985): 220–29. For his use of the resulting repudiation of the nonpropositional to criticize "the philosophy of reflection," see his *Self-Consciousness and Self-Determination* (Cambridge: MIT Press, 1986), especially the claim that "the phenomenon of justification and the question of justifying what is considered true is actually nowhere to be found in Hegel" (p. 294). On the attempts of "the philosophy of reflection" to work at a subpropositional level, to get behind sentences to "the conditions of possibility" of sentences, see my "Strawson's Objectivity Argument," *Review of Metaphysics* 24 (Dec. 1970): 207–44. In that paper I try to show how Kant's search for "conditions of the possibility of experience" requires him to violate his own claim that we cannot know anything that is not a possible experience. I argue that the temptation to go transcendental (i.e., to search for noncausal conditions of possibility) is lessened (though not, alas, eliminated) once the "linguistic turn" is taken. Gasché, by contrast, believes that "the method of reflection" (the one common to Hegel, Heidegger and, on his view, Derrida) can survive the linguistic turn; he claims, for example, that Austin "hinged the entire representational function of language . . . on a constituting self-reflectivity of the linguistic act" (p. 76). I criticize the idea of transcendental argumentation at greater length in "Verificationism and Transcendental Arguments," *Noûs* 5 (1971): 3–14, and in "Transcendental Argument, Self-Reference, and Pragmatism" in *Transcendental Arguments and Science,* edited by Peter Bieri, Rolf-P. Horstmann and Lorenz Krüger (Dordrecht: D. Reidel, 1979), pp. 77–103.

16   "For Tugendhat, and the analytic tradition he represents, knowledge and truth can only be propositional. . . . [But] by eliminating altogether the ontological dimension of self-identity in self-consciousness (and, for that matter, in absolute reflection), one deprives oneself of the possibility of thinking the very foundations of propositional knowledge and truth, as well as of the very

confinement will forbid one to do something which needs to be done, and which Derrida may in fact have accomplished.

Whereas Gasché thinks that words like "différance" and "iterability" signify "infrastructures" – structures which it is Derrida's great achievement to have unearthed – I see these notions as merely abbreviations for the familiar Peircean-Wittgensteinian anti-Cartesian thesis that meaning is a function of context, and that there is no theoretical barrier to an endless sequence of recontextualizations. I think the problems with taking this Derridean jargon as seriously as Gasché does are the same as those which arise if one takes the jargon of *Being and Time* as a serious answer to questions of the form "How is the ontic possible? What are its *ontological* conditions?" If one thinks of writers like Hegel, Heidegger, and Derrida as digging down to successively deeper levels of noncausal conditions – as scientists dig down to ever deeper levels of causal conditions (molecules behind tables, atoms behind molecules, quarks behind atoms . . .) – then the hapless and tedious metaphilosophical question "How can we tell when we have hit bottom?" is bound to arise. More important, so will the question "Within what language are we to lay out arguments demonstrating (or even just making plausible) that we have *correctly* identified these conditions?"

The latter question causes no great embarrassment for physicists, since they can say in advance what they want to get out of their theorizing. But it *should* embarrass people concerned with the question of what *philosophical* vocabulary to use, rather than with the question of what vocabulary will help us accomplish some specific purpose (e.g., splitting the atom, curing cancer, persuading the populace). For either the language in which the arguments are given is itself an antecedently given one or it is a disposable ladder-language, one which can be forgotten once it has been *aufgehoben*. The former alternative is impossible if one's aim is to cast doubt on *all* final vocabularies previously available – an ambition common to Hegel, Heidegger and Derrida. Seizing the latter horn of the dilemma, however, requires admitting that the arguments which one uses must themselves be thrown away once they have achieved their purpose. But that would mean, on the normal understanding of the term, that these were not *arguments,* but rather suggestions about how to speak differently. Argumentation requires that the same vocabulary be used in premises and conclusions – that both be part of the same language-game. Hegelian *Aufhebung* is something quite different. It is what happens when we play elements of an old vocabulary off against each other in order to make us impatient for a new vocabulary. But that

idea of epistemic self-consciousness. . . . Without the presupposition of ontological or formal-ontological identity of being and thought, of subject and object, of the knower and what is known, there is no ground for any propositional attribution whatsoever" (Gasché, p. 77). On the "analytic" view I share with Tugendhat and Habermas, the very idea of a "ground" for "propositional attribution" is a mistake. The practice of playing sentences off against one another in order to decide what to believe – the practice of argumentation – no more requires a "ground" than the practice of using one stone to chip pieces off another stone in order to make a spear-point.

activity is quite different from playing old beliefs against other old beliefs in an attempt to see which survives. An existing language-game will provide "standard rules" for the latter activity, but *nothing* could provide such rules for the former. Yet Gasché tells us that "Derrida's work is a genuinely philosophical inquiry that takes the standard rules of philosophy very seriously."[17]

On my view, it is precisely *Aufhebung* that Derrida is so good at. But one could only think of this practice as *argumentative* if one had a conception of argument as subpropositional – one which allowed the unit of argumentation to be the word rather than the sentence. That is, indeed, a conception of argumentation which, notoriously, we find in Hegel's *Logic* – the text to which Gasché traces back "the philosophy of reflection." Hegel tried to give a sense to the idea that there are inferential relations among individual concepts which are not reducible to inferential relations among sentences which use the words signifying those concepts – that there is a "movement of the concept" for the philosopher to follow, not reducible to the reweaving of a web of belief by playing beliefs off against each other. Hegel thought that he followed this movement as he went from "Being" at the beginning of the *Logic* to "the Absolute Idea" at its end.

Nominalists like myself – those for whom language is a tool rather than a medium, and for whom a concept is just the regular use of a mark or noise – cannot make sense of Hegel's claim that a concept like "Being" breaks apart, sunders itself, turns into its opposite, etc., nor of Gasché's Derridean claim that "concepts and discursive totalities are already cracked and fissured by necessary contradictions and heterogeneities."[18] The best we nominalists can do with such claims is to construe them as saying that one can always make an old language-game look bad by thinking up a better one – replace an old tool with a new one by using an old word in a new way (e.g., as the "privileged" rather than the "derivative" term of a contrast), or by replacing it with a new word. But this need for replacement is *ours,* not the concept's. *It* does not go to pieces; rather, *we* set it aside and replace it with something else.

Gasché is quite right in saying that to follow Wittgenstein and Tugendhat in this nominalism will reduce what he wants to call "philosophical reflection" to "a fluidization or liquefaction (*Verflüssigung*) of all oppositions and particularities by means of objective irony."[19] Such liquefaction is what I am calling *Aufhebung* and praising Derrida for having done spectacularly well. We nominalists think that all that philosophers of the world-disclosing (as opposed to the problem-solving) sort can do is to fluidize old vocabularies. We cannot make sense of the notion of

---

17 Gasché, p. 122.
18 Gasché, p. 136.
19 Gasché, p. 139. Gasché thinks that the confusion of Derrida's enterprise with such a *Verflüssigung* is one of the "dominant misconceptions" of deconstruction. He views American Derrida-fans as especially prone to such misconceptions, in particular to the misconception that Derrida "literarizes" philosophy.

discovering a "condition of the possibility of language" – nor, indeed, of the notion of "language" as something homogeneous enough to have "conditions." If, with Wittgenstein, Tugendhat, Quine and Davidson, one ceases to see language as a medium, one will reject *a fortiori* Gasché's claim that "[language] must, in philosophical terms, be thought of as a totalizing medium."[20] That is only how a certain antinominalistic philosophical tradition – "the philosophy of reflection" – must think of it.

If one does think of it that way, to be sure, then one will have to worry about whether one has got hold of a true or a false totality. One will worry about whether one has burrowed, deeply enough (whether, for example, Derridean infrastructures, though doubtless deeper than mere Heideggerian *Existentiale,* may not conceal still deeper and more mysterious entities which underlie *them.*) But if, with Wittgenstein, one starts to think of vocabularies as tools, then totality is no longer a problem. One will be content to use lots of different vocabularies for one's different purposes, without worrying much about their relation to one another. (In particular, one will be more willing to accept a private–public split: using one set of words in one's dealings with others, and another when engaged in self-creation.) The idea of an overview of the entire realm of possibility (one made possible by having penetrated to the conditionless conditions of that realm) seems, from this Wittgensteinian angle, crazy. For we nominalists think that the realm of possibility expands whenever somebody thinks up a new vocabulary, and thereby discloses (or invents – the difference is beside any relevant point) a new set of possible worlds.

Nominalists see language as just human beings using marks and noises to get what they want. One of the things we want to do with language is to get food, another is to get sex, another is to understand the origin of the universe. Another is to enhance our sense of human solidarity, and still another may be to create oneself by developing one's own private, autonomous, philosophical language. It is possible that a single vocabulary might serve two or more of these aims, but there is no reason to think that there is any great big meta-vocabulary which will somehow get at the least common denominator of all the various uses of all the various marks and noises which we use for all these various purposes. So there is no reason to lump these uses together into something big called "Language," and then to look for its "condition of possibility," any more than to lump all our beliefs about the spatio-temporal world together into something called "experience" and then look, as Kant did, for *its* "condition of possibility." Nor is there any reason to lump all attempts to formulate great big new vocabularies, made by people with many different purposes (e.g., Plato, St. Paul, Newton, Marx,

---

20   Gasché, p. 45. For a discussion of Davidson's work as a break with the notion of language as medium, see the first chapter of my *Contingency, Irony, and Solidarity.*

Freud, Heidegger), into something called "the discourse of philosophy" and then to look for conditions of the possibility of that discourse.

How does one go about deciding whether to read Derrida my way or Gasché's way? How does one decide whether he is really a much-misunderstood transcendental "philosopher of reflection," a latter-day Hegel, or really a much-misunderstood nominalist, a sort of French Wittgenstein?[21] Not easily. Derrida makes noises of both sorts. Sometimes he warns us against the attempt to hypostatize something called "language." Thus early in *Of Grammatology* he says "This inflation of the sign 'language' is the inflation of the sign itself, absolute inflation, inflation itself" (p. 6). But, alas, he immediately goes on to talk in a grandiloquent, Hegel-Heidegger, "destiny of Europe" tone about how "a historico-metaphysical epoch *must* finally determine as language the totality of its problematic horizon."[22]

Derrida himself, I have to admit, used to use words like "rigorous" a lot. There is a lot in his early work which chimes with Gasché's interpretation.[23] But as he moves along from the early criticisms of Husserl through *Glas* to texts like the "Envois" section of *The Post Card*, the tone has changed. I should like to think of Derrida as moving away from the academic, "standard rules of philosophy" manner of his early work to a manner more like the later Wittgenstein's. Indeed, I should like to see his early work as something of a false start, in the same way that *Being and Time* is, in the light of Heidegger's later work, a false start, and as Wittgenstein thought his *Tractatus* to have been a false start.

But perhaps it is just too soon for a judgment to be rendered on whether Gasché or I am looking at Derrida from the right angle, or whether we both may not be somewhat squinty-eyed. For Derrida is, to put it mildly, still going strong. Still, it may be a service to those coming to Derrida for the first time to have a choice between opposed readings at their disposal.

21 See Henry Staten, *Wittgenstein and Derrida* (Lincoln: Univ. of Nebraska Press, 1984): "The deconstructive critique of language could even be phrased as a *denial that there is language*" (p. 20).
22 I have criticized Derrida's tendency to adopt this tone in "Deconstruction and Circumvention." For a more general criticism of the Heideggerian, un-"playful" side of Derrida, see Barbara Herrnstein Smith, "Changing Places: Truth, Error and Deconstruction," in her *Contingencies of Value* (Cambridge: Harvard Univ. Press, 1988). Smith argues that " 'the metaphysics of Western thought' *is* thought, all of it, root and branch, everywhere and always" and that "as figure and ground change places, the unravelling of Western metaphysics weaves another Western metaphysics" (p. 118). I agree, and take the point to be that each generation's irony is likely to become the next generation's metaphysics. Metaphysics is, so to speak, irony gone public and flat – liquefaction congealed, providing a new ground on which to inscribe new figures. From my angle, the attempt to make Derrida into somebody who has discovered some "philosophical truths" is a premature flattening-out of Derrida's irony. I think that he ought to be kept fluid a while longer before being congealed (as eventually he must be) into one more set of philosophical views, suitable for doxographic summary.
23 Gasché himself expresses doubt (p. 4) that his way of reading Derrida works for some of Derrida's later writings.

De Man and the American Cultural Left

Paul de Man was one of the most beloved and influential teachers of recent times. He was the person primarily responsible for the movement which we now call "deconstruction." The special twist which de Man put on certain Heideggerian and Derridean themes has been the single most influential contribution to what is sometimes called, by its enemies, "the politicization of the humanities" in American universities. De Man's interpretations of these men's work laid the foundation for the attempt, widespread among American academics in recent years, to reinvigorate leftist social criticism by deploying new philosophico-literary weapons. This attempt is central to the activities of what Henry Gates has called "the American Cultural Left," defined by him as "a Rainbow Coalition" of deconstructionists, feminists, people working in gay and ethnic studies, and so on.

Members of the Cultural Left typically believe that we have recently acquired a radically new understanding of the nature of language and of literature. They think that this shift is comparable in importance to the shift from Aristotelian to Galilean mechanics, and that it has similarly important moral and political consequences. For the Cultural Left, "reading" — in the special sense which de Man gave to that term — has become a watchword in the same way that "scientific method" was a watchword in the 1920s and 1930s. In that period, everyone from H.G. Wells to John Dewey was telling us that life and politics would become better if only we could adopt the attitude and the habits of the natural scientist. We are now being told the same sort of thing about the attitude and habits of the literary critic. For example, J. Hillis Miller, one of de Man's closest friends and followers, has said that "the millenium [of universal peace and justice among men] would come if all men and women became good readers in de Man's sense."[1]

To see how Miller could be led to say such a thing, consider the following passages from de Man. In his 1967 essay "Criticism and Crisis" de Man says:

the statement about language, that sign and meaning can never coincide, is what is precisely taken for granted in the kind of language called literary. Literature, unlike everyday language, begins on the far side of this knowledge; it is the only form of language free from the fallacy of unmediated expression.[2]

---

1 J. Hillis Miller, *The Ethics of Reading* (New York: Columbia University Press, 1987), p. 58.
2 Paul de Man, *Blindness and Insight*, 2nd ed. (Minneapolis: University of Minnesota Press, 1983), p. 17.

Slightly later in the same essay, de Man identifies freedom from the fallacy of unmediated expression with the discovery "of desire as a fundamental pattern of being that discards any possibility of satisfaction." The consciousness that results from this discovery, de Man continues,

consists of the presence of a nothingness. Poetic language names this void with ever-renewed understanding and . . . it never tires of naming it again. This persistent naming is what we call literature.[3]

To see the point of these passages, one needs to see what de Man means by "the fallacy of unmediated expression," the fallacy of thinking that "sign and meaning can coincide." Committing this fallacy is roughly the same thing as being what Derrida calls "logocentric." Logocentrists believe that language sometimes accurately represents something nonlinguistic, that sometimes sign and meaning coincide, in the sense that the sign perfectly represents something else – its meaning. The meaning, in turn, is a thought in somebody's mind which itself may perfectly represent something nonmental. For logocentrists, language is at its best when it is perfectly transparent to reality – "identical with its object," as Aristotle and Hegel put it.

Those who do not commit the fallacy of unmediated expression discard these metaphors of transparency and identity and accept Saussure's claim that language is a "play of differences." They believe that signs have meaning by virtue of their relations to other signs – relations of similarity and dissimilarity, rather than by their coincidence with something mental. They further believe that all thought is in language, so that thoughts too have meaning only by virtue of their relations to other thoughts. For antilogocentrists, therefore, truth is not a matter of transparency to, or correspondence with, reality, but rather a matter of relating thoughts or signs to one another.

Antilogocentrism is a special case of antiessentialism, of the radical holism common to Wittgenstein, Quine, Dewey, Davidson, and Derrida. Logocentrism is simply essentialism as applied to sentences and beliefs. Once one drops the essentialist idea that things have both intrinsic and relational properties – properties which they have "in themselves" and properties which they have merely in relation to, e.g., human desires and interests – then a Saussurian notion of language and a Davidsonian antirepresentationalist account of knowledge follow naturally. To claim that language is a play of differences, with Saussure, is just to say, with Wittgenstein, that the meaning of a word is its use in the language, and to add with Quine that the unit of empirical significance is the whole of science. One can generalize Quine's and Wittgenstein's points by saying that the significance of a sentence, like that of a belief or a desire, is its place in a web of other sentences, or beliefs or desires. To say this is to emphasize

3 Ibid., p. 18.

the context-sensitivity of signs and of thoughts – to treat them not as quasi-things but as nodes in a web of relations. But that is simply to describe them as antiessentialists wish *everything* – tables, quarks, people, social institutions – to be described.

De Man puts his own special twist on Derridean polemic against logocentrism and on antiessentialist redescriptions when he says, in an essay on Derrida's interpretation of Rousseau, that "Rousseau escapes from the logocentric fallacy precisely to the extent that his language is *literary*."[4] De Man thinks that literature has *always* been antiessentialist. For him, culture has always been divided into two uses of language: the literary use of language in which language reveals its true, relational nature, on the one hand, and commonsensical, scientific, and philosophical uses of language on the other. The latter uses of language *conceal* this nature.

This startling claim that literature has always been making a philosophical point connects with de Man's claim that literature has always offered us a way of living which "discards any possibility of satisfaction."[5] For de Man, the fact that language is a play of relations is just one more example of the more general fact that desire is, in its inmost nature, unsatisfiable. That is why he says that the attempt to "do away with literature" is the attempt to avoid facing "the nothing-ness of human things."[6] Here de Man echoes Sartre's claim that "man is a futile passion" – futile because he is the being who has no essence but who nevertheless insists on attributing an essence to himself. De Man shares Sartre's sense of human life as a perpetual oscillation. At one pole of this oscillation is the desire to attain a God's-eye view, to incarnate the very logos of reality, internalize the intrinsic nature of things. At the other pole is the thought that this attempt is impossible because there is no such logos and no such nature. What is original with de Man is the claim that the sense of the "nothingness of human things," of the impossibil-ity of realizing the central human desire – has always been evident in what he calls "literary language." For de Man, literature has always hinted at what Nietz-sche, Heidegger, Sartre, and Derrida have now made philosophically explicit: that instead of thinking of ourselves, logocentrically, as *knowers,* we must now think of ourselves as confronting a void – an abyss which cannot be known but can only, in de Man's words, be "named with ever-renewed understanding." Instead of thinking of ourselves as living according to the constraints set by the nature of physical reality and the dictates of moral imperatives, we must think of ourselves as "[unable] to escape from a condition that is felt to be unbearable." It is, de Man says, the "distinctive character of literature" to make this inability manifest.[7]

4 Ibid., p. 138.
5 Ibid., p. 17.
6 Ibid., p. 18.
7 Ibid., p. 162.

The sort of pluralist and pragmatic antiessentialism which I take over from Dewey agrees with all of de Man's antilogocentric, Derridean premises, but denies that they entail his existentialist, Sartrean conclusions. We pragmatists do not see the end of logocentrism or the death of God as requiring us to adopt a new self-image. For us, no argumentative roads lead from antiessentialist philosophy to the choice of such an image. Nor do any argumentative roads lead from this kind of philosophy to any particular brand of politics. The absence of an intrinsic human nature, and thus of built-in moral obligations, seems to us pragmatists compatible with any and every decision about what sort of life to lead, or what sort of politics to pursue. The repudiation of the traditional logocentric image of the human being as Knower does not seem to us to entail that we face an abyss, but merely that we face a range of choices.

Sartre's point that we have a tendency to repudiate and evade this freedom of choice is perfectly just, but there is no reason to think that when we recognize this tendency we have thereby discovered the nature of what it is to be human. On a pragmatist view, antiessentialists like Sartre and de Man should not turn essentialist at the last moment by claiming to have discovered such a nature. Sartre should not have said "Man's essence is to have no essence," but should have confined himself to saying "Human beings no more have an essence than anything else does." De Man should not have assimilated the Saussurian-Derridean antiessentialist account of how signs function to the claim that desire "as such" is intrinsically unsatisfiable, that this unsatisfiability is the *essence* of desire. Some desires are satisfiable and some are not. The *logocentrists'* desires may not be satisfiable, but other people have other desires which are satisfiable: for example, the desire for individual self-creation and the desire for social justice.

Like Heidegger and Derrida, de Man treats the end of essentialism and logocentrism as an event of world-historical significance. We pragmatists treat it as merely the latest stage in a gradual and continuous shift in human beings' sense of their relation to the rest of the universe — a change which led from worshiping Gods to worshiping sages to worshiping empirical scientific inquirers. With luck, this process will end by leaving us unable to *worship* anything. But the resulting inability to love one thing with all one's heart, soul, and mind, will not entail the inability to rejoice in a lot of different things. It will not necessarily produce a condition we find unbearable, nor a void, nor an abyss. So we pragmatists see no reason to set up an altar to Literature — to the Dark God whose voice is in the literariness of language — on the spot where we once worshiped the radiant, effulgent Logos. Pragmatists would prefer to have no high altars, and instead just have lots of picture galleries, book displays, movies, concerts, ethnographic museums, museums of science and technology, and so on — lots of cultural options but no privileged central discipline or practice.

One reason we pragmatists have this preference is that we see the sort of cultural pluralism which rejects metaphors of centrality and depth as chiming with democratic politics — with the spirit of tolerance which has made constitutional democracies possible. We see this tolerance as saying that public policy and public institutions must be neutral on questions of what is central to human life, questions about the goal or point of human existence. Contemporary democratic societies are built around the assumption that we have to develop institutions which are suitable for people who have wildly different ideas on such topics — for example, worshipers of God, of science, of literature, and of nothing in particular.

Although we antiessentialists obviously cannot deduce the truth of antiessentialism from its suitability for democratic societies, much less claim that it is a necessary foundation for such societies, we do regard this suitability as a point in its favor. The American Cultural Left, however, influenced by Foucault as well as de Man, sees the contemporary democratic states, including our own, as either imperialist powers or disciplinary societies or both. They do not regard harmony between Dewey's antiessentialism and American institutions as a recommendation, for they do not think much of those institutions. They see philosophical views which suggest consensual, reformist politics of the sort Dewey favored as "complicit" with the "discourses of power" which are the invisible regulators of life in the bourgeois democracies. Just as the Marxists of the 1930s thought of Dewey as "the philosopher of American imperialism," so the contemporary Cultural Left views us pragmatists as at best socially irresponsible and at worst apologists for a repressive ideology.[8]

The contemporary American Cultural Left would like to recapture the drive and direction which the left of the 1930s thought that it had gotten from Marxism. Like that older left, our Cultural Left wants its own special talents and competences — the sorts of talents which suit one for philosophy, history, or literary criticism, and the sort of competences which one acquires through advanced study in such disciplines — to be directly applicable to political purposes. As Lentricchia puts it, leftists whose only political outlets are sit-ins, picketing, and the like "are being crushed by feelings of guilt and occupational alienation."[9]

For professors of literature who want a way of making their specialized skill and knowledge politically relevant, of getting leftist politics into their classrooms and their books, the writings of the later de Man are a godsend. Just as Sartre became disgusted by the apolitical tone of what he had written in the 1930s and 1940s,

8 Frank Lentricchia, in his *Criticism and Social Change* (Chicago: University of Chicago Press, 1983) explains why leftist teachers of literature need to relate their academic work to their politics, and criticizes pragmatism as inadequate for their purposes. The criticisms of pragmatism which Lentricchia makes are typical of the American Cultural Left. Lentricchia sees my own work, e.g., as tending toward a "divorce of culture from political power" (p. 19), a claim echoed by Jonathan Culler, who says that the "complacency" of my pragmatism "seems altogether appropriate to the age of Reagan" (*Framing the Sign* [Norman, Okla.: University of Oklahoma Press, 1988], p. 55). (In later sections of his book however (particularly pp. 38–52), Lentricchia offers criticisms of de Man which parallel my own.)
9 Ibid., p. 7.

and proclaimed in 1960 that "existentialism is only an enclave within Marxism," so de Man, as he grew older and more influential, became sensitive to criticism of his work as merely a new aestheticism. In an essay published in 1982 he claimed that

more than any other mode of inquiry, including economics, the linguistics of literariness is a powerful and indispensable tool in the unmasking of ideological aberrations, as well as a determining factor in accounting for their occurrence. Those who reproach literary theory for being oblivious to social and historical (that is to say ideological) reality are merely stating their fear at having their own ideological mystifications exposed by the tool they are trying to discredit. [10]

In an interview given the year before his death, de Man went a step further, claiming that the sort of close reading which he attempted and taught was *indispensable* to political thought. Then he said

I have always maintained that one could approach the problems of ideology and by extension the problems of politics *only* [italics added] on the basis of critical-linguistic analysis. [11]

These two passages have set the theme for much of the writing of the American Cultural Left. This left has come to take for granted that what Lentricchia calls its sense of "occupational alienation" can in fact be overcome. It can be overcome because the sort of thing one learns in graduate study in the humanities, and in particular in the study of literature, is precisely what is needed to enable one to "approach the problems of politics."

From a pragmatist point of view, there is a grain of truth in this claim, but only a grain. It is true that the study of literature sensitizes one to the way in which any phenomenon may be described in a lot of different ways. So readers of literature become aware of rhetoric, of the fact that what seems true will depend upon the interplay between the language used and an audience's expectations. Literary study helps one realize that today's literal and objective truth is just the corpse of yesterday's metaphor. Those who study and teach the history of literature are in a good position to see how the vocabularies of moral and political deliberation can be changed by the literary imagination, the way in which poets have occasionally functioned as unacknowledged legislators. In the course of their teaching, they can occasionally see deep changes taking place in the students' image of themselves or of their society. Witnessing such changes makes it easy for teachers of literature to take seriously Stephen Dedalus's desire "to forge in the smithy of my soul the uncreated conscience of my race." It also lets them understand that Lincoln was not just making a bad joke when he told Harriet Beecher Stowe that she had brought about the Civil War. Again, their

10 De Man, *The Resistance to Theory* (Minneapolis: University of Minnesota Press, 1986), p. 11.
11 Ibid., p. 121.

role in promulgating and enforcing a literary canon makes it easy for them to see that such a canon can function as a repressive force — how decisions about which books to assign can make it harder for students to think about what is wrong with their previous socialization, and thus to think about what is wrong with their society.

Having granted all these points, however, we pragmatists still want to insist that what de Man says in the passages I have cited is absurd. It is just not the case that one has to have a Saussurian-Wittgensteinian-Derridean understanding of the nature of language in order to think clearly and usefully about politics. One does not have to be an antiessentialist in philosophy in order to be politically imaginative or politically useful. Philosophy is not *that* important for politics, nor is literature. Lots of people who accept theocentric or Kantian logocentric accounts of moral obligation unconsciously and uncritically — starting with Kant himself — have done very well at political thinking. They have been invaluable to social reform and progress. The same can be said of lots of essentialists — for example, all those people who still think that either natural or social science can change our self-image for the better by telling us what we really, essentially, intrinsically, are.

Even though we pragmatists commend our antiessentialism and antilogo-centrism on the ground of its harmony with the practices and aims of a democratic society, we do not want to claim that accepting and applying such doctrines is *necessary* for overcoming social and economic repression. After all, a lot of such repression is so blatant and obvious that it does not take any great analytic skills or any great philosophical self-consciousness to see what is going on. It does not, for example, take any "critical-linguistic analysis" to notice that millions of children in American ghettos grew up without hope while the U.S. government was preoccupied with making the rich richer — with assuring a greedy and selfish middle class that it was the salt of the earth. Even economists, plumbers, insurance salesmen, and biochemists — people who have never read a text closely, much less deconstructed it — can recognize that the immiseration of much of Latin America is partially due to the deals struck between local plutocracies and North American banks and governments.

We pragmatists view the "critique of ideology" as an occasionally useful tactical weapon in social struggles, but as one among many others. We see no evidence to confirm de Man's claim that those familiar with "the linguistics of literariness" are likely to be more useful than, say, statisticians or muckraking journalists. Suggesting that this sort of linguistics is somehow central or essential to political thought seems to us like suggesting that, say, antisubmarine mines are central or essential to modern warfare. Only an admiral who had spent too long in the bureau that lets contracts for new kinds of mines would make the latter claim. Only a professor of literature suffering from a really extreme case of "occupational alienation" would make the sort of claims which de Man makes. Only someone who takes both literature and philosophy far too seriously would say, as Hillis Miller does, that

Language promises, but what it promises is itself. This promise it can never keep. It is this fact of language, a necessity beyond the control of any user of language, which makes things happen as they do happen in the material world of history.[12]

Language can be described, and has been usefully described by de Man and Derrida, as making promises it cannot keep. This description is genuinely enlightening when one is thinking about the attempts of essentialist intellectuals to penetrate through appearance to reality, to find the area where the *ultimate* levers of power are concealed, the vocabulary which finally puts *everything* in the right perspective. But history is not a conspiracy of essentialist intellectuals, nor are such intellectuals the principal instruments of social injustice. Lots of different things, ranging from the assignment of textbooks through the greed of legislators and the obsessions of dictators to the outbreak of epidemics, "make things happen as they do happen in the material world of history." To take Derrida's and de Man's useful and original antiessentialist redescription of language as the key to morality and politics is one more example of turning essentialist at the last minute.

This sort of simplistic and self-deceptive hypostatization of language or of literature is, however, a natural result of loving, or hating, one thing with all one's heart and soul and mind. It is a natural result of trying to bring everything together – one's most private emotional needs and one's public responsibilities, one's secret self-image and one's shame at the leisure and wealth that permit one to devote oneself to the cultivation of that self-image. So the worship of some such hypostatization is the characteristic temptation of the intellectuals. The intellectuals are people whose talents suit them for the task of redescription – the task of finding new metaphors, words in which to formulate new beliefs and desires. They are the people who are not content with the vocabulary into which they were socialized, and who are able to invent a new one. They are self-creators, in the sense that they can escape from the moral and political vocabulary into which they were socialized and become new people by reshaping their self-image. But just insofar as they retain a sense of the needs of other human beings, they feel alienated from these others – all those who do not speak the new language which the intellectual has invented in the course of reinventing herself. They also feel guilty insofar as they cannot relate their own projection of self-invention to the needs of those less capable of redescription and reinvention.

One way to get out from under this sense of guilt and alienation is illustrated by Nietzsche's occasional attempts to proclaim himself superhuman, and therefore entitled to neglect the needs of mere humans. Another, much more common way,

---

12 *The Ethics of Reading,* p. 35.

illustrated by other passages in Nietzsche, is to hypostatize the central term of one's newly created vocabulary, to treat this term ("Reason," "the movement of History," "Language") as the One True Name of God. For this strategy helps one see oneself as a prophet, or perhaps even a redeemer. It helps one see one's own inner transfiguration as auguring the transformation of the human world, and in particular of the social arrangements which have left the needs of others unsatisfied.

Marxists are notorious for adopting this latter alternative, and Aron was right to call Marxism "the opium of the intellectuals." But from my antiessentialist angle, the hallucinatory effects of Marxism, and of the post-Marxist combination of de Man and Foucault currently being smoked by the American Cultural Left, are just special cases of the hallucinatory effects of all essentialist thought. Once this hallucinatory quality was best illustrated by science worship — by the people who told us that the millennium would come when we took a scientific approach to value-choice and conflict-resolution. Nowadays it is best illustrated by literature-worship — by the people who say the sorts of absurd things which I have quoted.

Still, saying absurd things is perfectly compatible with being a force for good. The Cultural Left has come in for a lot of flak lately — particularly from people who write for *The New Criterion* and the *National Review* and who are more interested in bashing liberals than in social justice. I hope that what I am saying about the Cultural Left will not be confused with what these people are saying. They go on about how the literature departments of American colleges and universities are being taken over by unscrupulous intellectual charlatans whose political goals outweigh their intellectual responsibilities. From my point of view, any leftist political movement — any movement which tries to call our attention to what the strong are currently doing to the weak — is a lot better than no left. Dialectical materialism was a pretty incoherent and silly philosophical system, and it eventually fell into the hands of mad tyrants. But it got quite a bit of good done while it lasted. Now that Marxism no longer looks plausible even in Paris, leftists who feel the need for a powerful philosophical backup are resorting to de Man and Foucault. But they are still doing a lot more good than most of their critics are doing.

Irving Howe has remarked, with some justice, that this Cultural Left is interested in taking over, not the government, but the English Department. But we should remember that in the 1920s and 1930s lots of Deweyan pragmatists were more interested in taking over the sociology and political science departments than in taking over the government. They had considerable success in doing so, and so students in social science courses were assigned books which made them more aware of the suffering caused by American institutions. The success of de Manians in taking over literature departments will have a similar effect. For the curricular emphases which they initiate will, in the course of a generation or so, trickle down into the high schools, and the conventional wisdom inculcated into young Americans will be changed.

Let me offer a couple of examples of such changes. Henry Gates, Deborah McDowell, and other specialists in Afro-American literature have helped rescue from oblivion Zora Neale Hurston's novel *Their Eyes Were Watching God*. People who got Ph.D. degrees in English during the 1980s are as likely to have read this novel as those who got their Ph.D.'s in the 1950s were to have read *The Diary of Anne Frank,* or as those who got their Ph.D.'s in the 1920s were to have read *The Mill on the Floss*. When I was in high school, I was assigned *The Mill on the Floss*. My fifteen-year-old daughter is currently being assigned *The Diary of Anne Frank*. I think it quite likely that any granddaughter I may have will, while in high school, be assigned *Their Eyes Were Watching God*. If she is, she will be a lot better informed about American history, rural poverty, and being black than I was at her age, and will be a more useful citizen in consequence.

Another example: while attending a rally of the Cultural Left at Duke University I heard Eve Klossofsky Sedgwick describe the prohibiting of gay high school teachers from counseling gay high school students about their gayness as "child abuse." My first reaction was that this was merely the sort of hyperbolic metaphor suitable for pep rallies, not to be taken literally. But by the time Sedgwick had finished her lecture I had literalized her metaphor. The examples she gave convinced me that this prohibition was, in fact, child abuse. While wondering what might undo the prohibition (which before hearing Sedgwick had struck me as as commonsensical as, when in high school, I had found antisodomy statutes) it occurred to me that gays might someday organize celebrations in the schools of one of the big events in American gay history – the Stonewall Riots. Maybe, in the early twenty-first century, it will be as commonplace for high schools to commemorate Stonewall as it is for them to celebrate Martin Luther King's birthday. (If this suggestion seems implausible, think how implausible the idea of celebrating King's birthday would have seemed to J. Edgar Hoover at the time of Selma.)

If either of the speculations I have offered come true, it will be because people like Gates and Sedgwick have patiently, over many years, plugged away despite the mockery and hostility of many of their professional colleagues. It is true that such struggles are not much like throwing cobblestones from barricades, or like risking the Gulag for publishing poems in *samizdat*. Still, unless some of today's academics are willing to struggle against such mockery and hostility, the education of the next generation of Americans will suffer a great deal. So will the moral tone of American public life. In exchange for the hope of such goods, one can afford to suppress a good deal of exasperation at de Man's hypostatizations.

If the sort of thing that Gates and Sedgwick are doing is to count as the politicization of the humanities, then we shall have to count what Locke and Hobbes did as the politicization of philosophy, what the founders of American sociology did as the politicization of social science, and what Shelley and the younger Wordsworth did as the politicization of literature. One point on which the Cultural Left is absolutely right to insist is that the social sciences and the humanities will, unless they become completely moribund, always be politicized, one way or another. There is no way to keep these disciplines alive if they become separated from the process of moral and political deliberation.

The only sense in which we want *un*politicized scholarship is that we do not want unpolitical scholars, or scholars of unpopular political persuasions, to be interfered with by those whose political views dominate their departments or their universities. But that is a matter of academic freedom and collegial good manners, not a matter of keeping the academy separate from political struggle. Threats to freedom and civility are, obviously, as frequent from the left as from the right. Doubtless American literature departments will, as the cultural leftists age from a band of Young Turks into an entrenched Old Guard, see many instances of injustice to junior faculty who have no taste for leftist politics, or who are dismissive of the political vocabulary of their elders. There are already indications that leftist political correctness is becoming a criterion for faculty hiring. But, with luck, these injustices will be no worse than those which contemporary academic leftists endured from exponents of "traditional humanistic values" in the course of their own rise to power.

PART III

Freud and moral reflection

The mechanical mind: Hume and Freud

Freud thought of himself as part of the same "decentering" movement of thought to which Copernicus and Darwin belonged. In a famous passage, he says that psychoanalysis "seeks to prove to the ego that it is not even master in its own house, but must content itself with scanty information of what is going on unconsciously in its mind." He compares this with the realization that "our earth was not the centre of the universe but only a tiny fragment of a cosmic system of scarcely imaginable vastness" and with the discovery, by Darwin, of our "ineradicable animal nature."[1]

Copernicus, Darwin, and Freud do have something important in common, but Freud does not give us a clear idea of what that is. It is not evident that successive decenterings add up to a history of humiliation; Copernicus and Darwin might claim that by making God and the angels less plausible, they have left human beings on top of the heap. The suggestion that we have discovered, humiliatingly, that humanity is less important than we had thought is not perspicuous. For it is not clear what "importance" can mean in this context. Further, the claim that psychoanalysis has shown that the ego is not master in its own house is unhelpful, for the relevant sense of "mastery" is unclear. Does our sense of our importance, or our capacity for self-control, really depend on the belief that we are transparent to ourselves? Why should the discovery of the unconscious add humiliation to the discovery of the passions?

I think one gets a better idea of the similarity Freud was trying to describe by contrasting a world of natural kinds with a world of machines – a world of Aristotelian substances with a world of homogenous particles combining and disassociating according to universal laws. Think of the claim that "man is a natural kind" not as saying that human beings are at the center of something, but that they *have* a center, in a way that a machine does not. A substance that exemplifies an Aristotelian natural kind divides into a central essence – one that provides a built-in purpose – and a set of peripheral accidents. But an artifact's formal and final causes may be distinct; the same machine, for example, may be

---

1 *The Standard Edition of the Complete Psychological Works of Sigmund Freud,* trans. James Strachey (London: Hogarth Press, 1966), 16:284–285. Future references to Freud will be to this edition (abbreviated *S.E.*), and will be inserted in the text.

used for many different purposes. A machine's purpose is not built in.[2] If humanity is a natural kind, then perhaps we can find our center and so learn how to live well. But if we are machines, then it is up to us to invent a use for ourselves.

What was decisive about the Copernican Revolution was not that it moved us human beings from the center of the universe, but that it began, in Dyksterhuis's phrase, the "mechanization of the world picture."[3] Copernicus and Newton between them made it hard to think of the universe as an edifying spectacle. When an infinite universe of pointless corpuscles replaced a closed world, it became hard to imagine what it would be like to look down upon the Creation and find it good.[4] The universe began to look like a rather simple, boring machine, rambling off beyond the horizon, rather than like a bounded and well-composed tableau. So the idea of a center no longer seemed applicable. Analogously, the result of Darwin's and Mendel's mechanization of biology was to set aside an edifying hierarchy of natural kinds. Viewing the various species of plants and animals as the temporary results of interactions between fortuitous environmental pressures

2   There can be such a thing as a "purer" Aristotelian substance – one that realizes its essence better because it is less subject to irrelevant accidental changes. (Indeed, Aristotle arranges substances in a hierarchy according to their degree of materiality, their degree of susceptibility to such changes – a hierarchy with "pure actuality" at the top.) But there is no such thing as a purified machine, though there may be another machine that accomplishes the same purpose more efficiently. Machines have no centers to which one can strip them down; stripped-down versions of machines are different machines, machines for doing or producing different things, not more perfect versions of the same machine.

3   The Copernican model of the heavens could not have been accepted without also accepting the corpuscularian mechanics of Galileo and Descartes. That mechanics was the entering wedge for a Newtonian paradigm of scientific explanation – one that predicted events on the basis of a universal homogenous microstructure, rather than revealing the different natures of the various natural kinds. The reason why "the new philosophy" cast all in doubt was not that people felt belittled when the sun took the place of the earth but that it had become hard to see what, given Galilean space, could be meant by the universe having a center. As it became harder to know what a God's-eye view would be like, it became harder to believe in God. As it became harder to think of the common-sense way of breaking up the world into "natural" kinds as more than a practical convenience, it became harder to make sense of the Aristotelian essence–accident distinction. So the very idea of the "nature" of something as setting the standards that things of that sort ought to fulfill began to blur.

4   In particular, it became difficult to see what the point of *man* could be – difficult to preserve anything like Aristotle's "functional" concept of man, well described by Alasdair MacIntyre as follows: "Moral arguments within the classical, Aristotelian tradition – whether in its Greek or its medieval versions – involve at least one central functional concept, the concept of *man* understood as having an essential nature and an essential purpose or function. . . . Aristotle takes it as a starting-point for ethical inquiry that the relationship of 'man' to 'living well' is analogous to that of 'harpist' to 'playing the harp well'. . . . But the use of 'man' as a functional concept is far older than Aristotle and it does not initially derive from Aristotle's metaphysical biology. It is rooted in the forms of a social life in which the theorists of the classical tradition give expression. For according to that tradition, to be a man is to fill a set of roles, each of which has its own point and purpose: a member of a family, a citizen, soldier, philosopher, servant of God. It is only when man is thought of as an individual prior to and apart from all roles that 'man' ceases to be a functional concept" (MacIntyre, *After Virtue* [Notre Dame, Ind.: Notre Dame University Press, 1981], p. 56). I take up MacIntyre's suggestion that we need to recapture such a concept in the final section of this essay.

and random mutations made the world of living creatures as pointless as Newtonian mechanics had made cosmology. Mechanization meant that the world in which human beings lived no longer taught them anything about how they should live.

In trying to see how Freud fits into this story of decentering-as-mechanization, one should begin by noting that Freud was not the first to suggest that, having mechanized everything else, we mechanize the mind as well. Hume had already treated ideas and impressions not as properties of a substratal self but as mental atoms whose arrangement *was* the self. This arrangement was determined by laws of association, analogues of the law of gravitation. Hume thought of himself as the Newton of the mind, and the mechanical mind he envisaged was – viewed from above, so to speak – just as morally pointless as Newton's corpuscularian universe.

Hume, however, suggested that the mechanization of neither nature nor the mind mattered for purposes of finding a self-image. With a sort of proto-pragmatist insouciance, he thought that talk about the atoms of Democritus, Newton's shining lights, and his own "impressions and ideas" offered, at most, a handy way of describing things and people for purposes of predicting and controlling them. For moral purposes, for purposes of seeing life as having a point, such talk might be irrelevant. Like Blake, Hume was prepared to say that the view from above – the view of the Baconian predictor and controller – was irrelevant to our sense of centeredness. His pragmatical reconciliation of freedom and determinism, like his reconciliation of armchair skepticism with theoretical curiosity and practical benevolence, is an invitation to take the mechanization of the mind lightly – as no more than an intriguing intellectual exercise, the sort of thing that a young person might do in order to become famous.

It is tempting to respond to Freud in the same way that Hume responded to his own mechanizing efforts: to say that for purposes of moral reflection a knowledge of Freudian unconscious motivation is as irrelevant as a knowledge of Humean associations or of neurophysiology. But this response is unconvincing. Unlike Hume, Freud *did* change our self-image. Finding out about our unconscious motives is not just an intriguing exercise, but more like a moral obligation. What difference between Hume's and Freud's ways of extending mechanization to the mind accounts for Freud's relevance to our moral consciousness?

If one views Freud's dictum that the ego is not master in its own house as saying merely that we often act in ways that could not have been predicted on the basis of our introspectible beliefs and desires, Freud will be merely reiterating a commonplace of Greek thought. If one views it as the claim that the mind can, for purposes of prediction and control, be treated as a set of associative mechanisms, a realm in which there are no accidents, Freud will be saying little that Hume had not said. So one must find another interpretation. One gets a clue, I think, from the fact that the phrase "not even master in its own house" is to the point only if some other person is behaving as if he or she were in charge. The phrase is an appropriate response to the incursion of an unwanted guest – for example, to the onset of schizophrenia. But it is not an appropriate reaction, for example, to an explanation of the dependence of our mood on our endocrine system. For glands are not, so to speak, quasi people with whom to struggle. Nor are neurons, which is why the possible identity of the mind with the brain is of no moral interest. Physiological discoveries can tell us how to predict and control ourselves – including how to predict and control our beliefs and desires – without threatening or changing our self-image. For such discoveries do not suggest that we are being shouldered aside by somebody else.

Psychological mechanisms will seem more decentering than physiological mechanisms only if one is of a naturally metaphysical turn of mind, insistent on pressing the questions, "But what am I *really?* What is my *true* self? What is *essential* to me?" Descartes and Kant had this sort of mind and so, in our day, do reductionist metaphysicians such as B. F. Skinner and antireductionist champions of "subjectivity" and "phenomenology" such as Thomas Nagel and Richard Wollheim. But the mechanization of nature made protopragmatists of most people, allowing them to shrug off questions of essence. They became accustomed to speaking one sort of language for Baconian purposes of prediction and control and another for purposes of moral reflection. They saw no need to raise the question of which language represented the world or the self as it is "in itself."[5] Yet Freudian discoveries are troubling even for pragmatists. Unlike the atoms of Democritus or Hume, the Freudian unconscious does not look like something that we might usefully, to achieve certain of our purposes, describe ourselves as. It looks like somebody who is stepping into our shoes, somebody who has different purposes than we do. It looks like a person using us rather than a thing we can use.

This clue – the fact that psychological mechanisms look most disturbing and decentering when they stop looking like mechanisms and start looking like persons – has been followed up by Donald Davidson. In a remarkable essay called "Paradoxes of Irrationality," Davidson notes that philosophers have always been upset by Freud's insistence on "partitioning" the self. They have tended to reject Freud's threatening picture of quasi selves lurking beneath the threshold of consciousness as an unnecessarily vivid way of describing the incoherence and confusion

5 Nonintellectuals' conviction that what the intellectuals talk about does not really matter was greatly strengthened when the new Enlightenment intellectuals informed them that the previous batch of intellectuals – the priests – had been *completely* wrong. One consequence of the mechanization of nature, and of the resulting popularity of a pragmatic, Baconian attitude toward knowledge-claims, was a heightened cynicism and indifference about the questions that intellectuals discuss. This is why metaphysical issues about "the nature of reality" and "the true self" have less resonance and popular appeal than religious heresies once did, and why philosophical questions raised within Comte's "positive," postmetaphysical perspective have even less. People always thought the priests a bit funny, but also a bit awe-inspiring. They thought German idealists, and Anglo-Saxon positivists, *merely* funny. By contrast, they take psychoanalysts seriously enough to attempt to imitate them, as in the development of parlor analysis and of psychobabble.

that may afflict a single self. They hope thereby to remain faithful to the common-sense assumption that a single human body typically contains a single self. Davidson defends Freudian partitioning by pointing out that there is no reason to say "You unconsciously believe that p" rather than "There is something within you which causes you to act as if you believed that p," unless one is prepared to round out the characterization of the unconscious quasi self who "believes that p" by ascribing a host of other beliefs (mostly true, and mostly consistent with p) to that quasi self. One can only attribute a belief to something if one simultaneously attributes lots of other mostly true and mostly consistent beliefs. Beliefs and desires, unlike Humean ideas and impressions, come in packages.[6]

Davidson puts these holistic considerations to work as follows. He identifies (not explicitly, but, if my reading of him is right, tacitly) being a person with being a coherent and plausible set of beliefs and desires. Then he points out that the force of saying that a human being sometimes behaves irrationally is that he or she sometimes exhibits behavior that cannot be explained by reference to a single such set. Finally, he concludes that the point of "partitioning" the self between a consciousness and an unconscious is that the latter can be viewed as an alternative set, inconsistent with the familiar set that we identify with conciousness, yet sufficiently coherent internally to count as a person. This strategy leaves open the possibility that the same human body can play host to two or more persons. These persons enter into causal relations with each other, as well as with the body whose movements are brought about by the beliefs and desires of one or the other of them. But they do not, normally, have conversational relations. That is, one's unconscious beliefs are not *reasons* for a change in one's conscious beliefs, but they may *cause* changes in the latter beliefs, just as may portions of one's body (e.g., the retina, the fingertips, the pituitary gland, the gonads).

To see the force of Davidson's suggestion is to appreciate the crucial difference between Hume and Freud. This is that Hume's mental atoms included only subpropositional components of beliefs – mostly names of perceptible and intro-spectible qualia. The mechanization of the self that Hume suggested, and that associationist psychology developed, amounted to little more than a transposition into mentalistic terminology of a rather crude physiology of perception and memory. By contrast, Freud populated inner space not with analogues of Boylean corpuscles but with analogues of persons – internally coherent clusters of belief and desire. Each of these quasi persons is, in the Freudian picture, a part of a single unified *causal* network, but not of a single person (since the criterion for individuation of a person is a certain minimal coherence among its beliefs and

---

6   Even if, as Hume thought, there is a possible universe consisting only of one sense-impression, we cannot make sense of the idea of a universe consisting only of the belief that, for example, Caesar crossed the Rubicon. Further, there is no such thing as an incoherent arrangement of Humean mental atoms. But there is such a thing as a set of beliefs and desires so incoherent that we cannot attribute them to a single self.

desires). Knowledge of all these persons is necessary to predict and control a human being's behavior (and in particular his or her "irrational" behavior), but only one of these persons will be available (at any given time) to introspection.

The rational unconscious as conversational partner

If one accepts this Davidsonian explanation of Freud's basic strategy, then one has taken a long step toward seeing why psychoanalysis can aptly be described as a decentering. For now one can see Freudian mechanisms as having, so to speak, a human interest that no physiological or Humean mechanism could have. One can see why it is hard to dismiss the Freudian unconscious as just one more useful, if paradoxical, redescription of the world that science has invented for purposes of saving the phenomena – the sort of redescription that can be ignored by everyday, practical purposes (as, for example, one ignores heliocentrism). The suggestion that some unknown persons are causing us (or, to stress the alienation produced by this suggestion, causing our bodies) to do things we would rather not do is decentering in a way that an account of heavenly bodies (or of the descent of man) is not. One will be thrown off base by this suggestion even if one has no interest in Aristotelian, metaphysical questions about one's "essence" or one's "true self." One can be entirely pragmatical in one's approach to life and still feel that something needs to be *done* in response to such a suggestion.

To take Freud's suggestion seriously is to wish to become acquainted with these unfamiliar persons, if only as a first step toward killing them off. This wish will take the place, for a pragmatical Freudian, of the religious and metaphysical desire to find one's "true center." It initiates a task that can plausibly be described as a moral obligation – the task whose goal is summed up in the phrase "where id was, there shall ego be." This goal does not require the Aristotelian notion that one's ego is more "natural" or more truly "oneself" than one's id. But adopting this goal does restore a point to the imperative "Know thyself," an imperative that one might have thought inapplicable to the self-as-machine.

On Freud's account of self-knowledge, what we are morally obligated to know about ourselves is not our essence, not a common human nature that is somehow the source and locus of moral responsibility. Far from being of what we share with the other members of our species, self-knowledge is precisely of what divides us from them: our accidental idiosyncrasies, the "irrational" components in our-selves, the ones that split us up into incompatible sets of beliefs and desires. The study of "the nature of the mind," construed as the study either of Humean association of ideas or of Freudian metapsychology, is as pointless, for purposes of moral reflection, as the study of the laws of celestial motion. What *is* of interest is the study of the idiosyncratic raw material whose processing Humean and Freud-ian mechanisms are postulated to predict, and of the idiosyncratic products of this processing. For only study of these concrete details will let us enter into conversational relations with our unconscious and, at the ideal limit of such conversation, let us break down the partitions.

The view of Freud that I am proposing will seem plausible only if one makes a clear distinction between two senses of "the unconscious": (1) a sense in which it stands for one or more well-articulated systems of beliefs and desires, systems that are just as complex, sophisticated, and internally consistent as the normal adult's conscious beliefs and desires; and (2) a sense in which it stands for a seething mass of inarticulate instinctual energies, a "reservoir of libido" to which consistency is irrelevant. In the second sense, the unconscious is just another name for "the passions," the lower part of the soul, the bad, false self. Had this been the only sense Freud gave to the term, his work would have left our strategies of character-development, and our self-image, largely unchanged. What is novel in Freud's view of the unconscious is his claim that our unconscious selves are not dumb, sullen, lurching brutes, but rather the intellectual peers of our conscious selves, possible conversational partners for those selves. As Rieff puts it, "Freud democratized genius by giving everyone a creative unconscious."[7]

This suggestion that one or more clever, articulate, inventive persons are at work behind the scene — cooking up our jokes, inventing our metaphors, plotting our dreams, arranging our slips, and censoring our memories — is what grips the imagination of the lay reader of Freud. As Freud himself said, if psychoanalysis had stuck to the neuroses, it would never have attracted the attention of the intellectuals.[8] It was the application of psychoanalytical notions to normal life that first suggested that Freud's ideas might call for a revision in our self-image. For this application breaks the connection between the Platonic reason—passion distinction and the conscious—unconscious distinction. It substitutes a picture of sophisticated transactions between two or more "intellects" for the traditional picture of one "intellect" struggling with a mob of "irrational" brutes.

The Platonic tradition had thought of articulate beliefs — or, more generally, propositional attitudes — as the preserve of the higher part of the soul. It thought of the lower parts as "bodily," as animallike, and in particular as prelinguistic. But a witty unconscious is necessarily a linguistic unconscious. Further, if "rational" means "capable of weaving complex, internally consistent, networks of belief" rather than "capable of contemplating reality as it is," then a witty unconscious is also a *rational* unconscious — one that can no more tolerate inconsis-

7   Philip Rieff, *Freud: The Mind of the Moralist* (New York: Harper and Row, 1966), p. 36.

8   "The importance of psycho-analysis for psychiatry would never have drawn the attention of the intellectual world to it or won it a place in *The History of our Times*. This result was brought about by the relation of psycho-analysis to normal, not to pathological, mental life" (Freud, *S.E.* 19:205; see also 18:240). Even if analytic psychiatry should some day be abandoned in favor of chemical and microsurgical forms of treatment, the connections that Freud drew between such emotions as sexual yearning and hostility on the one hand, and between dreams and parapraxes on the other, would remain part of the common sense of our culture.

tency than can consciousness.[9] So we need to distinguish the unconscious as "the deepest strata of our minds, made up of instinctual impulses," strata that know "nothing that is negative, and no negation," in which "contradictories coincide" (*S.E.* 14:296), from the unconscious as the sensitive, whacky, backstage partner who feeds us our best lines. The latter is somebody who has a well-worked-out, internally consistent view of the world – though one that may be hopelessly wrong on certain crucial points. One needs to distinguish Freud's banal claim that "our intellect is a feeble and dependent thing, a plaything and tool of our instincts and affects" (*S.E.* 14:301) – which is just a replay of Hume's claim that "reason is, and ought to be, the slave of the passions"[10] – from his interesting and novel claim that the conscious–unconscious distinction cuts across the human–animal and reason–instinct distinctions.

If one concentrates on the latter claim, then one can see Freud as suggesting that, on those occasions when we are tempted to complain that two souls dwell, alas, in our breast, we think of the two as one more-or-less sane and one more-or-less crazy human soul, rather than as one human soul and one bestial soul. On the latter, Platonic model, self-knowledge will be a matter of self-purification – of identifying our true, human self and expelling, curbing, or ignoring the animal self. On the former model, self-knowledge will be a matter of getting acquainted with one or more crazy quasi people, listening to their crazy accounts of how things are, seeing why they hold the crazy views they do, and learning something from them. It will be a matter of self-enrichment. To say "Where id was, there will ego be" will not mean "Whereas once I was driven by instinct, I shall become autonomous, motivated solely by reason." Rather, it will mean something like: "Once I could not figure out why I was acting so oddly, and hence wondered if I were, somehow, under the control of a devil or a beast. But now I shall be able to see my actions as rational, as making sense, though perhaps based on mistaken premises. I may even discover that those premises were not mistaken, that my unconscious knew better than I did."[11]

9 See Davidson, "Paradoxes of Irrationality," in *Philosophical Essays on Freud,* ed. B. Wollheim and J. Hopkins (Cambridge: Cambridge University Press, 1982), especially his discussion of "the paradox of rationality" at p. 303.

10 *Any* associationist psychology will make *that* claim. For it is a corollary of the claim that reason is not a faculty of contemplating essence but only a faculty of inferring beliefs from other beliefs. Since the initial premises of such inferences must then be supplied by something other than reason, and if the only faculty that can be relevantly opposed to "reason" is "passion," then Hume's claim follows trivially. But it would, of course, be more consistent with the mechanistic vocabulary of associationist psychology to drop talk of faculties and, in particular, to drop the terms "reason" and "passion." Once the mind becomes a machine instead of a quasi person, it no longer has faculties, much less higher and lower ones. Hume is interlacing the old vocabulary of faculties with the results of the new associationism for the sake of shock value.

11 This way of stating the aim of psychoanalytic treatment may seem to make everything sound too sweetly reasonable. It suggests that the analyst serves as a sort of moderator at a symposium: he or she introduces, for example, a consciousness which thinks that Mother is a long-suffering object of pity to an unconscious which thinks of her as a voracious seductress, letting the two hash out

The advantage of this way of thinking of the passions is that it enables one to take a similar view of conscience. For just as this view humanizes what the Platonic tradition took to be the urges of an animal, so it humanizes what that tradition thought of as divine inspiration. It makes conscience, like passion, one more set of human beliefs and desires – another story about how the world is, another Weltanschauung. Most important, it makes it *just* another story – not one that (in the case of the passions) is automatically suspect nor one that (in the case of conscience) is automatically privileged. It treats, so to speak, the three different stories told by the id, the superego, and the ego as alternative extrapolations from a common experience – in particular, experience of childhood events. Each story is an attempt to make these events coherent with later events, but the stimuli provided by such events are (usually) so diverse and confusing that no *single* consistent set of beliefs and desires is able to make them all hang together.

To view these three (or more) stories as on a par, as alternative explanations of a confusing situation, is part of what Rieff calls "Freud's egalitarian revision of the traditional idea of an hierarchical human nature."[12] To adopt a self-image that incorporates this egalitarian revision is to think that there is no single right answer to the quesion "What *did* happen to me in the past?" It is also to think that there is no such answer to the question "What sort of person am I now?" It is to recognize that the choice of a vocabulary in which to describe either one's childhood or one's character cannot be made by inspecting some collection of "neutral facts" (e.g., a complete videotape of one's life history). It is to give up the urge to purification, to achieve a stripped-down version of the self, and to develop

the pros and cons. It is of course true that the facts of resistance forbid the analyst to think in conversational terms. He or she must instead think in terms of Freud's various topographic-hydraulic models of libidinal flow, hoping to find in these models suggestions about how to overcome resistance, what meaning to assign to novel symptoms, and so forth.

But it is also true that the patient has no choice but to think in conversational terms. (This is why self-analysis will usually not work, why treatment can often do what reflection cannot.) For purposes of the patient's conscious attempt to reshape his or her character, he or she cannot use a self-description in terms of cathexes, libidinal flow, and the like; topographic-hydraulic models cannot form part of one's self-image, any more than can a description of one's endocrine system. When the patient thinks about competing descriptions of his or her mother, the patient has to think dialectically, to grant that there is much to be said on both sides. To think, as opposed to react to a new stimulus, simply *is* to compare and contrast candidates for admission into one's set of beliefs and desires. So, while the analyst is busy thinking causally, in terms of the patient's reactions to stimuli (and in particular the stimuli that occur while the patient is on the couch), the patient has to think of his or her unconscious as, at least potentially, a conversational partner.

These two ways of thinking seem to me alternative tools, useful for different purposes, rather than contradictory claims. I do not think (despite the arguments of, for example, Paul Ricoeur and Roy Schafer) that there is a tension in Freud's thought between "energetics" and "hermeneutics." Rather, the two seem to me to be as compatible as, for example, microstructural and macrostructural descriptions of the same object (e.g., Eddington's table). But to defend my eirenic attitude properly I should offer an account of "resistance" that chimes with Davidson's interpretation of the unconscious, and I have not yet figured out how to do this. (I am grateful to George Thomas, Seymour Rabinowitz, and Cecil Cullender for pointing out this difficulty to me.)

12 Philip Rieff, *The Triumph of the Therapeutic* (New York: Harper and Row, 1966), p. 56.

what Rieff calls "tolerance of ambiguities . . . the key to what Freud considered the most difficult of all personal accomplishments: a genuinely stable character in an unstable time."[13] On the view I am offering, Freud gave us a new technique for achieving a genuinely stable character: the technique of lending a sympathetic ear to our own tendencies to instability, by treating them as alternative ways of making sense of the past, ways that have as good a claim on our attention as do the familiar beliefs and desires that are available to introspection. His mechanistic view of the self gave us a vocabulary that lets us describe all the various parts of the soul, conscious and unconscious alike, in homogenous terms: as equally plausible candidates for "the true self."

But to say that all the parts of the soul are equally plausible candidates is to discredit both the idea of a "true self" and the idea of "the true story about how things are." It is to view the enlightened, liberated self – the self that has finally succeeded in shaping itself – as a self that has given up the need to "see things steadily and see them whole," to penetrate beyond shifting appearances to a constant reality. Maturity will, according to this view, consist rather in an ability to seek out new redescriptions of one's own past – an ability to take a nominalistic, ironic view of oneself. By turning the Platonic parts of the soul into conversational partners for one another, Freud did for the variety of inter-pretations of each person's past what the Baconian approach to science and philosophy did for the variety of descriptions of the universe as a whole. He let us see alternative narratives and alternative vocabularies as instruments for change, rather than as candidates for a correct depiction of how things are in themselves.

Much of what I have been saying is summarized in Freud's remark, "If one considers chance to be unworthy of determining our fate, it is simply a relapse into the pious view of the Universe which Leonardo himself was on the way to overcoming when he wrote that the sun does not move" (S.E. 11:137).[14] This recommendation that we see chance as "not unworthy of determining our fate" has as a corollary that we see ourselves as having the beliefs and emotions we do, including our (putatively) "specifically moral" beliefs and emotions, because of some very particular, idiosyncratic things that have happened in the history of the race, and to ourselves in the course of growing up. Such a recognition produces the ability to be Baconian about oneself. It lets one see oneself as a Rube Goldberg machine that requires much tinkering, rather than as a substance with a precious essence to be discovered and cherished. It produces what Whitehead called "the virtues which Odysseus shares with the foxes" – rather than, for example, those

---

13 Ibid., p. 57.

14 It is interesting that in the passage cited Freud is referring back to a passage (S.E. 11:76) where he credits Leonardo not only with anticipating Copernicus but with having "divined the history of the stratification and fossilization in the Arno valley," a suggestion that Leonardo anticipated Lyell (and so, in a way, Darwin) as well.

which Achilles shares with the lions, or those which Plato and Aristotle hoped to share with the gods.

From this Baconian angle, the point of psychoanalysis is the same as that of reflection on the sort of character one would like to have, once one ceases to take a single vocabulary for granted and begins the attempt to revise and enlarge the very vocabulary in which one is at present reflecting. The point of both exercises is to find new self-descriptions whose adoption will enable one to alter one's behavior. Finding out the views of one's unconscious about one's past is a way of getting some additional suggestions about how to describe (and change) oneself in the future. As a way of getting such suggestions, psychoanalysis differs from reading history, novels, or treatises on moral philosophy only in being more painful, in being more likely to produce radical change, and in requiring a partner.

Purification and self-enlargement

Because morality is associated both with human solidarity and with tragedy, my claim that attention to personal idiosyncrasy "remoralizes" a mechanistic self may seem paradoxical. One might protest, in the spirit of Kant, that the whole point of morality is self-forgetfulness, not making an exception of oneself, seeing oneself as counting for no more than any other human being, being motivated by what is common to all humanity. To emphasize idiosyncrasy is to emphasize the comic variety of human life rather than the tragedies that morality hopes to avert.

The appearance of paradox results from the fact that "morality" can mean either the attempt to be just in one's treatment of others or the search for perfection in oneself. The former is public morality, codifiable in statutes and maxims. The latter is private morality, the development of character. Like Freud, I am concerned only with the latter. Morality as the search for justice swings free of religion, science, metaphysics, and psychology. It is the relatively simple and obvious side of morality — the part that nowadays, in the wake of Freud, is often referred to as "culture" or "repression." This is the side of morality that instructs us to tell the truth, avoid violence, eschew sex with near relations, keep our promises, and abide by the Golden Rule.

The story of progress in public morality is largely irrelevant to the story of the mechanization of the world view.[15] Galileo, Darwin, and Freud did little to help or hinder such progress. They have nothing to say in answer either to the Athenian question "Does justice pay?" or to the Californian question "How much

15   The Enlightenment attempt to connect the two by seeing both feudalism and Aristotelian science as instances of "prejudice and superstition" was a self-deceptive neo-Aristotelian attempt to preserve the idea of man as an animal whose essence is rationality, while simultaneously identifying rationality with certain newly created institutions.

repression need I endure?" Freud, in particular, has no contribution to make to social theory. His domain is the portion of morality that cannot be identified with "culture"; it is the private life, the search for a character, the attempt of individuals to be reconciled with themselves (and, in the case of some exceptional individuals, to make their lives works of art).[16]

Such an attempt can take one of two antithetical forms: a search for purity or a search for self-enlargement. The ascetic life commended by Plato and criticized by Nietzsche is the paradigm of the former. The "aesthetic" life criticized by Kierkegaard is the paradigm of the latter. The desire to purify oneself is the desire to slim down, to peel away everything that is accidental, to will one thing, to intensify, to become a simpler and more transparent being. The desire to enlarge oneself is the desire to embrace more and more possibilities, to be constantly learning, to give oneself over entirely to curiosity, to end by having envisaged all the possibilities of the past and of the future. It was the goal shared by, for example, de Sade, Byron, and Hegel.[17] On the view I am presenting, Freud is an apostle of this aesthetic life, the life of unending curiosity, the life that seeks to extend its own bounds rather than to find its center.

For those who decline the options offered by de Sade and Byron (sexual experimentation, political engagement), the principal technique of self-enlargement will be Hegel's: the enrichment of language. One will see the history of both the race and oneself as the development of richer, fuller ways of formulating one's desires and hopes, and thus making those desires and hopes themselves – and thereby oneself – richer and fuller. I shall call such a development the "acquisition of new vocabularies of moral reflection." By "a vocabulary of moral reflection" I mean a set of terms in which one compares oneself to other human beings. Such vocabularies contain terms like magnanimous, a true Christian, decent, cowardly, God-fearing, hypocritical, self-deceptive, epicene, self-destructive, cold, an antique Roman, a saint, a Julien Sorel, a Becky Sharpe, a red-blooded American, a shy gazelle, a hyena, depressive, a Bloomsbury type, a man of respect, a grande dame. Such terms are possible answers to the question "What is he or she like?" and thus possible answers to the question "What am *I* like?" By summing up patterns of behavior, they are tools for criticizing the character of

16 Here I am agreeing with Rieff against, for example, Fromm and Marcuse: "Psychoanalysis is the doctrine of the private man defending himself against public encroachment. He cultivates the private life and its pleasures, and if he does take part in public affairs it is for consciously private motives" (Rieff, *The Mind of the Moralist*, p. 278). Rieff seems to me right in saying that Freud had little to say about how and whether society might be made "less repressive": "Like those who worked for shorter hours but nevertheless feared what men might do with their leisure, Freud would have welcomed more constructive releases from our stale moralities, but did not propose to substitute a new one. Our private ethics were his scientific problem: he had no new public ethics to suggest, no grand design for the puzzle of our common life" (ibid., p. 38).

17 See Hans Blumenberg's discussion of "theoretical curiosity," and especially his contrast between the medieval criticism of curiosity and Bacon's praise of it, in *The Legitimacy of the Modern Age*, trans. Robert Wallace (Cambridge: MIT Press, 1983).

others and for creating one's own. They are the terms one uses when one tries to resolve moral dilemmas by asking "What sort of person would I be if I did this?"

This question is, of course, not the only question one asks when reflecting about what to do. One also asks, for example, "How would I justify myself to so-and-so?" and "Would this action violate the general rule that . . . ?" But answers to these questions will reflect the vocabulary of moral reflection at one's disposal. That vocabulary helps one decide to which sort of people to justify oneself. It puts some flesh on abstract rules like the categorical imperative and "Maximize human happiness!" It is distinctions between such vocabularies, rather than between general principles, that differentiate the moralities of communities, historical epochs, and epochs in the life of the curious intellectual. The availability of a richer vocabulary of moral deliberation is what one chiefly has in mind when one says that we are, morally speaking, more sensitive and sophisticated than our ancestors or than our younger selves.

Much could be said about how the addition of specifically psychoanalytic concepts to religious and philosophical concepts (and to the invocation of historical and literary archetypes) has influenced contemporary patterns of moral deliberation.[18] My theme, however, is different. I want to focus on the way in which Freud, by helping us see ourselves as centerless, as random assemblages of contingent and idiosyncratic needs rather than as more or less adequate exemplifications of a common human essence, opened up new possibilities for the aesthetic life. He helped us become increasingly ironic, playful, free, and inventive in our choice of self-descriptions. This has been an important factor in our ability to slough off the idea that we have a true self, one shared with all other humans, and the related notion that the demands of this true self — the specifically moral demands — take precedence over all others. It has helped us think of moral reflection and sophistication as a matter of self-creation rather than self-knowledge. Freud made the paradigm of self-knowledge the discovery of the fortuitous materials out of which we must construct ourselves rather than the discovery of the principles to which we must conform. He thus made the desire for purification seem more self-deceptive, and the quest for self-enlargement more promising.

By contrast, the history of modern philosophy has centered on attempts to preserve an enclave of nonmechanism, and thus to keep alive the notion of a "true self" and the plausibility of a morality of self-purification. Descartes was willing to follow Galileo in dissolving all the Aristotelian natural kinds into so many vortices of corpuscles, with one exception. He wanted the mind to remain exempt from this dissolution. The mind and its faculties (notably intellect, conceived of as immediate, nondiscursive grasp of truth) were to remain as Platonism and Christianity had conceived of them. This enclave of nonmechanism that Descartes

18 See, for example, Adam Morton, "Freudian Commonsense," in *Philosophical Essays on Freud* (cited above in n. 9). I think that Morton asks just the right questions, although I have doubts about the character–personality distinction that he draws.

claimed to have descried became the preserve of a subject called "metaphysics."[19] Kant recognized the ad hoc and factitious character of this Cartesian attempt to keep the world safe for nonmechanism, and so he developed a different, more drastic, strategy to achieve the same end. He was willing to put mind and matter on a par, and to follow Hume in dissolving what he called "the empirical self" into predictable associations of mental atoms. But he distinguished that self from the true self, the moral self, the part of the self that was an agent, rather than a subject of scientific inquiry.

This still smaller and more mysterious enclave of nonmechanism became the preserve of a subject called "moral philosophy." Kant tried to make morality a nonempirical matter, something that would never again have anything to fear from religion, science, or the arts, nor have anything to learn from them.[20] For, Kant explained, the reason why the New Science had described a world with no moral lesson, a world without a moral point, was that it described a world of appearance. By contrast, the true world was a world that was, so to speak, nothing but point: nothing but a moral imperative, nothing but a call to moral purity.

One result of Kant's initiative was to impoverish the vocabulary of moral philosophy and to turn the enrichment of our vocabulary of moral reflection over to novelists, poets, and dramatists.[21] The nineteenth-century novel, in particular, filled a vacuum left by the retreat of one-half of moral philosophy into idealist metaphysics and the advance of the other half into politics.[22] Another result was

19 Consider Leibniz's novel and influential use of the terms *physics* and *metaphysics* to name the study of mechanism and of nonmechanism, respectively – to distinguish between the area in which Newton was right and the area in which Aristotle and the scholastics had been right.

20 As J. B. Schneewind has pointed out to me, this remark is accurate only for Kant's early thinking on morality. Later in his life the purity and isolation claimed for morality in the *Grundlagen* became compromised in various ways. It was, however, the early writings on morality that became associated with Kant's name, and that his successors were concerned to criticize.

21 See Iris Murdoch, *The Sovereignty of Good* (New York: Schocken Books, 1971), p. 58: "It is a shortcoming of much contemporary moral philosophy that it eschews discussion of the separate virtues, preferring to proceed directly to some sovereign concept such as sincerity, or authenticity, or freedom, thereby imposing, it seems to me, an unexamined and empty idea of unity, and impoverishing our moral language in an important area." Murdoch's claim that "the most essential and fundamental aspect of our culture is the study of literature, since this is an education in how to picture and understand human situations" (p. 34) would have meant something different two hundred years ago. For then the term *literature* covered Hume's *Enquiries* and his *History* as well as novels, plays, and poems. Our modern contrast between literature and moral philosophy is one result of the development that Murdock describes: "Philosophy . . . has been busy dismantling the old substantial picture of the 'self,' and ethics has not proved itself able to rethink this concept for moral purposes. . . . Moral philosophy, and indeed morals, are thus undefended against an irresponsible and undirected self-assertion which goes easily hand-in-hand with some brand of pseudo-scientific determinism. An unexamined sense of the strength of the machine is combined with an illusion of leaping out of it. The younger Sartre, and many British moral philosophers, represent this last dry distilment of Kant's view of the world" (pp. 47–48).

22 The latter phenomenon is exemplified by, for example, Bentham and Marx – philosophers who have been responsible for much good in the public sphere but who are useless as advisers on the development of one's moral character.

what Alasdair MacIntyre calls the invention of "the individual" – a moral self who existed "prior to and apart from all roles,"[23] who was independent of any social or historical context. To say that the moral self exists apart from all roles means that it will remain the same no matter what situation it finds itself in, no matter what language it uses to create its self-image, no matter what its vocabulary of moral deliberation may be. That, in turn, means that the moral self has no need to work out a sensitive and sophisticated vocabulary as an instrument to create its character. For the only character that matters is the one it already has. Once it began to seem (as it did to Kant) that we had always known a priori all there was to know about the "morally relevant" portion of human beings, the Hegelian urge to enrich our vocabulary of moral reflection began to seem (as it did to Kierkegaard) a merely "aesthetic" demand, something that might amuse a leisured elite but which had no relevance to our moral responsibilities.[24]

This account of modern philosophy can be summarized by saying that when modern science made it hard to think of man as a natural kind, philosophy responded by inventing an unnatural kind. It was perhaps predictable that the sequence of descriptions of this self that begins with Descartes should end with Sartre: the self as a blank space in the middle of a machine – an être-pour-soi, a "hole in being." By contrast, Freud stands with Hegel against Kant, in an attitude of Nietzschean exuberance rather than Sartrean embarrassment. He offers us a way to reinvent the search for enlargement, and thereby reinvents the morality of character. I can summarize my account of how he does this in five points:

1. Whereas everybody from Plato to Kant had identified our central self, our conscience, the standard-setting, authoritative part of us, with universal truths, general principles, and a common human nature, Freud made conscience just one more, not particularly central, part of a larger, homogenous machine. He identified the sense of duty with the internalization of a host of idiosyncratic, accidental episodes. On his account our sense of moral obligation is not a matter of general ideas contemplated by the intellect, but rather of traces of encounters between particular people and our bodily organs. He saw the voice of conscience not as the voice of the part of the soul that deals with generalities as opposed to the part that deals with particulars, but rather as the (usually distorted) memory of certain very particular events.

2. This identification did not take the form of a reductive claim that morality was "nothing but . . ." delayed responses to forgotten stimuli. Since Freud was willing to view *every* part of life, every human activity, in the same terms, there was no contrast to be drawn between the "merely" mechanical and reactive

---

23 See the passage from MacIntyre quoted in note 4 above.

24 For a contemporary account of the contrast between the Kantian and the Hegelian attitudes, see Alan Donagan, *A Theory of Morality* (Chicago: University of Chicago Press, 1977), chap. 1, on "Hegel's doctrine of the emptiness of the moral point of view" (p. 10).

character of moral experience and the free and spontaneous character of something else (e.g., science, art, philosophy or psychoanalytic theory).

3. Nor did this identification of conscience with memory of idiosyncratic events take the form of the claim that talk about such events was a ("scientific") substitute for moral deliberation. Freud did not suggest that we would see ourselves more clearly, or choose more wisely, by restricting our vocabulary of moral reflection to psychoanalytic terms. On the contrary, Freud dropped the Platonic metaphor of "seeing ourselves more clearly" in favor of the Baconian idea of theory as a tool for bringing about desirable change.[25] He was far from thinking that psychoanalytic theory was the *only* tool needed for self-enlargement.

4. This Baconian attitude was the culmination of the mechanizing movement that had begun in the seventeenth century. That movement had replaced the attempt to contemplate the essences of natural kinds with the attempt to tinker with the machines that compose the world. But not until Freud did we get a usable way of thinking of *ourselves* as machines to be tinkered with, a self-image that enabled us to weave terms describing psychic mechanisms into our strategies of character-formation.

5. The increased ability of the syncretic, ironic, nominalist intellectual to move back and forth between, for example, religious, moral, scientific, literary, philosophical, and psychoanalytical vocabularies without asking the question "And which of these shows us how things *really* are?" – the intellectual's increased ability to treat vocabularies as tools rather than mirrors – is Freud's major legacy. He broke some of the last chains that bind us to the Greek idea that we, or the world, have a nature that, once discovered, will tell us what we should do with ourselves. He made it far more difficult than it was before to ask the question "Which is my true self?" or "What is human nature?" By letting us see that even in the enclave which philosophy had fenced off, there was nothing to be found save traces of accidental encounters, he left us able to tolerate the ambiguities that the religious and philosophical traditions had hoped to eliminate.

"The Rich Aesthete, the Manager, and the Therapist"

My account of Freud as a Baconian has taken for granted that the move from Aristotelian to Baconian views of the nature of knowledge, like that from an ethics of purity to one of self-enrichment, was desirable. My enthusiasm for the mechanization and decentering of the world is dictated by my assumption that the ironic, playful intellectual is a desirable character-type, and that Freud's

25 Rieff makes this contrast between Platonic and Baconian attitudes, saying that the latter, the "second theory of theory," views theory as "arming us with the weapons for transforming reality instead of forcing us to conform to it. . . . Psychoanalytic theory belongs to the second tradition" (*Triumph of the Therapeutic*, pp. 55–56). This view of Freud's aim is central to my account of his achievement, and I am much indebted to Rieff's work.

importance lies in his contribution to the formation of such a character. These assumptions are challenged by those who see the mechanization of nature as a prelude to barbarism. Such critics emphasize, as I have, the link between a pragmatic, tinkering approach to nature and the self, and the aesthetic search for novel experiences and novel language. But they condemn both.

The most thoroughly thought-out, if most abstract, account of the relation between technology and aestheticism is offered by Heidegger.[26] But the more concrete criticisms of modern ways of thinking offered by Alasdair MacIntyre in *After Virtue* are more immediately relevant to the topics I have been discussing. MacIntyre would agree, more or less, with my description of the connections between Baconian ways of thought and Nietzschean values. But he takes the fact that the paradigmatic character-types of modernity are "the Rich Aesthete, the Manager, and the Therapist" (p. 29) to show that these ways of thought, and these values, are undesirable. In MacIntyre's view, the abandonment of an Aristotelian "functional concept of man" leads to "emotivism" — the obliteration of any genuine distinction between manipulative and non-manipulative social relations" (p. 22).

MacIntyre is, I think, right in saying that contemporary moral discourse is a confusing and inconsistent blend of notions that make sense only in an Aristotelian view of the world (e.g., "reason," "human nature," "natural rights") with mechanistic, anti-Aristotelian notions that implicitly repudiate such a view. But whereas MacIntyre thinks we need to bring back Aristotelian ways of thinking to make our moral discourse coherent, I think we should do the opposite and make the discourse coherent by discarding the last vestiges of those ways of thinking.[27] I would welcome a culture dominated by "the Rich Aesthete, the Manager, and the Therapist" so long as *everybody* who wants to gets to be an aesthete (and, if not rich, as comfortably off as most — as rich as the Managers can manage, guided by Rawls's Difference Principle).

Further, I think that we can live with the Freudian thought that everything everybody does to everyone else (even those they love blindly and helplessly) can be described, for therapeutic or other purposes, as manipulation. The postulation of

26 See Heidegger's essays "The Question Concerning Technology" and "The Age of the World View" in *The Question Concerning Technology and Other Essays*, trans. W. Lovitt (New York: Harper and Row, 1977). I suggest a Deweyan response to Heidegger's view of technology at the end of "Heidegger, Contingency, and Pragmatism," above. MacIntyre would join me in repudiating Heidegger's attack on technology but would retain Heidegger's account of the shift in moral consciousness that followed upon the abandonment of an Aristotelian world view.

27 It is tempting to say that I would accept MacIntyre's claim that the only real choice is between Aristotle and Nietzsche, and then side with Nietzsche. But the choice is too dramatic and too simple. By the time MacIntyre gets rid of the nonsense in Aristotle (e.g., what he calls the "metaphysical biology"), Aristotle does not look much like himself. By the time I would finish discarding the bits of Nietzsche I do not want (e.g., his lapses into metaphysical biology, his distrust of Hegel, his *ressentiment*, etc.) he would not look much like Nietzsche. The opposition between these two ideal types is useful only if one does not press it too hard.

unintrospectible systems of beliefs and desires ensures that there will be a coherent and informative narrative to be told in those terms, one that will interpret all personal and social relations, even the tenderest and most sacred, in terms of "making use of" others. Once those extra persons who explain akrasia and other forms of irrationality are taken into account, there are, so to speak, too many selves for "selflessness" to seem a useful notion. But the increased ability to explain, given by Freud's postulation of additional persons, hardly prevents us from drawing the common-sense distinction between manipulating people (i.e., consciously, and deceptively, employing them as instruments for one's own purposes) and not manipulating them. The availability of a description for explanatory purposes does not entail its use in moral reflection, any more than it precludes it.

MacIntyre construes "emotivism" as the only option left, once one abandons the Aristotelian idea of man, because he retains a pre-Freudian[28] division of human faculties. In terms of this division, "desire" or "will" or "passion" represents the only alternative to "reason" (construed as a faculty of seeing things as they are in themselves). But dividing people up this way begs the question against other ways of describing them — for example, Freud's way. Freud (at least according to the Davidsonian interpretation I have developed here) drops the whole idea of "faculties," and substitutes the notion of a plurality of sets of beliefs and desires. MacIntyre's definition of "emotivism" ("the doctrine that all evaluative judgments and more specifically all moral judgments are *nothing but* expressions of preference, expressions of attitude or feeling" [p. 11]) makes sense only if there is something else such judgments might have been — for example, expressions of a correct "rational" grasp of the nature of the human being.

Moral psychology, like moral discourse, is at present an incoherent blend of Aristotelian and mechanist ways of speaking. I would urge that if we eradicate the former, "emotivism" will no longer be an intelligible position. More generally, if we take Freud to heart, we shall not have to choose between an Aristotelian "functional" concept of humanity, one that will provide moral guidance, and Sartrean "dreadful freedom." For the Sartrean conception of the self as pure freedom will be seen as merely the last gasp of the Aristotelian tradition — a self-erasing expression of the Cartesian determination to find *something* nonmechanical at the center of the machine, if only a "hole in being."[29] We shall not need a picture of "the human self" in order to have morality — neither of a nonmechanical enclave nor of a meaningless void where such an enclave ought to have been.

It seems a point in my favor that MacIntyre does not answer the question of whether it is "rationally justifiable [*pace* Sartre] to conceive of each human life as a

---

28 Or, more generally, premechanist (and thus pre-Humean: see note 10 on Hume and faculty psychology).

29 Metaphysicians like Sartre would, to paraphrase Nietzsche, rather have a metaphysics of nothingness than no metaphysics. This was a trap around which Heidegger circled in his early work but eventually walked away from, leaving Sartre to take the plunge.

unity" (p. 189) by saying (with Aristotle) "yes, because the function of man is. . . ." Rather, he offers us "a concept of a self whose unity resides in the unity of a narrative which links birth to life to death as narrative beginning to middle to end" (p. 191).[30] MacIntyre tacitly drops the Aristotelian demand that the themes of each such narrative be roughly the same for each member of a given species, and that they stay roughly constant throughout the history of the species. He seems content to urge that in order for us to exhibit the virtue of "integrity or constancy" we must see our lives in such narrative terms. To attempt that virtue is just what I have been calling "the search for perfection," and I agree that this search requires the construction of such narratives. But if we do drop the Aristotelian demand, contenting ourselves with narratives tailored ad hoc to the contingencies of individual lives, then we may welcome a Baconian culture dominated by "the Rich Aesthete, the Manager, and the Therapist" — not necessarily as the final goal of human progress, but at least as a considerable improvement on cultures dominated by, for example, the Warrior or the Priest.

On my account of Freud, his work enables us to construct richer and more plausible narratives of this ad hoc sort — more plausible because they will cover *all* the actions one performs in the course of one's life, even the silly, cruel, and self-destructive actions. More generally, Freud helped us see that the attempt to put together such a narrative — one that minimizes neither the contingency nor the decisive importance of the input into the machine that each of us is — must take the place of an attempt to find the function common to all such machines. If one takes Freud's advice, one finds psychological narratives without heroes or heroines. For neither Sartrean freedom, nor the will, nor the instincts, nor an internalization of a culture, nor anything else will play the role of "the true self." Instead, one tells the story of the whole machine *as* machine, without choosing a particular set of springs and wheels as protagonist. Such a story can help us, if anything can, stop the pendulum from swinging between Aristotelian attempts to discover our essence and Sartrean attempts at self-creation *de novo*.

This suggestion that our stories about ourselves must be stories of centerless mechanisms — of the determined processing of contingent input — will seem to

30 There seems to be a tension in MacIntyre's *After Virtue* between the early chapters, in which it is suggested that unless we can identify a telos common to all members of our species we are driven to the "emotivist" view that "all moral judgments are *nothing but* expressions of preference" (p. 11), and chapters 14–15. In the latter chapters, which MacIntyre thinks of as a rehabilitation of Aristotelianism (see p. 239), nothing is done to defeat the suggestion that all moral judgments are nothing but choices among competing narratives, a suggestion that is compatible with the three paradigmatically Aristotelian doctrines that MacIntyre lists on pp. 183–186 of his book. By dropping what he calls "Aristotle's metaphysical biology" (p. 183), MacIntyre also drops the attempt to evaluate "the claims to objectivity and authority" of "the lost morality of the past" (p. 21). For unless a knowledge of the function of the human species takes us beyond MacIntyre's Socratic claim that "the good life for man is the life spent in seeking for the good life for man" (p. 204), the idea of one narrative being more "objective and authoritative" than another, as opposed to being more detailed and inclusive, goes by the board.

strip us of human dignity only if we think we need *reasons* to live romantically, or to treat others decently, or to be treated decently ourselves. Questions like "Why should I hope?" or "Why should I not use others as means?" or "Why should my torturers not use me as a means?" are questions that can *only* be answered by philosophical metanarratives that tell us about a nonmechanical world and a nonmechanical self — about a world and a self that have centers, centers that are sources of authority. Such questions are tailored to fit such answers. So if we renounce such answers, such metanarratives, and fall back on narratives about the actual and possible lives of individuals, we shall have to renounce the needs that metaphysics and moral philosophy attempted to satisfy. We shall have to confine ourselves to questions like, "If I do this rather than that now, what story will I tell myself later?" We shall have to abjure questions like, "Is there something deep inside my torturer — his rationality — to which I can appeal?"

The philosophical tradition suggests that there is, indeed, something of this sort. It tends to take for granted that our dignity depends on the existence of something that can be opposed to "arbitrary will." This thing, usually called "reason," is needed to give "authority" to the first premises of our practical syllogisms. Such a view of human dignity is precisely what Freud called "the pious view of the Universe." He thought that the traditional oppositions between reason, will, and emotion — the oppositions in terms of which MacIntyre constructs his history of ethics — should be discarded in favor of distinctions between various regions of a homogenous mechanism, regions that embody a plurality of persons (that is, of incompatible systems of belief and desire). So the only version of human dignity that Freud lets us preserve is the one MacIntyre himself offers: the ability of each of us to tailor a coherent self-image for ourselves and then use it to tinker with our behavior. This ability replaces the traditional philosophical project of finding a coherent self-image that will fit the entire species to which we belong.

Given this revisionary account of human dignity, what becomes of human solidarity? In my view, Freud does nothing for either liberal or radical politics, except perhaps to supply new terms of opprobrium with which to stigmatize tyrants and torturers.[31] On the contrary, he diminishes our ability to take seriously much of the traditional jargon of both liberalism and radicalism — notions such as "human rights" and "autonomy" and slogans such as "man will prevail" and "trust the instincts of the masses." For these notions and slogans are bound up with Aristotelian attempts to find a center for the self.

31 But diagnoses of the Freudian mechanisms that produce suitable candidates for the KGB and the Gestapo, of the sort made popular by Adorno and others who talk about "authoritarian personalities," add little to the familiar pre-Freudian suggestion that we might have fewer bully boys to cope with if people had more education, leisure, and money. The Adorno-Horkheimer suggestion that the rise of Nazism within a highly developed and cultivated nation shows that this familiar liberal solution is inadequate seems to me unconvincing. At any rate, it seems safe to say that Freudo-Marxist analyses of "authoritarianism" have offered no better suggestions about how to keep the thugs from taking over.

On the other hand, Freud does nothing to diminish a sense of human solidarity that, rather than encompassing the entire species, restricts itself to such particular communal movements as modern science, bourgeois liberalism, or the European novel. If we avoid describing these movements in terms of metaphysical notions like "the search for truth," or "the realization of human freedom," or "the attainment of self-consciousness," histories of them will nevertheless remain available as larger narratives within which to place the narratives of our individual lives. Freud banishes philosophical metanarratives, but he has nothing against ordinary historical narratives. Such narratives tell, for example, how we got from Galileo to Gell-Man, or from institutions that defended merchants against feudal overlords to institutions that defend labor against capital, or from *Don Quixote* to *Pale Fire*.

Letting us see the narratives of our own lives as episodes within such larger historical narratives is, I think, as much as the intellectuals are able to do in aid of morality. The attempt of religion and metaphysics to do more – to supply a backup for moral intuitions by providing them with ahistorical "authority" – will always be self-defeating. For (given the present rate of social change) another century's worth of history will always make the last century's attempt to be ahistorical look ridiculous. The only result of such attempts is to keep the pendulum swinging between moral dogmatism and moral skepticism.[32] What metaphysics could not do, psychology, even very "deep" psychology, is not going to do either; we pick up Freud by the wrong handle if we try to find an account of "moral motivation" that is more than a reference to the historical contingencies that shaped the process of acculturation in our region and epoch.

Historical narratives about social and intellectual movements are the best tools to use in tinkering with ourselves, for such narratives suggest vocabularies of moral deliberation in which to spin coherent narratives about our individual lives. By contrast, the vocabulary Freud himself used in much of his writing – an individualist, Stoic vocabulary, charged with ironic resignation – does little for the latter purpose. It has too much in common with the vocabulary of the self-erasing narratives of Rameau's nephew, Dostoevsky's "Underground Man," and Sartre's Roquentin: stories about machines chewing themselves to pieces. By contrast, narratives that help one identify oneself with communal movements engender a sense of being a machine geared into a larger machine. This is a sense worth having. For it helps reconcile an existentialist sense of contingency and mortality with a Romantic sense of grandeur. It helps us realize that the best way of tinkering with ourselves is to tinker with something else – a mechanist way of saying that only he who loses his soul will save it.[33]

32 For a discussion of the causes and effects of such pendulum swings, see Annette Baier, "Doing without Moral Theory?," in her *Postures of the Mind* (Minneapolis: University of Minnesota Press, 1985).

33 This paper owes a great deal to the comments of J. B. Schneewind, Alexander Nehamas, and the late Irvin Ehrenpreis on a draft version.

Habermas and Lyotard on postmodernity

In *Knowledge and Human Interests* Habermas tried to generalize what Marx and Freud had accomplished by grounding their projects of "unmasking" in a more comprehensive theory. The strand in contemporary French thought which Habermas has frequently criticized in recent years starts off from suspicion of Marx and Freud, suspicion of the masters of suspicion, suspicion of "unmasking." Lyotard, for example, says that he will

use the term "modern" to designate any science that legitimates itself with reference to a metadiscourse of this kind [i.e., "a discourse of legitimation with respect to its own status, a discourse called philosophy"] making an explicit appeal to some grand narrative, such as the dialectics of the Spirit, the hermeneutics of meaning, the emancipation of the rational or working subject, or the creation of wealth.[1]

He goes on to define "postmodern" as "incredulity towards metanarratives," and to ask "Where, after the metanarratives, can legitimacy reside?"[2] From Lyotard's point of view, Habermas is offering one more metanarrative, a more general and abstract "narrative of emancipation"[3] than the Freudian and Marxian metanarratives.

For Habermas, the problem posed by "incredulity towards metanarratives" is that unmasking only makes sense if we "preserve at least one standard for [the] explanation of the corruption of *all* reasonable standards."[4] If we have no such standard, one which escapes a "totalizing self-referential critique," then distinctions between the naked and the masked, or between theory and ideology, lose their force. If we do not have these distinctions, then we have to give up the Enlightenment notion of "rational criticism of existing institutions," for "rational" drops out. We can still, of course, have criticism, but it will be of the sort which Habermas ascribes to Horkheimer and Adorno: "they abandoned any theoretical approach and practiced ad hoc determinate negation. . . . The praxis of negation is what remains of the 'spirit of . . . unremitting theory'."[5] Anything that Habermas will count as retaining a "theoretical approach" will be counted by

1 Jean-François Lyotard, *The Postmodern Condition: A Report on Knowledge,* trans. Geoff Bennington and Brian Massumi (Minneapolis: University of Minnesota Press, 1984), p. xxiii.
2 Ibid., pp. xxiv–xxv.
3 Ibid., p. 60.
4 Jürgen Habermas, "The Entwinement of Myth and Enlightenment: Re-reading *Dialectic of Enlightenment,*" *New German Critique* 26 (1982):28.
5 Ibid., p. 29.

an incredulous Lyotard as a "metanarrative." Anything that abandons such an approach will be counted by Habermas as more or less irrationalist because it drops the notions which have been used to justify the various reforms which have marked the history of the Western democracies since the Enlightenment, and which are still being used to criticize the socioeconomic institutions of both the Free and the Communist worlds. Abandoning a standpoint which is, if not transcendental, at least "universalistic," seems to Habermas to betray the social hopes which have been central to liberal politics.

So we find French critics of Habermas ready to abandon liberal politics in order to avoid universalistic philosophy, and Habermas trying to hang on to universalistic philosophy, with all its problems, in order to support liberal politics. To put the opposition in another way, the French writers whom Habermas criticizes are willing to drop the opposition between "true consensus" and "false consensus," or between "validity" and "power," in order not to have to tell a metanarrative in order to explicate "true" or "valid." But Habermas thinks that if we drop the idea of "the better argument" as opposed to "the argument which convinces a given audience at a given time," we shall have only a "context-dependent" sort of social criticism. He thinks that falling back on such criticism will betray "the elements of reason in cultural modernity which are contained in . . . bourgeois ideals," e.g., "the internal theoretical dynamic which constantly propels the sciences – and the self-reflexion of the sciences as well – *beyond* the creation of merely technologically explitable knowledge."[6]

Lyotard would respond to this last point by saying that Habermas misunderstands the character of modern science. The discussion of "the pragmatics of science" in *The Postmodern Condition* is intended to "destroy a belief that still underlies Habermas's research, namely that humanity as a collective (universal) subject seeks its common emancipation through the regularization of the 'moves' permitted in all language games, and that the legitimacy of any statement resides in its contribution to that emancipation." Lyotard claims to have shown that "consensus is only a particular state of discussion [in the sciences], not its end. Its end, on the contrary, is paralogy."[7] Part of his argument for this odd suggestion is that "Postmodern science – by concerning itself with such things as undecidables, the limits of precise control, conflicts characterized by incomplete information, '*fracta*', catastrophes, and pragmatic paradoxes – is theorizing its own evolution as discontinuous, catastrophic, non-rectifiable and paradoxical."[8]

I do not think that such examples of matters of current scientific concern do anything to support the claim that "consensus is not the end of discussion." Lyotard argues invalidly from the current concerns of various scientific disciplines to the claim that science is somehow discovering that it should aim at permanent

6 Ibid., p. 18.
7 Lyotard, *Postmodern Condition*, pp. 65–66.
8 Ibid., p. 60.

revolution, rather than at the alternation between normality and revolution made familiar by Kuhn. To say that "science aims" at piling paralogy on paralogy is like saying that "politics aims" at piling revolution on revolution. No inspection of the concerns of contemporary science or contemporary politics could show anything of the sort. The most that could be shown is that talk of the aims of either is not particularly useful.

On the other hand, Lyotard does have a point, the point he shares with Mary Hesse's criticism of Habermas's Diltheyan account of the distinction between natural science and hermeneutic inquiry. Hesse thinks that "it has been sufficiently demonstrated [by what she calls 'post-empiricist' Anglo-American philosophy of science] that the language of theoretical science is irreducibly metaphorical and unformalizable, and that the logic of science is circular interpretation, reinterpretation, and self-correction of data in terms of theory, theory in terms of data."[9] This kind of debunking of empiricist philosophy of science is happily appropriated by Lyotard. Unfortunately, however, he does not think of it as a repudiation of a bad account of science but as indicating a recent change in the nature of science. He thinks that science used to be what empiricism described it as being. This lets him accuse Habermas of not being up to date.

If one ignores this notion of a recent change in the nature of science (which Lyotard makes only casual and anecdotal attempts to justify), and focuses instead on Lyotard's contrast between "scientific knowledge" and "narrative," this turns out to be pretty much the traditional positivist contrast between "applying the scientific method" and "unscientific" political or religious or commonsensical discourse. Thus Lyotard says that a "scientific statement is subject to the rule that a statement must fulfill a given set of conditions in order to be accepted as scientific."[10] He contrasts this with "narrative knowledge" as the sort which "does not give priority to the question of its own legitimation, and . . . certifies itself in the pragmatics of its own transmission without having recourse to argumentation and proof." He describes "the scientist" as classifying narrative knowledge as "a different mentality: savage, primitive, under-developed, backward, alienated, composed of opinions, customs, authority, prejudice, ignorance, ideology."[11] Lyotard, like Hesse, wants to soften this contrast and to assert the rights of "narrative knowledge." In particular, he wants to answer his initial question by saying that once we get rid of the *meta*narratives, legitimacy resides where it always has, in the first-order narratives:

There is, then, an incommensurability between popular narrative pragmatics, which provides immediate legitimation, and the language game known as the question of legitimacy. . . . Narratives . . . determine criteria of competence and/or illustrate how they are

9   Mary Hesse, *Revolutions and Reconstructions in the Philosophy of Science* (Bloomington, Ind.: Indiana University Press, 1980), p. 173.
10 Lyotard, *Postmodern Condition*, p. 8.
11 Ibid., p. 27.

to be applied. They thus define what has the right to be said and done in the culture in question, and since they are themselves a part of that culture, they are legitimated by the simple fact that they do what they do.[12]

This last quotation suggests that we read Lyotard as saying: the trouble with Habermas is not so much that he provides a metanarrative of emancipation as that he feels the need to legitimize, that he is not content to let the narratives which hold our culture together do their stuff. He is scratching where it does not itch. On this reading, Lyotard's criticism would chime with the Hesse-Feyerabend line of criticism of empiricist philosophy of science, and in particular with Feyerabend's attempt to see scientific and political discourse as continuous. It would also chime with the criticisms offered by many of Habermas's sympathetic American critics, such as Bernstein, Geuss, and McCarthy. These critics doubt that studies of communicative competence can do what transcendental philosophy failed to do in the way of providing "universalistic" criteria.[13] They also doubt that universalism is as vital to the needs of liberal social thought as Habermas thinks it. Thus Geuss, arguing that the notion of an "ideal speech situation" is a wheel which plays no part in the mechanism of social criticism, and suggesting that we reintroduce a position "closer to Adorno's historicism," says:

If rational argumentation can lead to the conclusion that a critical theory [defined as "the 'self-consciousness' of a successful process of emancipation and enlightenment"] represents the most advanced position of consciousness available to us in our given historical situation, why the obsession with whether or not we may call it 'true'?[14]

Presumably by "rational argumentation" Geuss means not "rational by reference to an extra-historical, universalistic set of criteria" but something like "uncoerced except in the ways in which all discourse everywhere is inevitably coerced – by being conducted in the terms and according to the practices of a given community at a given time." He is dubious that we need a theoretical account which gets behind that vocabulary and those conventions to something "natural" by reference to which they can be criticized. As Geuss says, the "nightmare which haunts the Frankfurt School" is something like Huxley's Brave New World, in which

agents are actually content, but only because they have been prevented from developing certain desires which in the 'normal' course of things they would have developed, and which cannot be satisfied within the framework of the present social order.[15]

12   Ibid., p. 23.
13   See, for example, Thomas McCarthy, "Rationality and Relativism: Habermas's 'Overcoming' of Hermeneutics," in Habermas: Critical Debates, ed. John B. Thompson and David Held (London, 1982).
14   Raymond Geuss, The Idea of a Critical Theory: Habermas and the Frankfurt School (Cambridge, Mass.: MIT Press, 1982), p. 94.
15   Ibid., p. 83.

To take the scare-quotes out from around "normal," one would have to have just the sort of metanarrative which Lyotard thinks we cannot get. But we think we need this only because an overzealous philosophy of science has created an impossible ideal of ahistorical legitimation.

The picture of social progress which Geuss's more historical line of thought offers is of theory as emerging at dusk, the belated "self-consciousness" of emancipation rather than a condition for producing it. It thus has links with the antirationalist tradition of Burke and Oakeshott, as well as with Deweyan pragmatism. It departs from the notion that the intellectuals can form a revolutionary vanguard, a notion cherished even by French writers who claim to have dispensed with Marx's metanarrative. On this account of social change, there is no way for the citizens of *Brave New World* to work their way out from their happy slavery by theory, and, in particular, by studies of communicative competence. For the narratives which go to make up their sense of what counts as "rational" will see to it that such studies produce a conception of undistorted communication which accords with the desires they presently have. There is no way for us to prove to ourselves that we are not happy slaves of this sort, any more than to prove that our life is not a dream. So whereas Habermas compliments "bourgeois ideals" by reference to the "elements of reason" contained in them, it would be better just to compliment those untheoretical sorts of narrative discourse which make up the political speech of the Western democracies. It would be better to be frankly ethnocentric.

If one is ethnocentric in this sense, one will see what Habermas calls "the internal theoretical dynamic which constantly propels the sciences . . . beyond the creation of technologically exploitable knowledge" not as a *theoretical* dynamic, but as a social practice. One will see the fact that modern science is more than engineering not as the result of an ahistorical teleology – e.g., an evolutionary drive towards correspondence with reality, or the nature of language – but merely as a particularly good example of the social virtues of the European bourgeoisie, of the increasing self-confidence of a community dedicated to (in Blumenberg's phrase) "theoretical curiosity." Modern science will look like something which a certain group of human beings invented, in the same sense in which these same people can be said to have invented Protestantism, parliamentary government, and Romantic poetry. What Habermas calls the "self-reflection of the sciences" will thus consist not in the attempt to "ground" scientists' practices (e.g., free exchange of information, normal problem-solving, and revolutionary paradigm-creation) in something larger or broader, but rather of attempts to show how these practices link up with, or contrast with, other practices of the same group or of other groups. When such attempts have a critical function, they will take the form of what Habermas calls "ad hoc determinate negation."

Habermas thinks that we need not be restricted, as Horkheimer and Adorno were, to such merely socio-historical forms of social criticism. He views

Horkheimer, Adorno, Heidegger, and Foucault as working out new versions of "the end of philosophy":

no matter what name it [philosophy] appears under now – whether as fundamental ontol-ogy, as critique, as negative dialectic, or genealogy – these pseudonyms are by no means disguises under which the traditional [i.e., Hegelian] form of philosophy lies hidden; the drapery of philosophical concepts more likely serves as the cloak for a scantily concealed end of philosophy.[16]

Habermas's account of such "end of philosophy" movements is offered as part of a more sweeping history of philosophy since Kant. He thinks that Kant was right to split high culture up into science, morality, and art and that Hegel was right in accepting this as "the standard (*massgeblich*) interpretation of modernity."[17] He thinks that "The dignity specific to cultural modernism consists in what Max Weber has called the stubborn differentiation of value-spheres."[18] He also thinks that Hegel was right in believing that "Kant does not perceive the . . . formal divisions within culture . . . as diremptions. Hence he ignores the need for unification that emerges with the separations evoked by the principle of subjectiv-ity."[19] He takes as seriously as Hegel did the question "How can an intrinsic ideal form be constructed from the spirit of modernity, that neither just imitates the historical forms of modernity nor is imposed upon them from the outside?"[20]

From the historicist point of view I share with Geuss, there is no reason to look for an intrinsic ideal that avoids "just imitating the historical forms of moder-nity." All that social thought can hope to do is to play the various historical forms of modernity off against one another in the way in which, e.g., Blumenberg plays "self-assertion" off against "self-grounding."[21] But because Habermas agrees with Hegel that there is a "need for unification" in order to "regenerate the unifying power of religion in the medium of reason,"[22] he wants to go back to Hegel and start again. He thinks that in order to avoid the disillusionment with "the philosophy of subjectivity" which produced Nietzsche and the two strands of post-Nietzschean thought which he distinguishes and dislikes (the one leading to Foucault, and the other to Heidegger), we need to go back to the place where the young Hegel took the wrong turn.[23] That was the place where he still had "the option of explicating the ethical totality as a communicative reason embodied in

---

16 Jürgen Habermas, *The Philosophical Discourse of Modernity,* trans. Frederick Lawrence (Cambridge, Mass.: MIT Press, 1987), p. 53.
17 Ibid., p. 19.
18 Habermas, "Entwinement," p. 18.
19 Habermas, *Philosophical Discourse,* p. 19.
20 Ibid., p. 20.
21 Hans Blumenberg, *The Legitimacy of the Modern Age,* trans. Robert M. Wallace (Cambridge, Mass.: MIT Press, 1983), p. 184.
22 Habermas, *Philosophical Discourse,* p. 20.
23 Ibid., p. 30.

intersubjective life-contexts."[24] Habermas thinks that it was the lack of a sense of rationality as *social* that was missing from "the philosophy of the subject" which the older Hegel exemplified (and from which he believes the "end-of-philosophy" thinkers have never really escaped).

But whereas Habermas thinks that the cultural need which "the philosophy of the subject" gratified was and is real, and can perhaps be fulfilled by his own focus on a "communication community," I would urge that it is an artificial problem created by taking Kant too seriously. On this view, the wrong turn was taken when Kant's split between science, morals, and art was accepted as a *donnée*, as *die massgebliche Selbstauslegung der Moderne*. Once that split is taken seriously, then the *Selbstvergewisserung der Moderne*, which Hegel and Habermas both take to be the "fundamental philosophical problem," will indeed seem urgent. For once the philosophers swallow Kant's "stubborn differentiation," then they are condemned to an endless series of reductionist and antireductionist moves. Reductionists will try to make everything scientific, or political (Lenin), or aesthetic (Baudelaire, Nietzsche). Antireductionists will show what such attempts leave out. To be a philosopher of the "modern" sort is precisely to be unwilling either to let these spheres simply coexist uncompetitively, or to reduce the other two to the remaining one. Modern philosophy has consisted in forever realigning them, squeezing them together, and forcing them apart again. But it is not clear that these efforts have done the modern age much good (or, for that matter, harm).

Habermas thinks that the older Hegel "solves the problem of the self-reassurance of modernity too well," because the philosophy of Absolute Spirit "removes all importance from its own present age . . . and deprives it of its calling to self-critical renewal."[25] He sees the popularity of "end-of-philosophy" thought as an over-reaction to this over-success. But surely part of the motivation for this kind of thought is the belief that Hegel too was scratching where it did not really itch. Whereas Habermas thinks that it is with Hegel's own over-success that philosophy becomes what Hegel himself called "an isolated sanctuary" whose ministers "form an isolated order of priests . . . untroubled by how it goes with the world," it is surely possible to see this development as having been Kant's fault, if anybody's, and precisely the fault of his "three-sphere" picture of culture. On this latter view, Kant's attempt to deny knowledge to make room for faith (by inventing "transcendental subjectivity" to serve as a fulcrum for the Copernican revolution) was provoked by an unnecessary worry about the spiritual significance, or insignificance, of modern science. Like Habermas, Kant thinks that modern science has a "theoretical dynamic," one which can be identified with (at least a portion of) "the nature of rationality." Both think that by isolating and exhibiting this dynamic, but distinguishing it from other dynamics (e.g., "practi-

24   Ibid., p. 40.
25   Ibid., p. 42.

cal reason" or "the emancipatory interest"), one can keep the results of science without thereby disenchanting the world. Kant suggested that we need not let our knowledge of the world *qua* matter in motion get in the way of our moral sense. The same suggestion was also made by Hume and Reid, but unlike these pragmatical Scots, Kant thought that he had to back up this suggestion with a story which would differentiate and "place" the three great spheres into which culture must be divided. From the point of view common to Hume and Reid (who disagreed on so much else) no such metanarrative is needed. What is needed is a sort of intellectual analogue of civic virtue — tolerance, irony, and a willingness to let spheres of culture flourish without worrying too much about their "common ground," their unification, the "intrinsic ideals" they suggest, or what picture of man they "presuppose."

In short, by telling a story about Kant as the beginning of modern philosophy (and by emphasizing the difference between modern and premodern philosophy) one might make the kind of fervent end-of-philosophy writing Habermas deplores look both more plausible and less interesting. What links Habermas to the French thinkers he criticizes is the conviction that the story of modern philosophy (as successive reactions to Kant's diremptions) is an important part of the story of the democratic societies' attempts at self-reassurance. But it may be that most of the latter story could be told as the history of reformist politics, without much reference to the kinds of theoretical backup which philosophers have provided for such politics. It is, after all, things like the formation of trade unions, the meritocratization of education, the expansion of the franchise, and cheap newspapers, which have figured most largely in the willingness of the citizens of the democracies to see themselves as part of a "communicative community" — their continued willingness to say "us" rather than "them" when they speak of their respective countries. This sort of willingness has made religion progressively less important in the self-image of that citizenry. One's sense of relation to a power beyond the community becomes less important as one becomes able to think of oneself as part of a body of public opinion, capable of making a difference to the public fate. That ability has been substantially increased by the various "progressive" changes I have listed.

Weber was of course right in saying that some of these changes have also worked the other way (to increase our sense of being controlled by "them"). But Habermas is so preoccupied with the "alienating" effects of such changes that he allows himself to be distracted from the concomitant increase in people's sense of themselves as free citizens of free countries. The typical German story of the self-consciousness of the modern age (the one which runs from Hegel through Marx, Weber, and Nietzsche) focuses on figures who were preoccupied with the world we lost when we lost the religion of our ancestors. But this story may be both too pessimistic and too exclusively German. If so, then a story about the history of modern thought which took Kant and Hegel less seriously and, for example, the relatively untheoretical socialists more seriously, might lead us to a kind of "end-of-philosophy" thinking which would escape Habermas's strictures on Deleuze and Foucault. For these French writers buy in on the usual German story, and thus tend to share Habermas's assumption that the story of the realignment, assimilation, and expansion of the three "value-spheres" is essential to the story of the *Selbstvergewisserung* of modern society, and not just to that of the modern intellectuals.

In order to interpret this problem of the three spheres as a problem only for an increasingly "isolated order of priests," one has to see the "principle of the modern" as something other than that famous "subjectivity" which post-Kantian historians of philosophy, anxious to link Kant with Descartes, took as their guiding thread. One can instead attribute Descartes' role as "founder of modern philosophy" to his development of what I earlier called "an overzealous philosophy of science" – the sort of philosophy of science which saw Galilean mechanics, analytic geometry, mathematical optics, and the like, as having more spiritual significance than they in fact have. By taking the ability to do such science as a mark of something deep and essential to human nature, as the place where we got closest to our true selves, Descartes preserved just those themes in ancient thought which Bacon had tried to obliterate. The preservation of the Platonic idea that our most distinctively human faculty was our ability to manipulate "clear and distinct ideas," rather than to accomplish feats of social engineering, was Descartes' most important and most unfortunate contribution to what we now think of as "modern philosophy." Had Bacon – the prophet of self-assertion, as opposed to self-grounding – been taken more seriously, we might not have been struck with a canon of "great modern philosophers" who took "subjectivity" as their theme. We might, as J. B. Schneewind puts it, have been less inclined to assume that epistemology (i.e., reflection on the nature and status of natural science) was the "independent variable" in philosophical thought and moral and social philosophy the "dependent variable." We might thereby see what Blumenberg calls "self-assertion" – the willingness to center our hopes on the future of the race, on the unpredictable successes of our descendants – as the "principle of the modern." Such a principle would let us think of the modern age as defined by successive attempts to shake off the sort of ahistorical structure exemplified by Kant's division of culture into three "value-spheres."

On this sort of account, the point I claimed Lyotard shared with Feyerabend and Hesse – the point that there are no interesting epistemological differences between the aims and procedures of scientists and those of politicians – is absolutely fundamental. The recovery of a Baconian, non-Cartesian attitude towards science would permit us to dispense with the idea of "an internal theoretical dynamic" in science, a dynamic which is something more than the "anything goes that works" spirit which unites Bacon and Feyerabend. It would break down the opposition between what Habermas calls "merely technologically exploitable knowledge" and "emancipation," by seeing both as manifestations of what Blumenberg calls "theoretical curiosity." It would free us from preoccupation with the purported tensions between the three "value-spheres" distinguished by Kant and Weber, and between the three sorts of "interests" distinguished by Habermas.

In the present space, I cannot do more than gesture towards the various rosy prospects which appear once one suggests that working through "the principle of subjectivity" (and out the other side) was just a side-show, something which an isolated order of priests devoted themselves to for a few hundred years, something which did not make much difference to the successes and failures of the European countries in realizing the hopes formulated by the Enlightenment. So I shall conclude by turning from the one issue on which I think Lyotard has a point against Habermas to the many issues about which Habermas seems to me in the right.

The thrust of Habermas's criticism of thinkers like Foucault, Deleuze, and Lyotard is that they offer us no "theoretical" reason to move in one social direction rather than another. They take away the dynamic which liberal social thought (of the sort represented by Rawls in America and Habermas himself in Germany) has traditionally relied upon, viz., the need to be in touch with a reality obscured by "ideology" and disclosed by "theory." Habermas says of Foucault's later work that it

replaced the model of repression and emancipation developed by Marx and Freud with a pluralism of power/discourse formations. These formations intersect and succeed one another and can be differentiated according to their style and intensity. They cannot, however, be judged in terms of validity, which was possible in the case of the repression and emancipation of conscious as opposed to unconscious conflict resolutions.[26]

This description is, I think, quite accurate, as is his remark that "the shock" which Foucault's books produce "is not caused by the flash of *insight* into a confusion which threatens identity" but instead by "the affirmed de-differentiation and by the affirmed collapse of those categories which alone can account for category mistakes of existential relevance." Foucault affects to write from a point of view light-years away from the problems of contemporary society. His own efforts at social reform (e.g., of prisons) seem to have no connection with his exhibition of the way in which the "humane" approach to penal reform tied in with the needs of the modern state. It takes no more than a squint of the inner eye to read Foucault as a stoic, a dispassionate observer of the present social order, rather than its concerned critic. Because the rhetoric of emancipation — the notion of a kind of truth which is *not* one more production of power — is absent from his work, he can easily be thought of as reinventing American "functionalist" sociology. The extraordinary *dryness* of Foucault's work is a counterpart of the dryness which Iris Murdoch once objected to in the writing of British analytic philosophers.[27] It is a dryness produced by a lack of

26 Habermas, "Entwinement," p. 29.
27 See Iris Murdoch, "Against Dryness," reprinted (from *Encounter*, 1961) in *Revisions*, ed. Stanley Hauerwas and Alasdair MacIntyre (Notre Dame, Ind.: Notre Dame University Press, 1983).

identification with any social context, any communication. Foucault once said that he would like to write "so as to have no face." He forbids himself the tone of the liberal sort of thinker who says to his fellow-citizens: "*We* know that there must be a better way to do things than this; let us look for it together." There is no "we" to be found in Foucault's writings, nor in those of many of his French contemporaries.

It is this remoteness which reminds one of the conservative who pours cold water on hopes for reform, who affects to look at the problems of his fellow-citizens with the eye of the future historian. Writing "the history of the present," rather than suggestions about how our children might inhabit a better world in the future, gives up not just on the notion of a common human nature, and on that of "the subject," but on our untheoretical sense of social solidarity. It is as if thinkers like Foucault and Lyotard were so afraid of being caught up in one more metanarrative about the fortunes of "the subject" that they cannot bring themselves to say "we" long enough to identify with the culture of the generation to which they belong. Lyotard's contempt for "the philosophy of subjectivity" is such as to make him abstain from anything that smacks of the "metanarrative of emancipation" which Habermas shares with Blumenberg and Bacon. Habermas's socialization of subjectivity, his philosophy of consensus, seems to Lyotard just one more pointless variation on a theme which has been heard too often.

But although disconnecting "philosophy" from social reform – a disconnection previously performed by analytic philosophers who were "emotivist" in meta-ethics while being fiercely partisan in politics – is one way of expressing exasperation with the philosophical tradition, it is not the only way. Another would be to minimize the importance of that tradition, rather than seeing it as something which urgently needs to be overcome, unmasked, or genealogized. Suppose, as I suggested above, one sees the wrong turn as having been taken with Kant, or better yet, with Descartes, rather than (like Habermas) with the young Hegel or the young Marx. Then one might see the canonical sequence of philosophers from Descartes to Nietzsche as a distraction from the history of concrete social engineering which made the contemporary North Atlantic culture what it is now, with all its glories and all its dangers. One could try to create a new canon – one in which the mark of a "great philosopher" was awareness of new social and religious and institutional possibilities, as opposed to developing a new dialectical twist in metaphysics or epistemology. That would be a way of splitting the difference between Habermas and Lyotard, of having things both ways. We could agree with Lyotard that we need no more metanarratives, but with Habermas that we need less dryness. We could agree with Lyotard that studies of the communicative competence of a transhistorical subject are of little use in reinforcing our sense of identification with our community, while still insisting on the importance of that sense.

If one had such a de-theoreticized sense of community, one could accept the claim that valuing "undistorted communication" was of the essence of liberal politics without needing a theory of communicative competence as backup. Attention would be turned instead to some concrete examples of what was presently distorting our communication — e.g., to the sort of "shock" we get when, reading Foucault, we realize that the jargon we liberal intellectuals developed has played into the hands of the bureaucrats. Detailed historical narratives of the sort Foucault offers us would take the place of philosophical metanarratives. Such narratives would not unmask something created by power called "ideology" in the name of something not created by power called "validity" or "emancipation." They would just explain who was currently getting and using power for what purposes, and then (unlike Foucault) suggest how some other people might get it and use it for other purposes. The resulting attitude would be neither incredulous and horrified realization that truth and power are inseparable nor Nietzschean *Schadenfreude,* but rather a recognition that it was only the false lead which Descartes gave us (and the resulting overvaluation of scientific theory which, in Kant, produces "the philosophy of subjectivity") that made us think truth and power *were* separable. We could thus take the Baconian maxim that "knowledge is power" with redoubled seriousness. We might also be made to take seriously Dewey's suggestion that the way to re-enchant the world, to bring back what religion gave our forefathers, is to stick to the concrete. Much of what I have been saying is an attempt to follow up on the following passage from Dewey:

We are weak today in ideal matters because intelligence is divorced from aspiration. . . . When philosophy shall have cooperated with the force of events and made clear and coherent the meaning of the daily detail, science and emotion will interpenetrate, practice and imagination will embrace. Poetry and religious feeling will be the unforced flowers of life.[28]

I can summarize my attempt to split the difference between Lyotard and Habermas by saying that this Deweyan attempt to make concrete concerns with the daily problems of one's community — social engineering — the substitute for traditional religion seems to me to embody Lyotard's postmodernist "incredulity towards metanarratives" while dispensing with the assumption that the intellectual has a mission to be avant-garde, to escape the rules and practices and institutions which have been transmitted to her in favor of something which will make possible "authentic criticism." Lyotard unfortunately retains one of the Left's silliest ideas — that escaping from such institutions is automatically a good thing, because it insures that one will not be "used" by the evil forces which have "co-opted" these institutions. Leftism of this sort necessarily devalues consensus and communication, for insofar as the intellectual remains able to talk to people outside the avant-garde she "compromises" herself. Lyotard exalts the "sublime," and argues that Habermas's hope that the arts might serve to "explore a living

28   John Dewey, *Reconstruction in Philosophy* (Boston: Beacon Press, 1957), p. 164.

historical situation" and to "bridge the gap between cognitive, ethical and political discourses,"[29] shows that Habermas has only an "aesthetic of the beautiful."[30] On the view I am suggesting, one should see the quest for the sublime, the attempt (in Lyotard's words) to "present the fact that the unpresentable exists," as one of the prettier unforced blue flowers of bourgeois culture. But this quest is wildly irrelevant to the attempt at communicative consensus which is the vital force which drives that culture.

More generally, one should see the intellectual *qua* intellectual as having a special, idiosyncratic need – a need for the ineffable, the sublime, a need to go beyond the limits, a need to use words which are not part of anybody's language-game, any social institution. But one should not see the intellectual as serving a *social* purpose when she fulfills this need. Social purposes are served, just as Habermas says, by finding beautiful ways of harmonizing interests, rather than sublime ways of detaching oneself from others' interests. The attempt of leftist intellectuals to pretend that the avant-garde is serving the wretched of the earth by fighting free of the merely beautiful is a hopeless attempt to make the special needs of the intellectual and the social needs of her community coincide. Such an attempt goes back to the Romantic period, when the urge to think the unthinkable, to grasp the unconditioned, to sail strange seas of thought alone, was mingled with enthusiasm for the French Revolution. These two, equally laudable motives should be distinguished.

If we do distinguish them, then we can see each as a distinct motive for the kind of "end of philosophy" thinking Habermas deplores. The desire for the sublime makes one want to bring the philosophical tradition to an end because it makes one want to cut free from the words of the tribe. Giving these words a purer sense is not enough; they must be abjured altogether, for they are contaminated with the needs of a repudiated community. Such a Nietzschean line of thought leads to the kind of avant-garde philosophy which Lyotard admires in Deleuze. The desire for communication, harmony, interchange, conversation, social solidarity, and the "merely" beautiful wants to bring the philosophical tradition to an end because it sees the attempt to provide metanarratives, even metanarratives of emancipation, as an unhelpful distraction from what Dewey calls "the meaning of the daily detail." Whereas the first sort of end-of-philosophy thinking sees the philosophical tradition as an extremely important failure, the second sort sees it as rather unimportant excursus. Those who want sublimity are aiming at a postmodernist form of intellectual life. Those who want beautiful social harmonies want a postmodernist form of social life, in which society as a whole asserts itself without bothering to ground itself.

29 Lyotard, *Postmodern Condition*, p. 72.
30 Ibid., p. 79.

Unger, Castoriadis, and
the romance of a national future

Roberto Mangabeira Unger is a Brazilian philosopher. "Brazilian philosophy" has as little international resonance as "American philosophy" did a hundred years ago. But in 1882 Walt Whitman, comparing Carlyle's "dark fortune-telling of humanity and politics" with "a far more profound horoscope-casting of those themes – G. F. Hegel's," wrote as follows:

Not the least mentionable part of the case, (a streak, it may be, of that humor with which history and fate love to contrast their gravity) is that although neither of my great authorities [Carlyle and Hegel] during their lives consider'd the United States worthy of serious mention, all the principal works of both might not inappropriately be this day collected and bound up under the conspicuous title: *Speculations for the use of North America, and Democracy there, with the relations of the same to Metaphysics, including Lessons and Warnings (encouragements too, and of the vastest,) from the Old World to the New.*[1]

Try pasting that title on your copy of Unger's *Politics,* having first altered "North America" to "South America," "Old World" to "Northern Hemisphere," and "New" to "Southern." The result would not be inappropriate. Though few of our great authorities presently consider Brazil worthy of serious mention, spaces left blank in the minds of one century's authorities often get filled in, quite quickly and quite surprisingly, during the next. Try beginning your reading of Unger's book with pages 64–79 of the first volume ("The Exemplary Instability of the Third World" and "A Brazilian Example").[2] Remember that Unger – though he has put in many years of hard work here in North America, changing the curricula of many of our law schools and the self-image of many of our lawyers – is a man whose mind is elsewhere. For him, none of the rich North Atlantic democracies are home. Rather, they are places where he has gathered some lessons, warnings, and encouragements.

1   Walt Whitman, "Carlyle from American Points of View," in *Prose Works* (Philadelphia: David McKay, 1900), p. 171 (emphasis in the original).
2   The three volumes of Unger's *Politics: A work in Constructive Social Theory* (Cambridge: Cambridge University Press, 1987) are titled *Social Theory: Its situation and its Task* (hereafter *Social Theory*), *False Necessity: Anti-Necessitarian Social Theory in the Service of Radical Democracy* (hereafter *False Necessity*), and *Plasticity into Power: Comparative Historical Studies on the Institutional Conditions of Economic and Military Societies* (hereafter *Plasticity into Power*). Unger was born in Brazil in 1947, was educated there and in Europe, and has been Professor of Law at Harvard since 1972.

Whitman prefaced *Leaves of Grass* with a comparison between the closed-down character of Europe and the openness of the American future:

Let the age and wars of other nations be chanted, and their eras and characters be illustrated, and that finish the verse. Not so the great psalm of the republic. Here the theme is creative, and has vista.[3]

In *Democratic Vistas* he proclaims that that psalm has barely begun:

Far, far, indeed, stretch, in distance, our Vistas! How much is still to be disentangled, freed! How long it takes to make this American world see that it is, in itself, the final authority and reliance![4]

As his book goes along, Whitman continually looks from the gloriously possible to the sickeningly actual – from the American future to the facts of the Gilded Age – and back again. His naive hope invariably prevails over his sophisticated disgust. Compare Unger on Brazil in 1985:

Indefinition was the common denominator of all these features of the life of the state. . . . All this indefinition could be taken as both the voice of transformative opportunity and the sign of a paralyzing confusion. At one moment it seemed that new experiments in human association might be staged here; at the next, that nothing could come out of this disheartening and preposterous blend of structure, shiftlessness, and stagnation.[5]

Again,

At this time in world history, an attitude once confined to great visionaries had become common among decent men and women. They could no longer participate in political struggle out of a simple mixture of personal ambition and devotion to the power and glory of the state. They also had to feel that they were sharing in an exemplary experiment in the remaking of society. A person who entered Brazilian politics in this spirit wanted his country to do more than rise to wealth and power as a variant of the societies and polities of the developed west. He wished it to become a testing ground for . . . the options available to mankind.[6]

To get in the right mood to read passages like these, we rich, fat, tired North Americans must hark back to the time when our own democracy was newer and leaner – when Pittsburgh was as new, promising, and problematic as São Paulo is now. Irving Howe describes "the American newness" of one hundred and fifty years ago as a time when "people start to feel socially invigorated and come to think they can act to determine their fate."[7] He continues bleakly:

3 Whitman, 1855 Preface to *Leaves of Grass*, in *Prose Works*, p. 264.
4 Whitman, "*Democratic Vistas*," in *Prose Works*, p. 226.
5 Unger, *Social Theory*, pp. 69–70.
6 Ibid., pp. 75–76.
7 Irving Howe, *The American Newness: Culture and Politics in the Age of Emerson* (Cambridge, Mass.: Harvard University Press, 1986), p. 17.

"What is it like to live at such a time? The opposite of what it is like to live today."[8]

Howe's bleakness, which I and many of my contemporaries share, comes from the fear that what Unger calls "the cycles of reform and reaction" that make up politics in the United States are simply not up to the demands of the times. This bleakness is increased by our inability to imagine any better goal than the next cycle of reform. On the one hand, we recognize that, for example, "Automation is progressing much more rapidly than the decretinization of American senators."[9] On the other hand, we see these cycles of reform and reaction as the operation of free institutions — institutions it took two hundred years of hard work, and lots of good luck, to construct. These institutions, increasingly rackety and ineffectual as they are, seem to be all we have got, and all we can really imagine having. So we content ourselves with saying that, as institutions go, ours are a lot better than the actually existing competition. Unger has us dead to rights when he speaks of "the rich, polished, critical and self-critical but also downbeat and Alexandrian culture of social and historical thought that now flourishes in the North American democracies."[10] Our high culture, at the end of the twentieth century, resembles the culture that Whitman saw at the end of the nineteenth when he looked toward Europe.[11]

In *Politics,* Unger is reacting against this bleak defensiveness and resignation. He sometimes thinks of the tragic liberalism of us Alexandrians as an inexplicable failure of imagination, and sometimes as an exasperating weakness of will. What makes him different from most theorists who are critical of American liberalism is his orientation toward the future rather than the past — his hopefulness. Most radical critics of American institutions (for example, the admirers of Althusserian, Heideggerian, or Foucauldian social thought — the people for whom Harold Bloom has invented the sobriquet "The School of Resentment") would not be caught dead with an expression of hopefulness on their faces. Their reaction to American inertia and impotence is rage, contempt, and the use of what they call "subversive, oppositional discourse," rather than suggestions about how we might do things differently. Whereas people like Howe and myself would love to get some good ideas about what the country might do (and dream of the election of, if

---

8 Ibid., p. 17. At the end of this book (p. 89), Howe bravely says that " 'The newness' will come again. It is intrinsic to our life." Maybe it will, but I would not know how to write a scenario for its return.

9 Cornelius Castoriadis, *The Imaginary Institution of Society,* trans. Kathleen Blamey (Cambridge, Mass.: MIT Press, 1987), p. 83.

10 Unger, *Social Theory,* p. 223.

11 There was, in fact, more in Europe to see than Whitman, who was not very well informed, saw. See James Kloppenberg's account of the social democratic intellectuals in France, Germany, and Britain in the last decades of the nineteenth century: *Uncertain Victory: Social Democracy and Progressivism in European and American Thought, 1870–1920* (Oxford: Oxford University Press, 1986). I am not sure there is more in contemporary North American culture than Unger sees.

not another Lincoln, at least another FDR), the School of Resentment washes its hands of the American experiment. Since these people have also been disappointed, successively, in Russia, Cuba, and China, they now tend to wash their hands of *all* "structures and discourses of power" (the Foucauldian term for what we used to call "institutions").

By contrast, when Unger is not berating us for our lack of hope and failure of nerve, he is sketching alternative institutions — a rotating capital fund, a government department of destabilization, and so on. He predicts, accurately, that the people who still take Marxism as a model of what a social theory should look like will reject his suggestions as reformist tinkering, as inadequately oppositional. With equal accuracy, he predicts that we downbeat, Alexandrian, social democratic liberals will view them as utopian. Still, the distance between the Unger of *Politics* (as opposed to the Unger of a dozen years back, the author of *Knowledge and Politics*[12]) and us Alexandrians is a lot less than that between Unger and the School of Resentment. For our reaction is, more accurately: "Utopian, but, God knows, worth trying; still, you'll never get it into a Democratic, much less a Republican, platform."

This is where Brazil comes in. If Unger were your ordinary universalizing social theorist — as he sometimes, alas, makes himself out to be — names of particular countries would not be relevant. But he is rather (as the caption of an early, nasty review of *Politics* put it) "a preposterous political romantic"[13] — as preposterous as Whitman, albeit better read. Being a political romantic is not easy these days. Presumably it helps a lot to come from a big, backward country with lots of raw materials and a good deal of capital accumulation — a country that has started to lurch forward, even though frequently falling over its own feet. It must also help, ironically enough, to come from a country that cannot hope to achieve what the North Atlantic has achieved in the way of equality and decency by the same means: reliance on a free market in capital and on compromises between pressure groups. As Unger says, "For many third world countries the route of empowered democracy [that is, something like Unger's own alternative institutions] may

---

12 For the difference between the two books, see Unger's postscript to the second edition of his *Knowledge and Politics* (New York: The Free Press, 1984). As he says there, he has become "much less anxious to emphasize the dependence of liberal ideas upon certain basic conceptions of modern speculative philosophy that first took recognizable form in the seventeenth-century" and much more ready to grant that "the classic nineteenth century forms of liberalism" represent "one of the great modern secular doctrines of emancipation" (p. 339). This decreased emphasis on philosophical presuppositions seems to me an important step forward in Unger's thought. For an example of the over-philosophized description of "liberalism" which many readers, alas, took away from the first (1975) edition of *Knowledge and Politics*, see Michael Ryan, "Deconstruction and Social Theory" in *Displacement: Derrida and After*, ed. Mark Krupnick (Bloomington: Indiana University Press, 1983), p. 154.

13 Steven Holmes, "The Professor of Smashing: The Preposterous Political Romanticism of Roberto Unger," *The New Republic*, Oct. 19, 1983.

represent less the bolder alternative to social democracy than the sole practical means by which even social-democratic goals can be achieved."[14]

Unger writes that

Much in this work can be understood as the consequence of an attempt to enlist the intellectual resources of the North Atlantic world in the service of concerns and commitments more keenly felt elsewhere. In this way I hope to contribute toward the development of an alternative to the vague, unconvinced, and unconvincing Marxism that now serves the advocates of the radical project as their lingua franca. If, however, the arguments of this book stand up, the transformative focus of this theoretical effort has intellectual uses that transcend its immediate origins and motives.[15]

I am interpreting *Politics* in the light of the first two sentences of this passage. I have doubts, however, about the third sentence. As a pragmatist, I think philosophy is at its best when it is content to be "its own time apprehended in thought" and lets transcendence go.[16] As a Kuhnian, I have doubts about whether argument plays much of a role in scientific or political Gestalt-switches. Arguments (whose premises must necessarily be phrased in familiar vocabularies) often just get in the way of attempts to create an unfamiliar political vocabulary, a new *lingua franca* for those trying to transform what they see around them. If Unger is able to supply future leaders of Third World social movements with a non-Marxist and non-"behavioral science" *lingua franca* – one that will help them brush aside the conventional wisdoms offered by the KGB and the CIA – he will have done something so important as to dwarf argumentation. He will have done for Third World leaders of the next century what Dewey tried to do for the North American intelligentsia of the first, more optimistic, half of the twentieth. Among other things, he will have helped make them aware that, as Dewey put it, "philosophy can proffer nothing but hypotheses, and that these hypotheses are of value only as they render men's minds more sensitive to the life about them."[17]

Realizing that Unger is a *Brazilian* philosopher lets us Alexandrians convert our initial reaction to his book to something more like, "We hope to Heaven these imaginary institutions do sell in Brazil; if they should actually *work* there, maybe then we could sell them here. The Southern Hemisphere might conceivably, a generation hence, come to the rescue of the Northern." This amounts to saying that if there is hope, it lies in the Third World. But this is not to say, with

---

14 Unger, *False Necessity*, p. 395.
15 Unger, *Social Theory*, pp. 223–224.
16 The phrase comes from the Preface to Hegel's *Philosophy of Right*, trans. T.M. Knox (Oxford: Clarendon Press, 1952), p. 11. Hegel continues, "It is just as absurd to imagine that a philosophy can transcend its contemporary world as it is to fancy that an individual can overleap his own age, jump over Rhodes."
17 John Dewey, *Reconstruction in Philosophy* (Boston: Beacon Press, 1948), p. 22.

Winston Smith, "If there is hope, it lies in the proles."[18] For the Third World is
not an undifferentiated mass of immiserated men and women. It is a set of diverse
nations, and if it is ever to have hope it will be for a diverse set of national futures.

The School of Resentment sometimes suggests, following Lukacs and Foucault,
that the immiserated share a common "consciousness" – which can be set over
against all "discourses of power" or "ideologies."[19] This suggestion that there is
something "deep down" – something ahistorical and international – under what
we powerful, discursive types have been inscribing on the bodies of the weak
makes this school feel justified in toying with anarchism, with the idea that
everything would be all right if we could just get "power" off everybody's backs.[20]
Members of this School will be shocked and indignant to find that Unger does not
assume that the initial agents of transformation in the Third World will be
workers and peasants. He thinks they will be petty bourgeois functionaries:

In countries with a strong statist tradition the lower rungs of the governmental bureau-
cracy constitute the most likely agents for the development of such floating resources. For
example, in many Latin American nations whole sectors of the economy (e.g., agriculture)
are closely supervised and coordinated by economic bureaucrats: public-credit officers and
agronomists. . . . But the bureaucracies are typically mined by a multitude of more or less
well-intentioned, confused, unheroic crypto-leftists – middle-class, university-trained
youth, filled with the vague, leftist ideas afloat in the world. The ambiguities of estab-
lished rules and policies and the failures of bureaucratic control can supply these people
with excuses to deny a fragment of governmental protection to its usual beneficiaries and
make it available to other people, in new proportions or in new ways. . . . The result is to
create a floating resource – one the transformers can appropriate or fight about.[21]

"Well-intentioned, confused, university-trained young crypto-leftists" is a reasonable description of the thousands of recently graduated lawyers who, influenced by Unger and other members of the Critical Legal Studies Movement, are
now helping make institutions in the United States slightly more flexible and
decent. It is also a good description of the only allies Gorbachev is likely to have
in his effort to restructure Russian institutions – namely, the more Winston-like
members of the Outer Party. If Unger's description of his hoped-for allies seems

18 George Orwell, *1984*, in *The Penguin Complete Novels of George Orwell* (London: Penguin, 1951),
p. 783.
19 See Habermas's discussion of this link between Lukacs and Foucault in his *The Philosophical
Discourse of Modernity*, trans. Frederick Lawrence (Cambridge, Mass.: MIT Press, 1987), p. 280.
20 For an acute analysis of the sources of such fantasies, see Bernard Yack, *The Longing for Total
Revolution: Philosophical Sources of Social Discontent from Rousseau to Marx and Nietzsche* (Princeton:
Princeton University Press, 1986).
21 Unger, *False Necessity*, p. 410; compare *Social Theory*, p. 76: "It was also vital [in the Brazilian
context] to avoid the path toward isolation that had helped defeat or tame the European leftist
parties and to renounce the preconceptions about feasible class alliances underlying that path.
You could not, for example, assume that the only alternative to a politics of unremitting hostility
to the petty bourgeoisie or the salaried middle classes was an alliance with the national entrepre-
neurs and landowners against the foreigner."

wry and self-mocking, it is. He would *like* to identify himself with the victimized masses. Who, two thousand years after Christ and a hundred after Zola, would not? But in *Politics,* the romanticism of *Knowledge and Politics* is balanced by a calculation of current possibilities.

Toward the end of *The Critical Legal Studies Movement,* Unger admitted that

> there is a disparity between our intentions and the archaic social form that they assume: a joint endeavor undertaken by discontented, factious intellectuals in the high style of nineteenth-century bourgeois radicalism. For all who participate in such an undertaking, the disharmony between intent and presence must be a cause of rage. We neither suppress this rage nor allow it the last word, because we do not give the last word to the historical world we inhabit. We build with what we have and willingly pay the price for the inconformity of vision to circumstance.[22]

This paragraph is typical of Unger at his best, and illustrates what separates him from the School of Resentment. He does not give the last word to the time he lives in. He also lives in an imaginary, lightly sketched future. That is the sort of world romantics *should* live in; their living there is the reason why they and their confused, utopian, unscientific, petty bourgeois followers can, occasionally, make the actual future better for the rest of us.[23]

The School of Resentment, made up of people who can single-handedly deconstruct a large social theory faster than a Third World village can construct a small elementary school, does not take kindly to romance. These people are modernists, maybe even *post*modernists. They have celebrated all the eras and characters, and they like to finish their verses with a dying fall. Jeffers anticipated them when he wrote:

> While this America settles in the mold of its vulgarity,
> heavily thickening to empire
> And protest only a bubble in the molten mass, pops and
> sighs out, and the mass hardens,
> I sadly remember that the flower fades to make fruit,
> the fruit rots to make earth.

When these people do social theory, they push aside the tradition of Locke, Jefferson, Mill, Dewey, and Habermas and turn to a tradition that began with Hegel and is continued in Heidegger's downbeat story of the destiny of the West. Hegel made bud-flower-and-fruit his archetypal dialectical triad. His idea of a social theory was a retrospective narrative, written by someone whose "shape of life had grown old."[24] Such a scenario either ends with the present (as Hegel and

22 Unger, *The Critical Legal Studies Movement* (Cambridge, Mass.: Harvard University Press, 1986), pp. 118–19.

23 See Nancy Rosenblum, *Another Liberalism: Romanticism and the Reconstruction of Liberal Thought* (Cambridge, Mass.: Harvard University Press, 1987) for a good account of the relation between liberalism and romanticism.

24 See Hegel, *The Philosophy of Right,* p. 13.

Heidegger prudently ended theirs) or else forecasts (as Marx and Mao did) a new kind of human being – someone on whose body "power" has inscribed nothing, someone who will burst the bounds of all the vocabularies used to describe the old, tattered, palimpsests. Since the School of Resentment is, nowadays, mostly "Post-Marxist," it tends to favor the former sort of scenario. So it relishes phrases like "late capitalism," "the end of the metaphysics of presence," "after Auschwitz," and "post-X (for any previous value of X)." Its members outdo each other in belatedness. They tend to accept some version of the story of the West as a long slide downhill from better days (the time of "organic community" or "the *polis*" or some such – a time before "structures of power" started scrawling all over us). They see no redeeming features in the present, except perhaps for their own helpless rage. When Heidegger describes the West as successively discrediting the notions of "the supersensory world, the Ideas, God, the moral law, the authority of reason, progress, the happiness of the greatest number, culture, civilization,"[25] they nod in recognition. Ah yes, "the greatest happiness of the greatest number" – at least we now see through *that* pathetic apology for the Panoptic State.

If my criticism of this School seems harsh, it is because one is always harshest on what one most dreads resembling. We tragic liberals are ourselves easily seduced by the lines I quoted from Jeffers' "Shine, Perishing Republic."[26] We are continually tempted by the urge to sit back and grasp our time in thought rather than continuing to try to change it. Even though we can still manage two cheers for America – even America under Reagan – a romantic like Unger sees little difference between us and the School of Resentment. For the only difference between us and the Resenters is that we regret our lack of imagination, whereas they make a virtue of what they think a philosophico-historical necessity.

Our only excuse is, once again, to appeal to national differences – to say, in effect, "Maybe it's easier in Brazil, but it's pretty hard here." Political imagination is, almost always, national imagination. To imagine great things is to imagine a great future *for a particular community,* a community one knows well, identifies with, can make plausible predictions about.[27] In the modern world, this usually means one's nation. Political romance is, therefore, for the foreseeable future, going to consist of psalms of *national* futures rather than of the future of "mankind." Officially, to be sure, we are all supposed to be "past" nationalism, to

25 Heidegger, "The Word of Nietzsche: God is Dead" in *The Question Concerning Technology and Other Essays,* trans. W. Lovitt (New York: Harper and Row: 1977), p. 65.
26 Consider, for example, Gore Vidal's account, in his historical novels and polemical essays, of America's transition from Republic to Empire. Vidal is a paradigmatically Alexandrian figure, still trying to be a liberal, but unable to repress his excitement over the rumors about the barbarians.
27 Consider the nationalism that runs through E.P. Thompson's discussion of Perry Anderson in his *The Poverty of Theory* (Brighton: New Left Books, 1978), as well as through Orwell's *The Road to Wigan Pier.*

be citizens of the human race. We are all supposed to believe, with the Marxists, that nationalism is just "mystification." But Cornelius Castoriadis gives this pretense the treatment it deserves:

To say: 'The proof that nationalism was a simple mystification, *and hence something unreal,* lies in the fact that it will be dissolved on the day of world revolution,' is not only to sell the bearskin before we catch the bear, it is to say: 'You who have lived from 1900 to 1965 and to who knows when, and you, the millions who died in the two wars . . . all of you, you are *in*-existent, you have always been in-existent with respect to true history. . . . True history was the invisible Potentiality that *will be,* and that, behind your back, was preparing the end of your illusions.'[28]

Castoriadis and Unger are willing to work with, rather than deconstruct, the notions that already mean something to people presently alive – while nonetheless not "giving the last word to the historical world they inhabit."[29] That is another way in which both differ from the School of Resentment. The latter School is interested not in building with what we have, but in penetrating to the "repressed" reality behind the "ideological" appearances. Resenters admire in Marxism precisely what Unger and Castoriadis distrust: the insistence on getting the "underlying realities" right, on doing theory first and getting to political utopias later. Though members of this School accept in meta-theory the Heidegger-Derrida view – that the reality–appearance distinction is the archetypal "binary opposition" from whose clutches we must escape – in their theoretical practice they wallow in it.[30]

Castoriadis and Unger escape this temptation because they adopt the attitude toward philosophy which I earlier quoted from Dewey. The "anti-naturalism" of Unger's book comes down to the least common denominator of Hegel, Marx, and Dewey: the claim that "the formative contexts of social life . . . or the procedural frameworks of problem solving and interest accommodation . . . [are] nothing but frozen politics: conflicts interrupted or contained" plus the desire "to deprive these frameworks or contexts of their aura of higher necessity or authority."[31] This anti-naturalism fits together nicely with Castoriadis' claim that "the imaginary – as the social imaginary and as the imagination of the psyche – is the logical and ontological condition of 'the real.' "[32] Just as in the individual psyche, moral character is "conflict interrupted or contained," so is the moral character of a society – that is, its institutions.

Unger urges the "thesis that everything in our ideas about the world, including

---

28 Castoriadis, *The Imaginary Institution of Society,* p. 149.
29 See Unger, *The Critical Legal Studies Movement,* p. 119.
30 See the (by now vast) literature on how to combine the "totalizing" aims of Marxism with the antitotalizing aims of "postmodernism": for example, Martin Jay, *Marxism and Totality* (Berkeley: University of California Press, 1984), pp. 510–537.
31 Unger, *Social Theory,* p. 145.
32 Castoriadis, *The Imaginary Institution of Society,* p. 336.

our conceptions of contingency, necessity, and possibility, is sensitive to changes in our empirical beliefs."[33] This holistic, Quinean thesis provides what he calls "the philosophical setting of an antinaturalistic social theory."[34] "Setting" is the right word. It is not so much a "foundation" for such a theory as an excuse not to take philosophy as seriously as the Marxists or the Resenters take it. That thesis helps one accept Unger's claim that "everything is politics" — that if politics can create a new form of social life, there will be time enough later for theorists to explain how this creation was possible and why it was a good thing. Quinean holism helps assure romantics that we humans are lords of possibility as well as actuality — for possibility is a function of a descriptive vocabulary, and that vocabulary is as much up for political grabs as anything else.[35]

This latter point — the least common denominator of Quine, Wittgenstein, and Dewey — provides the backup for Castoriadis' claim that what matters in a social thinker is the bits to which argumentation is irrelevant:

What the greatest thinkers may have said that was truthful and fecund was always said *despite* what they thought of as being and as thinkable, not because of what they thought or in agreement with it. And, to be sure, it is in this *despite* that their greatness is expressed, now as ever.[36]

In other words, if there is social hope it lies in the imagination — in people describing a future in terms which the past did not use. "The *only* thing that is not defined by the imaginary in human needs," Castoriadis says, "is an approximate number of calories per day."[37] Every other "constraint" is the fossilized product of some past act of imagination — what Nietzsche called "truth," namely, "[a] mobile army of metaphors, metonyms and anthropomorphisms . . . a sum of human relations which have been enhanced, transposed, and embellished poetically and rhetorically, and which after long use seem firm, canonical, and obligatory to a people."[38]

Certain constraints may come to seem so firm, canonical and obligatory to a people that their sense of themselves as a community will not outlast the elimination of those constraints. This is what we tragic liberals fear may be the case in the

33 Unger, *Social Theory*, p. 180.
34 Ibid., p. 170, and compare p. 223.
35 I have developed this point about Romanticism in chapter 1 of *Contingency, Irony, and Solidarity* by reference to Donald Davidson's radicalization of Quine's holistic philosophy of language, and especially to his treatment of metaphor. Castoriadis makes the same point when he describes *legein*, the use of one vocabulary rather than another, as a "primordial institution," and says that "at this level identitary logic *cannot* seize hold of the institution, since the institution is neither necessary nor contingent, since its emergence is not determined but is that on the basis of which and by means of which alone something determined exists" (*The Imaginary Institution of Society*, p. 258).
36 Castoriadis, *The Imaginary Institution of Society*, p. 200.
37 Ibid., p. 265.
38 Nietzsche, "On Truth and Lie in an Extra-Moral Sense," in *The Viking Portable Nietzsche*, ed. and trans. Walter Kaufmann (New York: Viking Press, 1954).

contemporary United States – and, more generally, in the rich North Atlantic democracies. The institutions that empowered our past (for example, inheritable private property) may strangle our future – with the poor and weak getting strangled first, as usual. The institutions that are our only protection against quasi-fascist demagogues may also be the constraints which prevent us from renouncing our insolent greed. The only way to fight off the Pat Robertsons or the Militant Tendency may be to cooperate with the George Bushes and the Kenneth Bakers. The only way to elect a Democratic President or a Labor Prime Minister may be to promise spoils to corrupt trade unions. Maybe North Atlantic politics have frozen over to such a degree that the result of breaking the ice would be something even worse than what we have now. That, at least, is the spectre that haunts contemporary North Atlantic liberals.

We tragic liberals realize wistfully that back in the 1880s we too might have seen illimitable vistas. We might have been the young John Dewey rather than the aging Henry Adams. We might have read Carlyle without discouragement, Whitman without giggles, and Edward Bellamy with a wild surmise. Nowadays, despite our fears, we still insist that it was lucky for the United States – not just for its poets and professors but also for its miners and sharecroppers – that our predecessors *did* read them that way. For in the intervening hundred years things actually got a *lot* fairer, more decent, more equal. People who had read those books had a lot to do with *making* them so. A century after Whitman's death it may seem that, as Orwell said, "the 'democratic vistas' have ended in barbed wire."[39] But we covered a lot of ground before our century, and our hope, began to run out. Maybe the Brazilians (or the Tanzanians, or *somebody*) will be able to dodge around that barbed wire – despite all that the superpowers can do to prevent them.

Unger's book offers a wild surmise, a set of concrete suggestions for risky social experiments, and a polemic against those who think the world has grown too old to be saved by such risk-taking. It does not offer a theory about Society, or Modernity, or Late Capitalism, or the Underlying Dynamics of anything. So, if Unger is going to have an audience, it may not be in the rich North Atlantic democracies. The intellectuals here may continue to find him "preposterous," because he does not satisfy what we have come to regard as legitimate expectations. He does not make moves in any game we know how to play. His natural audience may lie in the Third World – where his book may someday make possible a new national romance. Maybe someday it will help the literate (that is, the petty bourgeois) citizens of some country to see vistas where before they saw only dangers – see a hitherto undreamt-of national future instead of seeing their country as condemned to play out the role that some foreign theorist has written for it.

---

39 Orwell, "Inside the Whale," in *The Collected Essays, Journalism and Letters of George Orwell*, vol. 1 (New York: Harcourt Brace Jovanovich, 1968), p. 500.

One of the most helpful ways to think about such a possibility is given by Castoriadis' analogy between the individual psyche and the social whole:

There comes a time when the subject, not because he has discovered the primal scene or detected penis envy in his grandmother, but through his struggle in his actual life and as a result of repetition, unearths the central signifier of his neurosis and finally looks at it in its contingency, its poverty and its *insignificance*. In the same way, for people living today, the question is not to understand how the transition from the neolithic clans to the markedly divided cities of Akkad was made. It is to understand – and this obviously means, here more than anywhere else, to act – the contingency, the poverty and the insignificance of this 'signifier' of historical societies, the division into masters and slaves, into dominators and dominated.[40]

From Castoriadis' angle, the efforts of nineteenth-century German philosophers (and of their ungrateful heirs, the contemporary School of Resentment) look like attempts to discover the primal scene, or to unmask grandmother's penis envy (and, more recently, grandfather's womb envy). The same doubts arise even about relatively unphilosophical social theory – social theory that ignores local (and, in particular, national) differences in favor of "underlying dynamics." Given Castoriadis' analogy, it is hard to believe that patient study of Man, or of Society, or of Capitalism, will tell us whether the division into dominators and dominated is "natural" or "artificial," or which, if any, contemporary societies are "ripe" for the elimination of this division, or what "factors" will determine whether or not this possibility will be realized. Such discussion seems as remote from the project of imagining a new national future as are hydraulic models of libidinal flow from what actually happens on the couch. Such models may help the analyst to make an incisive diagnostic remark, but they are of no help in predicting the wildly idiosyncratic and unpredictable incident in the "struggle of actual life" that suddenly permits that endlessly repeated remark to mean something to the patient. Nor do they help in predicting the course of the analysis from that point onward.

Both Unger's slogan "everything is politics" and Castoriadis' analogy help us see why, insofar as social theory declines to be romantic, it is inevitably retrospective, and thus biased towards conservatism. As Hegel said, it typically tells us about the rise of a form of life that has now grown old – about possibilities which are, by now, largely exhausted. It tells us about the structure of what, with luck, our descendants will regard as our neurosis, without telling us much about what they will regard as "normal." It abstracts from national histories, which is like abstracting from the particular family in which a particular patient grew up. It tends to dismiss as "irrational" whatever purely local factors falsify its generalizations and predictions. This is just as unhelpful as telling the patient that his resistance to the analyst is "irrational."

40 Castoriadis, *The Imaginary Institution of Society*, p. 155.

Liberal social theorists resist Unger's and Castoriadis' suggestion that release from domination, if and when it comes, will come not in the form of "rational development" but through something unforeseeable and passionate. Most of the twentieth century's political surprises, liberals rightly point out, have been unpleasant ones. Romanticism, after all, was common to Mussolini, Hitler, Lenin, and Mao — to all the leaders who summoned a nation to slough off its past in an act of passionate self-renewal, and whose therapy proved far worse than the disease — as well as to Schiller, Shelley, Fichte, and Whitman. So it is tempting for us liberals to say that the slogan "everything is politics" is too dangerous to work with, to insist on a role for "reason" as opposed to "passion."

The problem we face in carrying through on this insistence is that "reason" usually means "working according to the rules of some familiar language-game, some familiar way of describing the current situation." We liberals have to admit the force of Dewey's, Unger's, and Castoriadis' point that such familiar language-games are themselves nothing more than "frozen politics," that they serve to legitimate, and make seem inevitable, precisely the forms of social life (for example, the cycles of reform and reaction) from which we desperately hope to break free. So we have to find something else for "reason" to mean. This effort to reinterpret rationality is central to Habermas' work, and culminates in his distinction between "subject-centered reason" and "communicative reason" — roughly, the distinction between rationality as appeal to the conventions of a presently-played language-game and appeal to democratic consensus, to "argumentative procedures" rather than to "first principles."[41]

But the idea of "argumentative procedures" for changing our description of what we are doing — for example, changing our political vocabularies from Mill's to Marx's, or from Althusser's to Unger's — seems inapplicable to the way in which patients grasp the contingency, poverty and insignificance of the central signifiers of their neuroses. To say that the aim of social change should be a society in which such procedures are all that we need — in which passionate, romantic, only retrospectively arguable breaks with the past are no longer necessary — is like saying that the aim of psychoanalysis should be "normal functioning." Of course it should, but that does not make psychoanalysis a less hit-or-miss, a more rational, procedure. Of course we should aim at such a society, but that does not mean that the only sort of social change we should work for is the kind for which we can offer good arguments. Unger has no more idea than do his readers whether

---

41 At p. 314 of *The Philosophical Discourse of Modernity,* Habermas says, "Subject-centered reason finds its criteria in standards of truth and success that govern the relationships of knowing and purposively acting subjects to the world of possible objects or states of affairs. By contrast, as soon as we conceive of knowledge as communicatively mediated, rationality is assessed in terms of the capacity of responsible participants in interactions to orient themselves in relation to validity claims geared to intersubjective recognition. Communicative reason finds its criteria in the argumentative procedures for directly or indirectly redeeming claims to propositional truth, normative rightness, subjective truthfulness, and aesthetic harmony."

his rotating capital fund will work – any more than Madison had of whether the separation of powers would work, or than an analyst has of whether a given remark will get through to a given patient. The only "argument" such people can give for such experiments is "Let's give it a try; nothing *else* seems to work."

This was, to be sure, also Hitler's and Mao's "argument." But we should not use this resemblance between Unger and Mao to make Unger look bad or Mao good. Rather, we should realize that the notion of "argumentative procedures" is not relevant to the situation in which nothing familiar works and in which people are desperately (on the couch, on the barricades) looking for something, no matter how unfamiliar, which might work. What remains relevant is, roughly, freedom of speech. Whether a given romantic, once in power, allows such freedom (of newspapers, universities, public assemblies, electoral choices, and so on) is, though not an infallible index, the best index we have of whether he or she is likely to do his or her nation some good. To my mind, the cash-value of Habermas' philosophical notions of "communicative reason" and "intersubjectivity" consists in the familiar political freedoms fashioned by the rich North Atlantic democracies during the last two centuries. Such notions are not "foundations" or "defenses" of the free institutions of those countries; they *are* those institutions, painted in the philosopher's traditional "gray on gray." We did not learn about the importance of these institutions as a counterweight to the romantic imagination by thinking through the nature of Reason or Man or Society; we learned about this the hard way, by watching what happened when those institutions were set aside.

More generally, I doubt that any philosophical reworking of the notion of "rationality," or of any similar notion, is going to help us sort out the de Sades from the Whitmans, the Heideggers from the Castoriadises,[42] or the Hitlers from the Rosa Luxemburgs. "Everything is politics," in this context, means that what political history cannot teach, philosophy cannot teach either. The idea that

---

42 Habermas describes Castoriadis as combining "the late Heidegger and the early Fichte in a Marxist fashion" (ibid., pp. 329–330). The description is accurate enough as far as it goes. It will also do for Unger, inasmuch as he, like Castoriadis, can make good use of the late Heideggerian idea of "world-disclosure." Were Habermas to criticize Unger he would, I should imagine, do so along the same lines as he criticizes Castoriadis, and say that Unger too "assimilates intramundane praxis to a linguistic world-disclosure hypostatized into a History of Being" (ibid., p. 332).

A full reply to Habermas' criticisms of Castoriadis would require a separate paper. Here I can only remark that Castoriadis no more *assimilates* these two than the psychoanalyst assimilates the patient's day-to-day "struggle in his actual life" to the unconscious fantasies that dictate the terms in which the patient describes that struggle. It is one thing to say that the language we currently use for describing our individual or social situation is an imaginative product, and another to say that recognizing this fact is incompatible with taking this language seriously. It is just not the case that such recognition "prejudices the validity of linguistic utterance generally" (ibid., p. 331), nor that on Castoriadis' view "social praxis disappears in the anonymous hurly-burly of the institutionalization of ever new worlds from the imaginary dimension" (ibid., p. 330).

theorizing, or philosophical reflection, will help us sort out good from bad romantics is part of the larger idea that philosophy can anticipate history by spotting "objectively progressive" or "objectively reactionary" intellectual movements. This is as bad as Plato's idea (recently resurrected by Allan Bloom[43]) that philosophers can distinguish "morally healthy" from "morally debilitating" kinds of music. We cannot hope to avoid risky social experiments by discerning the presence or absence of dubious overtones (for example, "bourgeois ideology," "authoritarianism," "irrationalism," "the philosophy of subjectivity") in the discourse of those who advocate such experiments.

In order to conclude on a concrete note, I shall discuss one such experiment. Suppose that somewhere, someday, the newly-elected government of a large industrialized country decreed that everybody would get the same income, regardless of occupation or disability. Simultaneously, it instituted vastly increased inheritance taxes and froze large bank transfers. Suppose that, after the initial turmoil, it worked: that is, suppose that the economy did not collapse, that people still took pride in their work (as streetcleaners, pilots, doctors, canecutters, Cabinet ministers, or whatever), and so on. Suppose that the next generation in that country was brought up to realize that, whatever else they might work for, it made no sense to work for wealth. But they worked anyway (for, among other things, national glory). That country would become an irresistible example for a lot of other countries, "capitalist," "Marxist," and in-between. The electorates of these countries would not take time to ask what "factors" had made the success of this experiment possible. Social theorists would not be allowed time to explain how something had happened that they had pooh-poohed as utopian, nor to bring this new sort of society under familiar categories. All the attention would be focused on the actual details of how things were working in the pioneering nation. Sooner or later, the world would be changed.

Castoriadis, like Edward Bellamy a hundred years ago, advocates such an experiment, but he sensibly declines to offer an argument for it:

If . . . I have maintained for twenty-five years that an autonomous society ought immediately to adopt, in the area of "requittal", an absolute equality of all wages, salaries, incomes, etc., this springs neither from some idea about any natural or other "identity/equality" of men, nor from theoretical reasoning . . . this is a matter of the imaginary significations which hold society together and of the *paideia* of individuals.[44]

The success of such an experiment would be the analogue of a patient getting better as a result of coming to see "in his actual life and as a result of repetition,"

---

43 Allan Bloom, *The Closing of the American Mind* (New York: Simon and Schuster, 1987), p. 68.
44 Castoriadis, *Crossroads in the Labyrinth,* trans. K. Soper and M. Ryle (Cambridge, Mass.: MIT Press, 1984), p. 329. The equalization of incomes was central to the imagination of the so-called Old Left here in the North Atlantic. No passage in *Animal Farm* did more to create ex-Communists than the one about how the pigs managed to get all the milk and apples. But it is the sort of option that the more up-to-date, theoretical, and resentful Left rarely discusses.

the "contingency, poverty and insignificance" of "the central signifier of his neurosis." The French had heard incisive diagnoses many times, but one summer morning in 1789 they woke up conscious of the contingency, poverty, and insignificance of the three Estates, the lilies of Bourbon, and the Catholic Church – of the imaginary significations that had been holding their social life together and that had been essential to the meaning of "France." Things in France did not work out very well at first, but the world was, eventually, changed for the better. European national neuroses began to have different sorts of central signifiers.

A large part of the irrelevance to the Third World of the Cold War, and of talk about "capitalism" and "socialism," is that the obstacles to equalization of income, and to a *paideia* that is *not* centered around the attainment of wealth, are pretty well the same in the United States and in Russia.[45] More broadly, the imaginary significations that hold society together are pretty much the same in both places. No single change could do more to expose the contingency, poverty, and insignificance of some of the central signifiers of the national neuroses of both superpowers than some third country's success at equalizing incomes. To say, as I have been saying here, that if there is hope it lies in the imagination of the Third World, is to say that the best any of us here in Alexandria can hope for is that somebody out there will do something to tear up the present system of imaginary significations within which politics in (and between) the First and Second Worlds is conducted. It need not be equalization of incomes, but it has to be something *like* that – something so preposterously romantic as to be no longer discussed by us Alexandrians. Only some actual event, the actual success of some political move made in some actual country, is likely to help. No hopeful book by Unger or Habermas, any more than one more hopeless, "oppositional," unmasking book by the latest Resenter, is going to do the trick. Unger, however, has an advantage over the rest of us. His advantage is not that he has a "more powerful theory," but simply that he is aware of "the exemplary instability of the Third World"[46] in a way that most of us are not. His theoretical writing is shot through with a romanticism for which we Alexandrians no longer have the strength. His book has a better chance than most to be linked, in the history books, with some such world-transforming event.

45 This is the kernel of truth in all the loose, resentful, Heideggerian talk about Russia and America being "metaphysically speaking, the same" and in all the loose, resentful analogies between the Gulag and the "carceral archipelagoes" of the democracies. See Foucault's discussion of the latter analogy in *Power/Knowledge: Selected Interviews and Other Writings,* ed. Colin Gordon (Brighton: The Harvester Press, 1980), p. 134.
46 See Unger, *Social Theory,* p. 64.

Moral identity and private autonomy:
The case of Foucault

Vincent Descombes has pointed out that attempts to appropriate Foucault's work have given us an American Foucault and a French Foucault. The American Foucault, he says, "sought to define autonomy in purely human terms," without the Kantian notion of a universal law. This Foucault can be read, I have argued, as an up-to-date version of John Dewey.[1] Like Dewey, this Foucault tells us that liberal democracies might work better if they stopped trying to give universalistic self-justifications, stopped appealing to notions like "rationality" and "human nature" and instead viewed themselves simply as promising social experiments.

But, as Descombes says, the American Foucault is Foucault with most of the Nietzscheanism drained away. The French Foucault is the *fully* Nietzschean one. For this Foucault, Descombes says, the project of autonomy requires us to have "inhuman thoughts," to have no "worries about sharing our beliefs with our fellow citizens."[2] Insofar as the French Foucault has any politics, they are anarchist rather than liberal.

I think that the contrast Descombes draws catches a real tension between two of Foucault's mixed and complicated motives. This tension is one characteristic of the Romantic intellectual who is also a citizen of a democratic society. Such an intellectual finds her moral identity — her sense of her relations to most other human beings — in the democratic institutions which she inhabits. But she does not think that her *moral* identity exhausts her self-description. For she does not think her conduct toward other human beings is the most important thing about her. What is *more* important is her *rapport à soi*, her private search for autonomy, her refusal to be exhaustively describable in words which apply to anyone other than herself. This is the search summed up in Blake's exclamation: "I must create my own system, or be enslaved by another man's."

Blake and Baudelaire share with Nietzsche and Heidegger the need to have a self which is autonomous, in the sense of being self-invented. To invent one's own self one must indeed think, in Descombes's words, "inhuman thoughts" — in the sense that one must have thoughts which no human being has yet had, write

---

1 I have offered such a reading of Foucault in my *Consequences of Pragmatism* (Minneapolis: University of Minnesota Press, 1982), at pp. 203–208.
2 Vincent Descombes, review of *Foucault: A Critical Reader*, ed. David Hoy (Oxford: Blackwell, 1986), in *London Review of Books*, March 5, 1987, p. 3.

books unlike any books yet written. So one must cut the links which bind one's vocabulary to the vocabularies being used by one's fellow humans.

But cutting those links does not necessarily mean cutting the social bonds which, for purposes of public action, unite one with one's fellow citizens. Nor does it necessarily mean ceasing to use in good faith, for public purposes, the political vocabulary used by the mass of one's fellow citizens. Just as Kierkegaard's knight of faith looks like a bank clerk, and in public acts like one, so the Romantic intellectual can be, for public purposes, your ordinary bourgeois liberal. It is only when a Romantic intellectual begins to want his private self to serve as a model for other human beings that his politics tend to become antiliberal. When he begins to think that other human beings have a moral duty to achieve the same inner autonomy as he himself has achieved, then he begins to think about political and social changes which will help them do so. Then he may begin to think that he has a moral duty to bring about these changes, whether his fellow citizens want them or not.

Foucault was, much of the time, what one might call a "knight of autonomy." He wanted to invent his own self as much as Nietzsche did. But, unlike Nietzsche, he did not urge anybody else to engage in this effort. He did not think that human beings *in general* have a moral duty to be Baudelairean or Nietzschean self-inventors. He did not envisage a politics which would help, or force, them to become more autonomous. Like a good liberal, he was willing to leave them alone to be as self-inventive or as banal as they liked. In an interview he said, "The search for a form of morality acceptable by everyone in the sense that everyone would have to submit to it, seems catastrophic to me."[3] Much of the time, his only politics was the standard liberal's attempt to alleviate unnecessary suffering.

Only much of the time, however. At other times, Foucault ran together his moral and his ethical identity – his sense of his responsibility to others and his *rapport à soi*. At these times, like Nietzsche, he projected his own search for autonomy out into public space. In both his and Nietzsche's case, the results were bad. These were the times when Foucault wrote the passages which upset his American admirers: for example, "I think to imagine another system is to extend our participation in the present system."[4] That is the sort of passage about which Michael Walzer says, "The powerful evocation of the disciplinary system gives way to an antidisciplinarian politics that is mostly rhetoric and posturing."[5] Yet these are the "anarchist" passages which many of his French admirers seem to like best.

We liberals in the United States wish that Foucault could have managed, just

3 *Les Nouvelles*, June 28, 1984, p. 37. Quoted by Drefyus and Rabinow in their "What is Maturity?," in *Foucault: A Critical Reader*, ed. Hoy.
4 This quotation comes from a 1971 interview with *Actuel*. It appears at p. 230 of the English translation of that interview in *Language, Counter-Memory, Practise: Selected Essays and Interviews*, ed. Donald F. Bouchard (Ithaca, N.Y.: Cornell University Press, 1977).
5 *Foucault: A Critical Reader*, ed. Hoy, p. 65.

once, what Walzer rightly says he always resisted: "some positive evaluation of the liberal state." So do our Canadian and German counterparts. Habermas echoes Charles Taylor's complaint about Foucault's "amazing one-sidedness"[6] when he says that Foucault's history of the power formations which formed modern subjectivity "filters out all the aspects under which the eroticization and internalization of subjective nature also meant a gain in freedom and expression."[7] You would never guess, from Foucault's account of the changes in European social institutions during the last three hundred years, that during that period suffering had decreased considerably, nor that people's chances of choosing their own styles of life increased considerably.

So Walzer, Taylor, Habermas, and I have a similarly mixed reaction to Foucault. On the one hand there is admiration and gratitude. For Foucault highlighted a new set of dangers to democratic societies. He served such societies well by telling them about tendencies and patterns that they needed to watch out for. As Taylor rightly says, and as Habermas might agree, Foucault "offered the Frankfurt School an account of the inner connection between the domination of nature and the domination of man which is rather more detailed and more convincing than what they [the Frankfurt School] came up with themselves."[8] On the other hand, we liberal reformists think that Foucault's work is pervaded by a crippling ambiguity between "power" as a pejorative term and as a neutral, descriptive term. In the first sense, to quote Taylor again, " 'power' belongs in a semantic field from which 'truth' and 'freedom' cannot be excluded." In the second sense, the term has the vacuity with which Nietzsche, at his worst, endowed the term *Wille zur Macht*. In this broad and vacuous sense, any study of anything (of chemical or mathematical relationships, of chess playing, of social institutions) will be a study of "strategies of power," just as it will be a study of "the exploitation of structural possibilities." Both phrases are resounding only because they are empty.

When a first-rate thinker gets hung up on the ambiguity between a pejorative and an empty sense of a crucial term, we have reason to suspect that he is trying to do two things at once. Foucault was trying to serve human liberty, but he was also, in the interest of his personal autonomy, trying to be a faceless, rootless, homeless stranger to humanity and to history. As a citizen, he was trying to achieve the same political consequences which a good humanitarian bourgeois liberal would wish to achieve. As a philosopher trying to invent himself, he was, to quote Taylor yet again, "tossing aside the whole tradition of Augustinian inwardness."[9] This tradition says that one's *deepest* identity is the one which binds

6 Ibid., p. 81.
7 Habermas, *The Philosophical Discourse of Modernity*, trans. Frederick Lawrence (Cambridge, Mass.: MIT Press, 1987), p. 292.
8 *Foucault: A Critical Reader*, ed. Hoy, p. 77.
9 Ibid., p. 99.

one to one's fellow humans, that there is something common to all men, and that getting in touch with this common element is getting in touch with one's real self. Foucault, as I understand him, wanted to do good to his fellow humans while at the same time having an identity which had nothing whatever to do with them. He wanted to help people without taking their vocabulary as the one in which he spoke to himself. He wanted to help them while inventing a self which had nothing much (indeed, as little as possible) to do with theirs.

My own view is that this is a feasible, if difficult, project: that one *can* do both of the things Foucault was trying to do, one *can* be "a knight of autonomy." But I wish that Foucault had been more willing to *separate* his two roles — more willing to separate his moral identity as a citizen from his search for autonomy. Then he might have had more resistance to the temptation to which Nietzsche and Heidegger succumbed — the temptation to try to find a public, political counterpart of this latter, private search. This, I think, was the temptation which led to his quasi-anarchism, to his refusal to be "complicit" with "power," even when "power" is stretched so far that it loses any contrastive force and becomes vacuous. That anarchism seems to me the result of a misguided attempt to envisage a society as free of its historical past as the Romantic intellectual hopes to be free of her private past.

The Romantic intellectual's goal of self-overcoming and self-invention seems to me a good model (one among many other good models) for an individual human being, but a very bad model for a society. We should not try to find a societal counterpart to the desire for autonomy. Trying to do so leads to Hitlerlike and Maolike fantasies about "creating a new kind of human being." Societies are not quasi-persons, they are (at their liberal, social democratic best) compromises between persons. The point of a liberal society is not to invent or create anything, but simply to make it as easy as possible for people to achieve their wildly different private ends without hurting each other. To work out the details of the continually shifting compromises which make up the political discourse of such a society requires a banal moral vocabulary — a vocabulary which is no more relevant to one individual's private self-image than to another's. In a liberal society, our public dealings with our fellow citizens are not *supposed* to be Romantic or inventive; they are supposed to have the routine intelligibility of the marketplace or the courtroom.

Publicly discussable compromises require discourse in a common vocabulary, and such a vocabulary is required to describe the *moral* identities a liberal society asks its citizens to have. They are asked to have this moral identity for public purposes, and to have it irrespective of whatever other, private identities they may also have. Only if one refuses to divide the public from the private realm will one dream of a society which has "gone beyond mere social democracy," or dream of "total revolution." Only then will anarchism begin to seem attractive. Only then will one be tempted to use a pejorative term like "discourse of power" to describe the results of *any* social compromise, *any* political balancing act.

196

The attempt to break down the distinction between the private and the public sphere is characteristic of a long-standing tradition in social philosophy. This is the tradition which, with Plato, sees society as man writ large. Most philosophers in this tradition try to isolate some central, ahistorical, noncontingent core (e.g., "reason" or "a specifically moral motivation") within us, and to use the presence of this element within us as a justification for certain political arrangements, certain social institutions. Foucault inverts this attempt. Since he sees human subjectivity as a contingent product of contingently existing forces, he does not believe that there is any such ahistorical noncontingent core. So he concludes, at least in his anarchist moments, that every social institution is equally unjustifiable, that all of them are on a par. All of them exert "normalizing power." From the failure of the Platonic attempt to find something deep within us which will let us answer Thrasymachus, he comes close to concluding that there is no interesting difference between Pericles and Critias.

It seems to me that we should drop the assumption which Plato and Foucault share. This is the assumption that, unless there is some interesting connection between what matters most to an individual and her purported moral obligations to our fellow human beings, she has no such obligations. If we drop this assumption, we can say that Romantic intellectuals, religious mystics, sexual fetishists, and others whose private self has nothing much to do with their public self, are under the same moral obligations as all the rest of us. No deep philosophical reason can be given to explain the fact that they are under such obligations, so Thrasymachus can never be answered to Plato's satisfaction. But an inability to answer Thrasymachus has no political consequences of the sort which Nietzsche and Foucault are sometimes inclined to draw. A sense of human subjectivity as a centerless bundle of contingencies, of the sort which both Foucault and Dewey shared with Nietzsche, is compatible with *any* sort of politics, *including* liberal politics.

Foucault's projection of the desire for private autonomy out onto politics seems to me the inverse of the insistence by my fellow liberal, Habermas, on notions like "rationality" and "the true self." Habermas would like to ground moral obligation, and thus social institutions, on something universally human. Conversely, Foucault's radical, Nietzschean anti-Platonism leads him to infer from the absence of anything which might serve as such a ground the absence of the need for social institutions. I should prefer to split the difference between Foucault and his liberal critics by saying that Nietzsche and Foucault are right against Plato, but that this anti-Platonism does nothing to show that there is something wrong with liberal societies. More generally, it does nothing to show that there is something wrong with whatever networks of power are required to shape people into individuals with a sense of moral responsibility.

Unlike Habermas, I do not think that Foucault needs to answer charges of "relativism." He does not have to answer Socratic questions like "why should domination be resisted?"[10] If one is willing, as Dewey and Foucault were, to give up the hope of universalism, then one can give up the fear of relativism as well. I agree with Ian Hacking that "it won't be long before the solemn clamor of the intellectuals about Foucault [asking 'where do you stand?'] sounds as quaint as the baying of the Edinburgh mob [around Hume, asking 'have you recanted your atheism?']."[11] I think Foucault should have answered the questions "Where do you stand?, What are your values?," in this way: "I stand with you as a fellow-citizen, but as a philosopher, I stand off by myself, pursuing projects of self-invention which are none of your concern. I am not about to offer philosophical grounds for being on your side in public affairs, for my philosophical project is a private one which provides neither motive nor justification for my political actions."

Such a reply would sound less shocking if one substituted "poet" for "philosopher." For as opposed to poets, philosophers are traditionally supposed to offer a "basis" for our moral obligations to others. They are supposed to have what Fraser calls "an adequate normative perspective."[12] Unlike poets, philosophers are supposed to be "rational," and rationality is supposed to consist in being able to exhibit the "universal validity" of one's position. Foucault, like Nietzsche, was a philosopher who claimed a poet's privileges. One of these privileges is to rejoin "What has universal validity to do with *me?*" I think that philosophers are as entitled to this privilege as poets, so I think this rejoinder sufficient.

Nevertheless, I think it is important to notice that one can ask that rhetorical question without going on to ask, as Nietzsche did, "What has the suffering of my fellow humans to do with me?" For one can be humane without being universalist, without believing either that it is "rational" to be concerned with the sufferings of others or that there is a "common humanity" which binds you to those others. One can want to relieve suffering without having an interesting answer when Socrates asks you *why* you desire this, and also without believing that this desire is the deepest and most important thing in your life. Foucault, I think, found himself in this position – the position which I have described as that of the "knight of autonomy." This meant that, whether he wanted to be or not, he was, among other things, a useful citizen of a democratic country – one who did his best to make that country's institutions fairer and more decent. I wish that he had been more comfortable with that self-description than he was.

10 See Habermas, *The Philosophical Discourse of Modernity*, p. 284, where he cites Nancy Fraser as posing this question.

11 *Foucault: A Critical Reader*, ed. Hoy, p. 238.

12 Nancy Fraser, "Foucault on Modern Power: Empirical Insights and Normative Confusions," *Praxis International* 1 (1981): 91. For a thoughtful reply to Fraser, Habermas, and Taylor on Foucault's behalf, see chapter 4 of David R. Hiley, *Philosophy in Question: Essays on a Pyrrhonian Theme* (Chicago: University of Chicago Press, 1988).

Index of names

Saussure, Ferdinand de, 5, 97, 130, 132, 135
Schafer, Roy, 151n
Schelling, Ferdinand, 28, 29n
Schiller, F. C. S., 189
Schneewind, J. B., 156n, 163n, 172
Schopenhauer, Arthur, 50–51, 61
Searle, John, 54n, 86n, 93n, 101, 104, 110–111
Sedgwick, Eve Klossofsky, 138
Sellars, Wilfrid, 14, 110, 116
Shelley, Percy Bysshe, 138, 189
Skinner, B. F., 146
Smith, Barbara Herrnstein, 109, 128n
Socrates, 24, 72, 108, 198
Spinoza, Baruch, 30, 90–91, 94, 100
Stalin, Joseph, 25, 69
Staten, Henry, 3, 59n, 128n
Sterne, Laurence, 73
Stevens, Wallace, 100
Stich, Stephen, 54n
Stowe, Harriet Beecher, 80, 134
Strauss, Leo, 49
Strawson, Peter, 112
Suslov, Mikhail Andreyevich, 81
Swift, Jonathan, 74, 79

Taylor, Charles, 67, 195, 198n
Thomas, George, 151n
Thompson, E. P. 184n

Thoreau, Henry David, 68n
Tillich, Paul, 19n
Tugendhat, Ernst, 124, 126–127

Unger, Roberto, 1, 177–186, 188–190, 192

Valéry, Paul, 24
Vidal, Gore, 184n
Voltaire, 74, 80

Walzer, Michael, 194–195
Weber, Max, 19n, 26, 169, 173
Wells, H. G., 129
Wheeler, Samuel, 3, 59n, 110n
Whitehead, Alfred North, 152
Whitman, Walt, 177–180, 187, 189
Williams, Bernard, 33
Wittgenstein, Ludwig, 3, 4, 5, 17, 35, 50–65, 91, 97, 99, 103–104, 110, 111n, 115, 124–128, 130, 135, 186
Wolff, Christian, 53
Wollheim, Richard, 146
Wordsworth, William, 138
Wundt, Wilhelm, 55

Yorck, Count von, 41, 42n

Zola, Emile, 183